ETHNIC SOLIDARITY FOR ECONOMIC SURVIVAL

ETHNIC SOLIDARITY FOR ECONOMIC SURVIVAL

KOREAN GREENGROCERS IN NEW YORK CITY

PYONG GAP MIN

Russell Sage Foundation • New York

The Russell Sage Foundation

Library of Congress Cataloging-in-Publication Data

Min, Pyong Gap, 1942–
   Ethnic solidarity for economic survival : Korean greengrocers in New York City / Pyong Gap Min.
      p. cm.
   Includes bibliographical references and index.
   ISBN 978-0-87154-577-0
   1. Korean American business enterprises—New York (State)—New York.
2. Korean American businesspeople—New York (State)—New York. 3. Korean Americans—New York (State)—New York. 4. New York (N.Y.)—Ethnic relations.
5. New York (N.Y.)—Emigration and immigration. I. Title.

HD2346.U52N5453 2008
381¢.456413008995707471—dc22

                                                                2007044180

Text design by Suzanne Nichols.

RUSSELL SAGE FOUNDATION
112 East 64th Street, New York, New York 10021

10 9 8 7 6 5 4 3 2 1

Contents

═ About the Author ═

Pyong Gap Min is professor of sociology at Queens College and the Graduate Center of the City University of New York.

= Acknowledgments =

Many people and organizations assisted me in a number of ways in collecting and analyzing data and writing this manuscript, and I would like to acknowledge the roles they played in completing this book project. First of all, I owe many thanks to a team of Korean, Chinese, and Indian undergraduate and graduate students who participated in the 2005–2006 telephone survey of Korean, Chinese, and Indian immigrants in New York City. I cannot list all the names of more than fifteen participants in the survey. But the following graduate students deserve mention here: Dong Wan Joo, Kathy Liu, Krittika Ghosh, Kristy Lai, Eun Sook Shim, Soniya Munshi, and Young Oak Kim. Young Oak selected the Korean sample and coordinated the entire telephone survey, while Kathy and Krittika helped select the Chinese and Indian samples, respectively. Young Oak and Kathy coded and analyzed survey data. They, along with He Huang, also analyzed census data. Of course, without the cooperation of those Chinese, Indian, and Korean immigrants who responded to the telephone survey, I would not have been able to collect survey data. When I encountered unexpected difficulties in completing the 2005–2006 telephone survey, Dean Savage, Alem Habtu, and Jimmy Moore at Queens College supported me with encouragement and advice. I also would like to express many thanks to Mehdi Bozorgmehr at City College for supporting my research activities and giving me encouragement for many years.

I owe my sincere gratitude to Dong Wan Joo for supporting my research for many years and assisting me in different ways in completing this book project. He joined Young Oak and me in conducting fieldwork and taking photos at Hunts Point Market, the office of the Korean Produce Association, and the Korean Harvest and Folklore Festivals. He also introduced me to several Korean greengrocers for personal interviews. I could not have completed this book project without the assistance and support of several former and current presidents and staff members of the Korean Produce Association. In particular, Young Tea Kim, the

2005 president of the KPA, and Hahn-gyoung Jo, executive director of the KPA, were kind enough to answer many questions about the history and structure of the KPA and Hunts Point Market and to allow me to use the KPA's annual and biannual reports, newsletters, and newspaper clippings. Five former presidents of the KPA—Chang Il Kim, Se Mok Lee, Joo Tae Yoo, Bo Young Jung, and In Suck Whang—provided valuable information about the KPA's activities in earlier years. Kenny Pak, the 2007 president of the KPA, morally supported my book project. In addition, Sung Soo Kim, director of the Korean Small Business Service Center, provided me with valuable information and newspaper articles.

This book would not have been possible without financial support by a number of organizations. A 2005–2007 grant from the National Science Foundation (Grant No: 0454239) enabled me to conduct the above-mentioned telephone survey and fieldwork. A 2005 mini-grant from the Korean-American Economic Development Center assisted me in getting additional fieldwork at the Hunts Point Market. I owe particular thanks to Paul Ciccantell and Patricia White, the Directors of the Sociology Program at the National Science Foundation. A 1990 PSC-CUNY Research Award made possible personal interviews with staff members of major Korean business associations in New York City and reviews of Korean newspaper articles published between 1977 and 1988. A 1991 Ford Foundation Diversity Initiative grant, originally awarded to Queens College, supported my survey study of Korean merchants in black neighborhoods and of black and white residents there in 1992. In addition, a Visiting Scholar Fellowship at Russell Sage Foundation in the 2006–2007 academic year gave me release time to complete this book. Any opinions, findings, and conclusions or recommendations expressed in this book are my own and do not necessarily reflect the views of these funding agencies.

The Russell Sage Foundation fellowship not merely gave me release time to write this book. It also included assistance with my research and writings by many staff members in a number of ways, and several of them deserve my recognition here. Eric Wanner, the president of the organization, and other key staff members made efforts to help visiting scholars concentrate in research and book writings as much as possible. No doubt, their efforts and policy helped me complete my book manuscript within a short period of time, and I would like to acknowledge my immense benefits from their efforts. Many other staff members did wonderful jobs in facilitating my research and making my stay there as comfortable as possible. But I owe thanks especially to Orly Clerge and Galo Falchettorre for assisting me with statistical analysis and Catherine Winograd for helping me with reference materials and proofreading and editing my manuscripts.

I would like to acknowledge that Ivan Light and Steven Gold provided useful comments for revising the manuscript and that their critical comments definitely helped improve the quality of the book. I also owe my gratitude to Eric Wanner and Suzanne Nichols at Russell Sage Foundation for firmly supporting the manuscript for publication from the beginning and processing it for the review and production quickly. I owe many thanks to Matthew Callan, the production editor at Russell Sage Foundation, whose easy-going attitude made my editorial and correction works comfortable and whose meticulous review of the manuscript has eliminated many technical errors included in the earlier version of the manuscript. I also need to indicate that Helen Glenn Court's super copy-editing work has made the book easy to read.

An earlier version of chapter 6 in this book originally appeared in the Fall 2007 issue of the *Du Bois Review*, entitled "Conflicts with Latino Employees and Reactive Solidarity." The revised version included in this book appears with their permission, for which I am grateful.

Finally, my acknowledgments would be incomplete without mentioning the significant role my wife, Young Oak, played in collecting and analyzing data for this book. She played the key part in conducting the telephone survey and the fieldwork at Hunts Point Market and black neighborhoods, analyzing survey data, and recruiting Korean immigrants for personal interviews cited in this book. She shared with me some agonizing moments while conducting the telephone survey, which we will remember for many years to come. I consider this book a product of our collaborative work, although I have not listed her as a coauthor.

= Chapter 1 =

Introduction

When members of a particular immigrant group concentrate in a particular trade, depend heavily on nonethnic suppliers, and serve exclusively nonethnic customers, they usually have a high level of business-related conflicts with other groups and government agencies and thus rely on ethnic collective action for economic survival. They need more than start-up capital, business information, and unpaid family members and co-ethnic employees to successfully establish and operate their businesses. They need to approach commercial activities collectively to neutralize external threats by establishing an ethnic trade association.

Because immigrant or ethnic entrepreneurship involves a moderate or high level of collective approach, it is important for social scientists to investigate the behaviors of immigrant-ethnic business associations and the results as well as the behaviors of individual immigrant merchants. In two classic anthropological studies, *Peddlers and Princes*[1] and *Custom and Politics in Urban Africa*,[2] the authors showed how migrant merchants in Asia and Africa were forced to organize collectively to protect their business interests. In his widely cited work, Abner Cohen documented in detail processes in which the Hausa, a migrant minority group in Nigeria, developed a complex political organization to prevent other ethnic groups from encroaching on Hausa trade and to coordinate the activities of Hausa members.[3]

Ivan Light's *Ethnic Enterprise in America,* published in 1972, remains the classic work on immigrant-ethnic entrepreneurship in the United States. In it, he showed how Chinese and Japanese immigrants in California were able to start their businesses using rotating credit associations, a communal technique of business capitalization, in the first half of the twentieth century. Although he highlighted the collectivistic approach to small businesses those immigrants took, he emphasized use of rotating credit associations as a major cause of business development rather than as its consequence. Researchers, predominantly sociologists, have subsequently examined ethnic resources or ethnic ties as the major factor in the

1

development of immigrant-ethnic entrepreneurship.[4] They have recently made a distinction between ethnic and class resources[5] and recognized "labor market disadvantages"[6] and "opportunity structure"[7] as major factors for the development of immigrant and ethnic businesses. Nevertheless, researchers interested in immigrant-ethnic entrepreneurship in the United States still seem to accept the ethnic resources hypothesis as the most popular one.

The concentration of group members in small business further enhances ethnic ties. Thus there is a mutual influence between ethnic ties and ethnic business. Since 1980, a growing number of social scientists have paid attention to the effects of ethnic business on ethnic ties.[8] Only few, however, have documented the effects of ethnic business on ethnicity in detail using empirical data.

I believe that they have not partly because a causal analysis of mutual effects is sometimes difficult. For example, many Korean immigrants have invited their parents or parents-in-law to the United States for babysitting and housework when starting small businesses, which typically are labor intensive and involve long hours of work for both partners. In this case, establishing the business has contributed to the extended family living arrangement[9] rather than the other way around. Many researchers are likely to consider the extended family a causal variable for the business when interpreting a high correlation between the two. Another example related to the business practices of Korean immigrants, which are tricky in a causal interpretation and closely related to the main objective of this book, is the abundance of business associations in the Korean immigrant community in New York and many collective actions they have taken. Many journalists, and even some researchers not familiar with the business-related intergroup conflicts that Korean merchants encounter, may attribute the presence of associations and their collective actions to Korean characteristics. However, Korean immigrant merchants engaged in several types of businesses were forced to establish associations mainly to protect their economic interests against outside groups and government agencies.

Ethnicity or ethnic identity is, of course, a prevalent term in this age of multiculturalism. Many researchers have also studied the ethnic phenomenon over the last three decades or so. Ethnicity has two interrelated but nonetheless separate components, which I label *ethnic attachment* and *ethnic solidarity*.[10] Ethnic attachment indicates the degree to which members of an immigrant-ethnic group are culturally, socially, and psychologically attached to the group. Ethnic solidarity refers to the extent to which members of an immigrant-ethnic group use ethnic collective action to protect economic, welfare and political interests. Ethnic attachment is based on individual, private identity, and ethnic solidarity is based on collective or political identity. Many researchers have failed to make this important distinction when conducting research on the ethnic phenomenon.[11]

Most of these limited studies have revealed positive effects of immigrant-ethnic entrepreneurship on cultural and social ethnic attachments. For example, Edna Bonacich and John Modell showed that Japanese Americans in the ethnic economy maintained Japanese cultural traditions and interacted socially with co-ethnic members to a greater extent than those in the general economy.[12] Jeffrey Reitz demonstrated that Chinese, Eastern European, and Southern European ethnic groups in Canada were more successful in retaining mother tongue and ethnic endogamy than other ethnic groups mainly because they were more actively involved in the ethnic economy.[13] Several studies have examined the effects of immigrant entrepreneurship on ethnic solidarity, the use of ethnic collective action.[14] Almost all these studies, though, are book chapters or sections of book chapters. Only one gives an extended coverage to the issue in a monograph.[15] Interestingly, all but Olzak's discuss the effects of Korean immigrants' business-related conflicts with other groups and government agencies on solidarity in New York City or Los Angeles.

Objectives

A high concentration of members of an immigrant group in businesses can enhance ethnic solidarity when the merchants depend on members of other groups, whether as customers, suppliers of merchandise, employees, or landlords. A group's dependency on other groups for commercial activities enhances its group solidarity mainly because commercial activities involve a great deal of intergroup conflicts. Korean merchants in several retail businesses, such as grocery or liquor, produce, and gift shops, depend heavily on minority customers, white suppliers, Latino employees, and white landlords.[16] Among all trade groups of Korean immigrant retailers, greengrocers in New York depend most on other groups. As a result, they have encountered multifaceted business-related intergroup conflicts and frequently used ethnic collective actions to protect themselves. The Korean produce retail business is thus an excellent empirical case on which to examine the effects of business-related intergroup conflicts on ethnic solidarity.

This book has three interrelated objectives. First, it intends to examine Korean greengrocers' business-related conflicts with white produce suppliers, black customers and residents, Latino employees, and various government agencies. I pay special attention to a recent decline in conflicts and the factors that have contributed to the decline. Many researchers have analyzed black boycotts of Korean stores in the 1980s and early 1990s, and the victimization of Korean merchants during the 1992 Los Angeles riots.[17] But no one has paid special attention to the recent dramatic drop in boycotts and other rejection of Korean stores in black neighborhoods.

Second and more significant, this volume examines Korean green-grocers' use of ethnic collective action in self-defense against white produce suppliers, black residents and boycott organizers, Latino employee picketing, and government regulations restricting commercial activities through its association, the Korean Produce Association (KPA). I look at group purchases, political and administrative lobbies, demonstrations, and boycotts. I focus on the Korean Produce Association because it has used ethnic collective action more than any other Korean business association.

This book also looks at the KPA's services to its members, the Korean community, and South Korea. The KPA is a sociologically interesting topic, not only because of its ethnic collective actions, but also because it has provided so many services, monetary and nonmonetary, to the Korean community in New York and to South Korea. To my knowledge, no previous study has examined in detail the role of a particular business association in providing various services to the immigrant-ethnic community or the homeland. The KPA's services are relevant to the literature on the economic and welfare impact of immigrant entrepreneurship on the immigrant community and its efforts to help South Korea are tied to the transnational literature.

As discussed in detail in chapter 5, the KPA, located at Hunts Point Market, the major produce wholesale market, single-handedly organized collective actions against white produce suppliers. Black boycotts, on the other hand, negatively affected all Korean business owners in black neighborhoods, though produce stores were the targets of four of the six long-term boycotts. As a result, not only the KPA, but also Korean merchants' associations in black neighborhoods, the Korean Association of New York (KANY), the Korean Consulate in New York, and many other Korean organizations and individuals participated in collective actions to terminate black boycotts. Because of the strong ethnic nature of Korean-black conflicts and Koreans' collective actions, chapter 5 analyzes the causes of black boycotts of Korean stores in black neighborhoods and ethnic collective action used by a number of Korean organizations, the KPA among them.

Korean produce retail stores in Manhattan were the main targets of Latino employee picketing. But picketing, like boycotts, influenced Korean merchants involved in other businesses as well. Given this, it is not surprising that several Korean organizations responded to the picketing and New York State Attorney General Spitzer's intervention on the basis of violations of labor regulations. For these reasons, chapter 6 also examines relationships between Korean store owners and Latino employees broadly, though it devotes a significant portion to local labor union and Latino pickets against Korean produce stores and the KPA's responses to them.

Theoretical and Other
Scholarly Contributions

This book documents the collective and organizational aspects of business operation among Korean greengrocers. Due to their experiences of greater external threats, Korean greengrocers in New York City used more ethnic collective action than any other Korean business group in the city. As I document elsewhere,[18] however, several other groups of Korean merchants in the city used ethnic collective action to some extent. Contemporary sociologists, because they approached immigrant entrepreneurship mainly as the result of individual immigrants' motivation and use of resources, have neglected to investigate collectivity and organizational dynamics involved in immigrant entrepreneurship.

This book systematically examines Korean greengrocers' conflicts with white suppliers, black customers, Latino employees, and government agencies. In the 1990s, after long-term black boycotts of Korean stores in New York City and the 1992 Los Angeles riots, many researchers actively pursued research on Korean-black conflicts. They have kept silent, however, about what has happened to Korean-black relations in recent years. In explaining the boycotts and their disappearance, I use a serial middleman minority theory, a revised version of middleman minority theory. It has an advantage over other perspectives in explaining the radical reduction.

This volume makes a distinction between ethnic attachment and ethnic solidarity. Korean greengrocers and other merchants have maintained a fairly high level of ethnic attachment over the past three decades, partly due to their involvement in the ethnic economy. The level of their ethnic solidarity has declined significantly in recent years, however, as their business-related intergroup conflicts have dissipated. When studying ethnic phenomena based on noneconomic sources, we can avoid confusion by making this distinction between ethnic attachment based on individual members' private identity and ethnic solidarity based on their collective, political identity.[19]

The Korean Produce Association has contributed extensive monetary and nonmonetary services to the Korean community. To examine the economic impact of small-business ownership, social scientists usually compare earnings of self-employed workers with those of employed workers based on census data. Earnings reported to the census, though, do not accurately reflect small business owners' economic conditions due to their tendency to underreport earnings. Chapter 7 of this volume explains how the KPA provided monetary and nonmonetary services to the Korean community. Successful Korean greengrocers also individually donate money for other ethnic organizations, as do other Korean business associations and owners, both services and donations. Accordingly, the concentration of Korean immigrants in small businesses has had positive effects on the Korean community as a whole.

This book also moderately contributes to transnational studies. A plethora of research addresses immigrants' transnational ties with their homelands. But almost all focus on individual immigrants' economic, social, political, and religious ties with homelands. Studies of organizational linkages are neglected. This book devotes chapter 7 to documenting the Korean Produce Association's strong linkages with government agencies and nonprofit organizations in South Korea, both in connection with its preparation of a major Korean cultural festival in New York City and its efforts to promote exports of Korean agricultural products to New York City.

This volume presents a history and contemporary overview of the Korean community in New York. No doubt, the produce retail business has been the most important of Korean immigrant businesses in New York and the Korean Produce Association has played a very influential role in the community. This book focuses on its use of ethnic collective action in the 1980s and early 1990s. It includes meaningful census and survey data on the socioeconomic background of Korean immigrants, their religious affiliations and frequency of participation in religious institutions, changes over time in their self-employment rate and industrial categories of businesses, and intergenerational transitions in occupational adjustments. To highlight the unique aspects of Korean immigrant business patterns in New York, I have compared Korean immigrants with Chinese, Indian, and Filipino immigrants in the same city, and with Jewish Americans historically.

Research Methods and Data Sources

It is my methodological principle that quantitative or qualitative data alone are not enough to capture the reality of the world, especially when studying particular immigrant-ethnic communities. I have thus used both quantitative (public documents and survey data) and qualitative (personal interviews, participant observations and newspaper articles) data in all of my major research projects. As usual, I have also used the following five data sources for this book: quantitative public documents, results of a major survey, personal interviews with Korean business owners and business leaders, participant observations, the KPA's various materials, and articles published in local Korean- and English-language newspapers. These data were collected in two time periods: 1991 to 1992 and 2005 to 2007.

In chapters 2 and 3, I largely used U.S. census data, especially the 2000 census, and annual Immigration and Naturalization Service immigration statistics for information on Korean immigration and settlement patterns, Korean immigrants' self-employment rate, industries of Korean immigrant businesses, and their educational levels. In chapter 3 forward, I used results of the 2005 telephone survey of Korean immigrants in New York

City's five boroughs based on the Kim sample technique for Korean business patterns.

In the spring of 1992, Korean, black, and white students interviewed three New York City subsamples: Korean merchants in black neighborhoods, black residents, and white residents. We randomly selected 150 Korean merchants from directories of Korean merchants' associations in three black neighborhoods in New York City: the Stuyvesant-Flatbush area, Brooklyn; Jamaica, Queens; and Harlem, Manhattan. Three Korean students interviewed ninety-five of them. We also randomly selected 500 households from New York City public telephone directories in the three areas that closely matched the addresses of the above selected Korean stores. Two black and two white students successfully completed 151 telephone interviews; ninety-seven respondents were black and fifty-one were white. Survey items focused on Korean-black mutual prejudice and stereotypes, black and white respondent views about Korean commercial activities in black neighborhoods, and all views about opportunity structure in American society.

Between March and May 2005, I conducted a major telephone survey of Korean, Chinese, and Indian immigrants in five boroughs of New York City, using the surname sampling technique, to examine business and ethnic attachment patterns among the three Asian immigrant groups. I used the Kim sampling technique for the Korean sample.[20] According to the Korean census, Kims comprise 21.8 percent of the population in Korea.[21] Kim is a uniquely Korean name and Kims represent the Korean population socioeconomically.[22] Thus we could select a sample of the Korean immigrant population by randomly selecting the Kim households listed in public telephone directories. We selected 800 Kim households listed in the 2004 public telephone directories in five boroughs of the New York central city. Many selected households were ineligible for the interview because they were either second or 1.5-generation Koreans or have no worker. Many other selected Kim households were unreachable either because they moved away or, more likely, because both partners worked long hours. Among the 530 eligible or reachable households (about two-thirds of the sample), 277 (52 percent) were successfully interviewed by Korean students.

We conducted in-depth personal or telephone interviews with more than sixty-six Korean immigrants in the two periods. In 1991 and 1992, I conducted ten personal interviews, three with staff members of local Korean merchants' associations and seven Korean merchants in the three black neighborhoods. Personal interviews focused on causes of Korean-black disputes in the stores, causes of black boycotts of Korean stores, and the efforts to moderate Korean-black boycotts. During the same period, I also interviewed nine staff members of Korean trade associations. My questions probed the histories of their associations, their memberships, budgets, major goals, major activities responding to Korean merchants' business-related intergroup conflicts, their lobbying activities of government agencies and politicians, and their services to their members and the Korean community.

In 2006 and 2007, I conducted in-depth interviews with twelve Korean merchants in the same three black neighborhoods and two Korean old-timers who used to have businesses in those black neighborhoods in the 1970s. My interviews focused on advantages for businesses in black neighborhoods in the earlier period and radical reductions of Korean-owned stores and black boycotts of Korean stores there in recent years. Between 2005 and 2007, Young Oak and I also interviewed sixteen current or former KPA staff members. We asked them about some or most of the following issues: the development of the Korean produce business in New York, the history of the KPA, their experiences with discrimination at HPM, the KPA's use of ethnic collective action, black boycotts of Korean produce stores, local union pickets against Korean produce stores, Korean-Latino relations, KPA services to the Korean community, and KPA efforts to help South Korea. We also asked them about their immigration history and establishment and operation of the produce business. In addition, we interviewed seven Korean greengrocers who had never served as staff members of the KPA. We asked some of the same questions asked of the KPA's staff members. Six of the twenty-three had their stores in a black neighborhood at the time of the interview or previously. They were asked some of the questions relating to Korean-black relations. The majority were interviewed face to face, but some were interviewed by telephone. I conducted sixteen interviews and Young Oak interviewed seven.

I also interviewed eleven leaders of other Koran associations (ten presidents of other Korean business associations and the president of the Korean Association of New York) and four nonproduce business owners who hired Latino employees. Leaders of business associations were asked about the same questions as those in 1991 and 1992. Only a few of the interviews with leaders of business owners other than KPA and the Korean Small Business Service Center presidents were used in this book, mostly in chapter 3. I also asked four nonproduce Korean merchants who hired three or more Latino employees about the degrees of their preference for Latino workers over native blacks and Mexican workers over other Latino employees, duration of Latino workers' employment, and their provision of formal rewards to and informal relations with Latino workers. I conducted all these fifteen interviews.

In chapters 2 and 3, I used several case histories to illustrate Korean immigration, settlement, and economic adjustment in New York City. Rather than formal interviews, I used—with their permission—personal stories of friends and relatives gleaned from casual conversations. I telephoned most of these individuals to clarify their stories of immigration and economic adjustment.

I have cited many excerpts from personal interviews with KPA staff members, greengrocers, leaders of other business associations, other Korean merchants, and immigrants not in business. I have used pseudonyms in many instances, but several real names as well, when the individuals approved my doing so. Because this book covers the history and contemporary trends of the Korean community in New York in general and greengrocers in particular, many informants suggested that I use their real names so that second- and third-generation children can read their stories.

Participant observations of Hunts Point Market and three black neighborhoods in New York City (Jamaica, Flatbush, and Harlem) in 1991 and 2005 through 2007 comprise the third major data source for this book. My 1991 observations were brief, limited to three or five hours involving one or two days. Those during the 2005 to 2007 period were more intensive. For several days, in the early hours of the morning, Young Oak, Dong Wan, and I observed Hunts Point Market, where Korean greengrocers and produce delivery drivers purchase merchandise and where the KPA office is located. We observed interactions between Korean greengrocers and delivery drivers and employees of white distributors. We also watched Koreans talking with one another over coffee at three Korean-owned coffee shops. We visited the KPA office several times, watching KPA leaders and members interacting there and interviewing one or two leaders on each visit. Young Oak and I also observed each of the three black neighborhoods for three or four days between 2006 and 2007. We counted the numbers of Korean-owned stores in two of the three black neighborhoods to compare with their numbers in 1991. We interviewed several Korean business owners, focusing on the changes in structure of those black neighborhoods, the number of Korean-owned stores, and Korean-black relations.

We also reviewed public documents of the KPA regarding its activities and services. They include the annual or biannual reports on its activities, newsletters, annual booklets on the Korean Harvest and Folklore Festival, and KPA press releases. I found that the KPA had lost some important public documents, but that whatever it kept was helpful to this study. The KPA's biannual reports include copies of many Korean newspaper articles that reported its activities. From particular pieces of KPA documents and newspaper articles, I located business-related intergroup conflicts or use of ethnic collective actions that occurred in particular years. I then called former staff members of the KPA who served in particular years to gather more detailed information about conflicts with white suppliers, the KPA's use of demonstrations, boycotts, and other ethnic collective activities, and the organization's monetary and nonmonetary services to the Korean community and Korea.

Finally, I reviewed media articles relating to Korean greengrocers' business-related intergroup conflicts and KPA's use of ethnic collective actions. I have regularly read three Korean dailies—the *Korean Times New York*, the *Korea Central Daily New York*, and the *Sage Gae Times*—since 1988 and selected all articles dealing with Korean immigrants' business-related intergroup conflicts and use of ethnic collective action by Korean business associations. Three graduate students also gathered all articles of the same nature published in the *New York Times*, the *Daily News*, the *New York Newsday*, the *New York Post*, and the *Amsterdam News* through LEXIS-NEXIS and PROQUEST. I have found these newspaper articles most useful in analyzing various cases of Korean merchants' and the Korean community's use of ethnic collective actions to deal with their business-related intergroup conflicts, especially in following the chronology of events. This is true especially because staff members of the KPA have a great deal of difficulty remembering details of particular boycotts, demonstrations, and other collective actions.

My use of multiple data sources, involving both qualitative and quantitative data, increases the validity of many of the arguments in this book. For example, based on participant observations, along with personal interviews with Korean business owners, we see a significant increase in the Latino and Caribbean immigrant populations in traditional African American neighborhoods, such as Harlem, over the past two decades. Review of demographics in the 1980, 1990, and 2000 U.S. censuses corroborates this finding. My fieldwork in black neighborhoods involving personal interviews with Korean merchants showed that the number of Korean-owned retail stores there has radically decreased. The three decennial census data support the significant reduction of Korean retail stores in a concomitant increase in the number of service-related businesses.

Structure of the Book

This book has eight chapters. Chapter 2 provides basic information about Korean immigration patterns, settlement patterns in New York City, and cultural and socioeconomic characteristics. Chapter 3 examines the high self-employment rate among Korean immigrants and major types of Korean-owned businesses. Its final section examines the effect of Korean immigrant participation in the ethnic economy on ethnic attachment. Chapter 4 examines the development and evaluation of Korean produce retail stores in New York and introduces Hunts Point Market and Korean Produce Association located there. More important, it examines Korean greengrocers and produce truck drivers' conflicts with produce suppliers at Hunts Point Market and the KPA's use of ethnic collective actions in self-defense. Chapter 5 covers black boycotts of Korean produce stores and

Korean reactive solidarity. Chapters 4 and 5 are perhaps the two most important chapters.

Chapter 6 examines Korean-Latino relations in New York City. It discusses Korean merchants' heavy reliance on Latino employees, local union and Latino worker pickets against Korean produce stores, and the KPA and the Korean community reactions. The final section offers a snapshot of the relations between Korean merchants and Latino customers. Chapter 7 analyzes the KPA's services to its members, the Korean community, and South Korea. With regard to the KPA's services to its members, it also analyzes the KPA's negotiations with government agencies and lobbies of administrators and politicians to moderate government regulations of small business activities. Chapter 8 provides a summary and the conclusion, discussing the theoretical and practical implications of major findings.

═ Chapter 2 ═

Immigration, Settlement
Patterns, and Backgrounds

T
his chapter describes Korean immigrants in New York City in terms
of their immigration and settlement patterns and socioeconomic
and religious backgrounds—the context for the business-related
intergroup conflicts and reactive solidarity among Korean greengrocers.
To highlight unique patterns of Koreans' immigration and settlement,
and population characteristics, I often compare Korean immigrants with
Chinese and Indians, the two other major Asian immigrant groups in
New York.

Koreans' Immigration and Growth
of the Korean Population

In 1960, there were only some 400 Koreans in New York, a significant proportion of them students at Columbia University, New York University,
and other schools in the region.[1] Other Koreans at the time included professionals, businessmen, wives of American servicemen, and employees
of the Korean Consulate. The Korean Foreign Students Association of
New York, organized by Korean students at Columbia University and
New York University in 1955, led the majority of Korean community activities. The Korean Association of New York was established in 1960 and
purchased an office building on 23rd Street between Sixth and Seventh
Avenues in Manhattan, which it still uses. According to Korean old-timers,
most Korean grocery stores, restaurants, and churches were located in
Manhattan in the early 1960s. Today, however, Queens—especially
Flushing—is the epicenter.

The Korean community in the United States is largely the by-product
of liberalized immigration laws. As shown in table 2.1, with the enforcement
of the 1965 Immigration Act, the annual number of Korean immigrants to
the United States gradually increased. The acceleration began in 1974 as
the number jumped to 28,000. Between 1976 and 1990, more than 30,000

Table 2.1   **Korean Immigrants and Settlement Intentions, 1965 to 2004**

Period	Immigrants	Percentage Intending to Live in	
		New York	New Jersey
1965 to 1969	17,869	—	—
1970 to 1974	92,745	12	4
1975 to 1979	148,645	9	3
1980 to 1984	162,178	10	4
1985 to 1989	175,803	11	4
1990 to 1994	112,215	14	6
1995 to 1999	75,579	12	8
2000 to 2004	89,871	9	7

Source: Immigration and Naturalization Service (1965–1978; 1979–2002).
Note: The fiscal year of 1976 includes immigrants admitted for fifteen months between July 1995 and September 1976 as INS changed the fiscal year from July through June to October through September.

Koreans entered the United States each year. Strong Korean-U.S. military, political, and economic linkages, which began during the Korean War (1950 to 1953), contributed to the increase in Korean immigrants to the United States. Although the Korean War ended in 1953, the military and political tensions between North and South Korea along the demilitarized zone continued until 2000, with approximately 40,000 American servicemen stationed in South Korea. Their presence led to the migration of many Korean women to the United States—about 6,000 per year in the late 1970s and early 1980s—through intermarriage. Most, after they had become naturalized citizens, brought their parents and siblings to the United States for permanent residence.[2] The annual total of Korean immigrants during the given period also includes many orphans adopted by American citizens— at the rate of about 3,000 per year.[3] In addition, the overpopulation in large cities in South Korea[4] and the oversupply of college graduates[5] were two major internal factors that pushed many Koreans to choose emigration to the United States.

After the peak year of 1987, Korean immigration began to gradually decline. The annual number went down below 20,000 in 1992 and held that low level until 2000. A number of positive changes in South Korea— a great increase in the standard of living, the replacement of military dictatorship by a civilian government in 1987, and a much lower probability of another civil war—have contributed to the drastic reduction in emigration. Wide publicity in Korea of Korean immigrants' difficulty in economic adjustment in the United States, especially after the 1992 Los Angeles riots, also discouraged Koreans from choosing emigration to the United States. About 2,300 Korean-owned stores in South Central Los Angeles were destroyed during the Los Angeles riots in April 1992.[6]

Many in Korea donated money to help the Korean victims of the riots. Given this, it is not surprising that 1992 was the turning point. In fact, many Korean immigrants returned to Korea in the years following the riots.

Because there were so few Korean immigrants in the New York-New Jersey area in the early 1960s, the vast majority being concentrated on the West Coast, not many Koreans were able to immigrate to the area as beneficiaries of family reunification. One of the major reasons the New York-New Jersey area attracted so many Korean immigrants immediately after the enforcement of the new immigration law was that the area had an expanding medical industry that needed many foreign medical professionals.[7] Far more Indian and Filipino medical professionals immigrated to the area than Koreans did,[8] but medical professionals and their family members still comprised a significant proportion of the Korean immigrants in the late 1960s and early 1970s. Illsoo Kim estimated that about 13,000 Korean medical professionals—physicians, nurses, pharmacists, and dentists—immigrated to the United States between 1965 and 1977, about 30 percent settling in the East Coast tri-state area.[9]

The Koreans who originally entered the United States as international students and changed their status to permanent residents comprised another important group in the New York-New Jersey area in the 1960s and 1970s. Many Korean graduate students came to this area to study at major colleges and universities in both New York and other areas on the East Coast. Some became professionals and managers in New York City after completing their master's or PhD programs. Those who did not complete their education or who completed it but could not find occupations commensurate with their education came to the city to start their own businesses. Others came to the area for professional or managerial positions after completing their education in other states. For example, Chin Ok Lee, one of my close friends, came to New York City in 1975 to start his career as an assistant professor at Cornell Medical College in Manhattan, after he had completed a PhD program in physiology at Indiana University and a postdoctoral fellowship at the University of Chicago.

The 1976 amendments to the 1965 Immigration Act that aimed to reduce the number of professional immigrants led to a dramatic decline in the number of Korean medical professionals.[10] Despite the reduction, the number of Korean immigrants continued to increase after 1975, mainly because those already admitted gradually became naturalized citizens and thus able to invite family members, including brothers and sisters, for permanent residence.

Beginning in 2001, the annual number of Korean immigrants substantially increased, an anomalously low number in 2003 aside, attributable mainly to the impact of the financial crisis that hit Korea in 1998. More than a million Koreans lost their jobs. Some consequently came to the United States as visitors and found temporary employment in Korean-owned stores. These undocumented residents have since changed their legal status to permanent residents. Under the impact of the financial crisis, an unusually high proportion of college graduates in Korea were unable to find meaningful occupations, which pushed many of them to come to the United States for a graduate education. Annual statistics on international students enrolled in higher educational institutions in the United States show that the number of Korean international students increased from about 41,000 in 1999 to about 59,000 in 2005.[11] Korea was the third largest source country of international students for higher education in the United States next to India and China, in the 2006–2007 academic year. Many Korean high school students, more than 10,000 per year, have also come to the United States for study, but their number is not included in the statistics on international students. If students enrolled in high schools are included, South Korea may be the largest source country of international students in American schools. Because a substantial proportion of these students are expected to change their status to permanent residents, the annual number of Korean immigrants is unlikely to remain below 20,000 in the near future.

The proportion of Korean immigrants settling in New York State ranged from 10 percent to 15 percent in the first half of the 1970s, but was reduced to 8 to 11 percent beginning in 1974. This reduction seems to be due to the 1976 revision of the immigration law that made it difficult for professionals to immigrate to the United States. The proportion increased after the Immigration Act of 1990 expanded professional immigration. Given that the New York area with its many prestigious colleges and universities has been a major hub for international students, the act has contributed significantly to fluctuations in the numbers of Korean immigrants in New York. The state is the second largest destination state for Korean immigrants after California.

A noteworthy trend in destinations over the years is that the proportion choosing New Jersey has gradually increased. In earlier years, only 3 to 4 percent of Korean immigrants settled in New Jersey each year, but beginning in 1989 approximately 5 to 11 percent did so. In the twenty-first century, Korean immigrants settled in New York and New Jersey in almost equal numbers. As the share in New Jersey has increased, the proportion in New York has declined. New Jersey as a destination state for Korean immigrants had ranked fifth but since the late 1990s has ranked third, overtaking Illinois and Texas, but still trailing California and New York.[12]

Two factors in particular have contributed to the increasing popularity of New Jersey to Korean immigrants. The most important is the establishment of two suburban Korean enclaves in Bergen County across the George Washington Bridge from New York City. Many Korean immigrants who had originally settled in Korean enclaves in Queens, attracted by good public schools and lower housing costs, re-migrated to several neighborhoods in Bergen County. They have created suburban Korean enclaves in

Table 2.2   Growth of Korean Populations, 1970 to 2005

Year	United States (A)	The New York– New Jersey CMSA (B)	B as Percentage of A
1970	69,130	—	—
1980	354,593	28,532 (SMSA)	8
1990	798,849	118,096	15
2000	1,076,872[a]	170,509[a]	16
	1,228,427[b]	172,404[b]	14
2005	1,262,387[a]	195,797[a]	16
	1,376,040[b]	201,066[b]	15

Sources: U.S. Census Bureau 1972; 1983, 125, 208; 1993, 31, 472; 2002, table 4.
[a] Number identifying as Korean alone.
[b] Number multiracial Korean.

Fort Lee and the Palisades Park, which have attracted more immigrants from Korea and New York City since the mid-1980s.[13] The other significant factor in the choice of New Jersey as a destination state is that many branches of Korean firms originally located in Manhattan moved to Bergen County. Most Koreans who work for Korean firms and Korean government agencies (in Manhattan), including the Korean Consulate, live in New Jersey. A large proportion have changed their status to permanent residents and invited their relatives.

As a result of the influx of Korean immigrants, the Korean population has witnessed a phenomenal growth since 1970. As shown in table 2.2, even if multiracial Koreans are excluded, the Korean American population increased from less than 70,000 in 1970 to 1.1 million in 2000, a 1,500 percent growth rate, and then reached about 1.3 million in 2005. Korean Americans, though, lead only Japanese Americans in population. They trail the other four major Asian groups—Chinese, Filipino, Asian Indian, and Vietnamese. This is primarily due to the fact that the immigration flow from Korea has moderated since the early 1990 but held steady or increased from China, India, the Philippines, and Vietnam.[14] The Korean American population is thus likely to comprise a smaller and smaller fraction of the Asian American population in the future.

As of 2005, approximately 200,000 single-race Korean Americans lived in the New York–Northern New Jersey–Long Island Consolidated Metropolitan Statistical Area. They account for 16 percent of the Korean population in the United States. The New York–New Jersey area is the second largest Korean population center next to southern California (the Los Angeles–Riverside–Orange County area), which is home to 24 percent of the population. The share of the Korean population in this area, relative to other areas, has grown over the past two decades, due mainly to the shift to New Jersey, especially to Bergen County. In the New York–New Jersey area, Korean Americans are the third largest Asian ethnic group next to Chinese and Asian Indians. Chinese and Asian Indians outnumber Koreans by large margins, 3.5 and 2.5 times, respectively. In New York the Filipino and Korean populations are comparable, but many New Yorkers believe the Korean population is much larger than the Filipino and even larger than the Indian. This image seems to have been created by the visibility of Korean-owned stores scattered across the New York–New Jersey area and by the prevalence of Korean churches with Korean-language signs.

Settlement Patterns and Enclaves in New York

Korean immigrants in New York, as well as in other cities, are less residentially concentrated and less enclave-oriented than their Chinese counterparts. They are more residentially concentrated, however, and have established more active immigrant enclaves and visible business districts than Asian Indian and Filipino immigrants.

Table 2.3 shows the distribution of Korean Americans in the New York–New Jersey metropolitan area, New York central city, and five boroughs based on the 2000 census (single race). About half of the Korean population in the New York–New Jersey–Long Island CMSA is in the New York central city, but only 38 percent of the total population is. White Americans, the majority of the population in the metropolitan area, are more widely dispersed in suburban counties than Korean Americans. Asian Americans as a whole show a higher level of concentration in the central city. In particular, Chinese Americans in the New York–New Jersey area, who make up about 40 percent of Asian Americans, are highly concentrated in the New York central city (72 percent). This is due to their greater tendency to concentrate in Chinese enclaves. Major suburban areas where large

Table 2.3   Distribution of Korean Population in 2000

	NY-NJ-CT CMSA (A)	New York City (B)	B as Percentage of A	Percentage Distribution of (B) in Five Boroughs				
				Q	M	BK	BR	SI
Total Population	21,199,865	8,008,278	38	28	19	31	17	6
Asian Americans	1,435,889	774,163	54	50	18	24	5	3
Koreans	170,509	86,473	51	72	13	7	4	4

Source: U.S. Census Bureau (2002).
Q = Queens; M = Manhattan; BK = Brooklyn; BR = Bronx; SI = Staten Island

numbers of Korean Americans are concentrated are two Long Island counties (Suffolk and Nassau), Bergen County in New Jersey, and two upstate New York counties (Westchester and Rockland).

Looking at the distribution of Koreans in New York City's five boroughs, 72 percent are concentrated in Queens, versus only 28 percent of the total population. Queens has many multiethnic neighborhoods thanks to the influx of Asian, Latino, and Caribbean immigrants over the last two decades.[15] Asian Americans as a whole are overrepresented in Queens, with about half of them settled there in 2000, accounting for 18 percent of the population in the borough. Although South Asian, Filipino, and Chinese immigrants are highly represented in many multiethnic neighborhoods in Queens, such as Elmhurst, Astoria, Jackson Heights, Woodside, Forest Hills and Rego Park, Koreans are substantially less so.

Instead, Korean immigrants have a greater tendency to cluster in heavily white middle class neighborhoods, such as Bayside, Little Neck, Oakland Gardens, and Douglaston in Queens Community District 11. In 2000, Asian Americans made up 27 percent of the population in this district and white residents 60 percent. The vast majority of Asian Americans settled in the district (85 percent) are Chinese (14,619) and Korean Americans (11,539). Korean and other Asian immigrants prefer District 11 partly because it is within the best school district (School District 26) in the city. According to my housing survey, Korean immigrants in this area encountered prejudice and harassment by white neighbors in the 1980s.[16] Now, however, Korean and other Asian residents feel comfortable living there because there are so many Asian immigrant families.

Chinese immigrants are also highly represented in these neighborhoods. I live in Bayside and my house is located between two Chinese-occupied houses and across from another. Not only in these more suburban middle class neighborhoods, but also in others in Queens, such as Flushing and Woodside, Chinese and Korean immigrants share neighborhoods. Some readers may believe that many Chinese and Korean immigrants share these neighborhoods mainly because of their middle class backgrounds. This, though, cannot completely explain the tendency of the Chinese and Korean immigrants to cluster in the same neighborhoods. Asian Indian immigrants as a group have even higher socioeconomic status than Chinese or Korean immigrants do, but relatively few are settled in Queens District 11.[17] They have established their own enclaves in other areas.[18] I believe mainly because of their cultural and physical similarities, Chinese and Korean immigrants tend to like each other, which is reflected in their selection of neighborhoods, friendship, dating, and intermarriage patterns.[19]

Korean immigrants in Queens are most highly concentrated in Flushing, a neighborhood encompassing two zip codes. As shown in table 2.4, about 20,000 Korean Americans, accounting for about 23 percent of all Korean Americans in New York City, resided in the Flushing neighborhood in

Table 2.4   Racial and Ethnic Composition in Flushing, 2000

	Number	Percentage
Total population	137,610	100.0
Non-Hispanic white	31,231	22.7
Hispanic	27,016	19.6
Black	6,043	4.4
Others[a]	5,068	3.7
Asian American	68,252	49.6
Chinese	33,641	24.4
Korean	19,627	14.6
Indian	9,402	6.8
Foreign-born	86,911	63.1

Source: Author's compilation from U.S. Census Bureau (2002).
[a] Others indicate Native Americans, Pacific Islanders, or people of mixed origin.

2000, where they accounted for 15 percent of the population. There are also, however, more Chinese and many Indian Americans in Flushing. Chinese Americans, numbering 34,000 in 2000, are the largest Asian group there, but account for only 9 percent of Chinese Americans in New York City. Flushing is the only neighborhood outside of the West Coast where Asian Americans are the majority of the population. White residents make up only about 20 percent.

Before Asian immigrants began to settle in the neighborhood in the 1960s, Flushing was nearly all white. In 1970, white Americans were by far the majority (96 percent) of the population in Community District 7, which encompasses Flushing, Whitestone, and College Point, and nonwhite, non-black residents made up less than 3 percent.[20] White residents in Flushing before 1970 were largely middle class people with heavily Italian, Jewish, and German ancestries. The development of many Long Island suburban neighborhoods since the 1960s and the New York City's financial crisis in the early 1970s led to the exodus of middle class whites from Flushing to Long Island. A long-time white resident in Flushing told me that many office buildings in downtown Flushing were empty in the early 1970s when Chinese, Korean, and Indian immigrants began to move there in large numbers.

New York City's Korean immigrants have created their largest enclave in Flushing, the center of the Korean community in New York City. Chinese immigrants have established the second largest Chinatown there, next to Chinatown in Lower East Side, Manhattan.[21] Both have established their business districts, or ethnic precincts, in downtown Flushing, using distinctive native-language commercial signs. The intersection of Roosevelt Avenue and Union Street is the core of the Korean business district that

Koreans commonly refer to as hanin sanga. Numerous Korean businesses with Korean-language signs are dotted along Union Street between 32th Avenue and 41st Avenue. Korean immigrants cannot expand their businesses west of Union Street because the next block, Main Street, is the heart of the business district of Flushing's Chinatown. Blocked from moving westward, Koreans have expanded their ethnic businesses eastward two and a half miles (about eighty blocks) along Northern Boulevard up to 220th Street toward Bayside. This expansion reflects the residential concentration of Korean immigrants about two miles on either side of Northern Boulevard between the two neighborhoods.

In late March 2005, I, along with Young Oak, counted Korean businesses in the Korean business district in Flushing, basing our counts on Korean commercial signs. We counted 405 in the heart of the Korean business district along Union Street and on avenues one or two blocks west and east of Union Street. All served primarily Korean customers with distinctive Korean cultural products. Considered the capital of the Korean community in New York City, the Korean business district in Flushing and the adjacent area house a number of offices of Korean cultural and social organizations. These include the Council of Korean Churches of Greater New York, (Korean) YWCA, the Korean American Family Service Center, Korean Youth Center, and a few Korean elderly centers. I counted another 240 Korean businesses along Northern Boulevard, covering about thirty blocks between Farrington Street and 165th Street. Korean-owned stores on Northern Boulevard stretch further eastward fifty-five more blocks to 220th Street in Bayside. On Northern Boulevard between 166th Street and 220th Street were another 220 Korean stores. The total number of Korean ethnic businesses geared to Koreans in the larger Flushing-Bayside Korean business district is 865. Korean businesses located in the Flushing-Bayside Korean enclave include restaurants, grocery stores, drinking places, beauty salons and barber shops, and many semi-professional and professional businesses. With Korean-language commercial signs, they serve mainly Korean customers (see table 3.5).

The proportion of New York City's Koreans in Manhattan increased from 9 percent in 1990 to 13 percent in 2000. The increase in Manhattan relative to other boroughs seems to be attributable to two factors: the increases in the number of young 1.5- and second-generation Koreans who work for various finance companies and in the number of international students enrolled in various colleges and universities. Most of these commute from neighborhoods in western Queens, such as Astoria, Woodside and Flushing, to avoid high rents in Manhattan. Many others, however, reside in Manhattan, paying higher rents there, to reduce their commuting time.

Another area of the city in which many Korean businesses with Korean-language signs and many Koreans are visible is Broadway. This is a rectangular eleven-block area in Manhattan from 24th Street to 35th Street between Sixth and Fifth Avenues. The intersection of 32nd Street and Broadway is considered its heart. In October 1995, the city named the district Koreatown and posted official signs (Korean Way) at the intersection. Approximately 400 Korean import and wholesale companies with Korean-language commercial signs were in this area in 1992.[22] The Korean-owned wholesale companies in the area have distributed wigs, handbags, clothing, toys, and other manufactured goods imported from South Korea and other Asian countries to Korean and other retailers in New York and other areas of the Northeast. When I conducted research in 2005, however, I found the number of Korean-owned wholesale stores in the Broadway Korean business district, which had numbered 400 in 1992, reduced to about 250. Intense competition with Chinese and Indian-owned wholesale stores, and rent hikes caused by urban renovations, forced some Korean stores in the area to close and others to move to New Jersey (see chapter 3).

Also in the Broadway district are many Korean professional and semi-professional businesses, such as accounting firms, travel agencies, and real estate agencies, which serve primarily the Korean importers and wholesalers there. There are also about forty Korean restaurants, several Korean nightclubs, two bakeries, a few bookstores, and other businesses in the Broadway area that cater to Korean ethnic tastes (see chapter 3). Although restaurants in Flushing serve exclusively Korean immigrant customers, those in Manhattan's Broadway area cater to young Koreans, 1.5- and second-generation Koreans and international students, as well as non-Korean customers. Some of these restaurants are popular among white and other Asian American customers. If you pass the heart of the Broadway Korean Business District between Broadway and 5th Avenue on 32nd Street, you will find long lines of customers, mostly young Korean and non-Korean, waiting in line outside restaurants. By serving more non-Korean customers, Korean restaurants in Manhattan have made a major contribution to publicizing Korean cuisines to New Yorkers. A Korean-owned hotel (the Stanford) located in the heart of the Broadway Korean business district accommodates many tourists from Korea. Various Korean tourist agencies start their buses from the Broadway Korean business district and pick up more Korean tourists in Flushing.

A few other places in Manhattan publicize the presence of Korean Americans and Korean culture in New York City. The Korean Association of New York, an umbrella organization, is located on 26th Street between Broadway and 6th Avenue. It holds many Korean ethnic meetings and observes Korean cultural and national holidays. In collaboration with the *Korea Times New York*, it has also organized the annual Korean parade and the Korean cultural festival in the Broadway Korean business district in October. The Korean Consulate is located in midtown between 57th Street and Park Avenue. The Korean Cultural Service within the Korean Consulate provides Korean art and calligraphy exhibitions and dance and music performances regularly. It also shows Korean movies once a month. Korean Buddhist leaders annually organize the Buddhist parade in May to celebrate the birth of Buddha. Although the Buddhist parade is presented as a multiethnic Buddhist festival, Korean Buddhists have played the leading role in organizing it. Finally, Lincoln Center and Carnegie Hall provide Korean classical and contemporary music and dance performances at regular intervals, at the rate of once every two weeks, attracting not only the Korean American but also the non-Korean audience.

Korean immigrants in New Jersey are highly concentrated in Bergen County, population 36,075 in 2000. In 2000, Korean Americans accounted for 36 percent (N = 6,065) of the population in Palisades Park and 31 percent (N = 5,978) in Fort Lee (Oh 2007, 85). Koreans in both neighborhoods have established two suburban enclaves. In January 2000, I counted 130 Korean stores that cater exclusively to Korean customers in the Fort Lee downtown area and another 120 in Palisades Park.[23] In addition, there are many Korean residents in three other municipalities in Bergen County—Cliffside Park, Ridgefield, and Leonia. In September 2004, the New Jersey Korean Community Center was established in Englewood. Transformed from a Korean senior center established in 2000, it provides various social services, and a number of cultural, educational and health programs, for Koreans, young and old. The classes include yoga, Tai Chi, Korean dancing, computing, knitting, drawing, and American history.

Edison is a medium-sized neighborhood in Middlesex County with a population of approximately 97,687 in 2000,[24] the majority of whom are white and about 23 percent Asian Indian. Although only a small number of Korean Americans live there, Joon Choi, a thirty-three-year-old second-generation Korean, was elected mayor of the municipality in 2005. This was possible mainly because Korean immigrants have been very active in politics in Bergen County. The Korean American Voters' Council, established in 1996 and the major Korean-American empowerment organization in the New York–New Jersey area, has its office in Fort Lee and has maintained close relations with Democratic Party political leaders in Bergen County and its adjacent counties. The strong linkages between the Korean American Voters' Council and Democratic Party leaders was the key to the nomination of Joon Choi as the Democratic Party's Edison municipality mayoral candidate. Because Edison is a predominantly Democratic area, Choi's nomination as the party's candidate almost guaranteed his victory in the main election. Two other Korean Americans have been elected as city council members in Bergen County, one representing Fort Lee and the other representing Palisades Park. The residential concentration of Korean immigrants in a few municipalities in Bergen County, their strong community organization, and small sizes of electoral districts in suburban municipalities have contributed to Korean Americans' success in electoral politics in New Jersey.

Cultural, Religious, and Socioeconomic Characteristics

In his work examining the adaptation of Cambodian and Hmong refugees in four American cities, Jeremy Hein criticizes immigrant scholars for having not paid enough attention to the history, politics, and culture of the homeland as significant contributing factors.[25] To highlight the significance of the variables related to the country of origin, he chose *Ethnic Origins* as the title of his book. I agree that the history, political situations, and culture of the home country have a significant influence on the adaptation of any immigrant group and that therefore immigrant scholars should include them as important analytic variables. Here I provide an overview of Korean immigrants' cultural, religious and historical backgrounds, and socioeconomic characteristics. This information is helpful in understanding Korean immigrants' reactive solidarity to business-related intergroup conflicts. They are also interesting in themselves.

Group Homogeneity and Confucian Traditions

Korean immigrants are highly homogeneous in their cultural and historical experiences, maybe more so than any other Asian group, with the exception of the Japanese. This homogeneity and lack of diversity are the basis of ethnic identity and group solidarity. Language is probably the most significant element of ethnicity, and Korean immigrants have only one language. This gives them a big advantage over multilingual Asian immigrant groups, such as Indians and Filipinos, in maintaining their ethnic ties. For example, because all Korean immigrants can speak, read, and write the Korean language fluently, they depend primarily on Korean-language dailies and television and radio programs for news, information, and leisure activities. Their almost exclusive dependence on ethnic media has strengthened their ties to the ethnic community and the home country, though it has hindered their integration to the larger society and their interactions with other groups.

Confucianism, which originated in China, was introduced to Korea in the fourth century. It began to have a powerful cultural influence in Korea during the Chosun Dynasty (1392 to 1910) when the government adopted it as a social, political, and economic philosophy. To establish and maintain order in the family, Confucius envisioned a hierarchical organization of family that emphasized children's loyalty, respect and devotion to their parents, and the wife's subordination to her husband. The phrase *filial piety* symbolizes this emphasis. The eldest son was supposed to live with his parents after marriage, providing them with financial support and health care. Further, filial piety was extended after the death of a parent as ancestor worship. Although urbanization, industrialization, and Westernization have led to great changes in family system in South Korea, the impact of Confucian ideology on family relations is still clearly felt. Korean families are more authoritarian in child socialization techniques, more patriarchal in marital relations, and more kin-oriented than American families, though there is a greater diversity in family life for younger generation Koreans. Significantly, most Koreans, including Christians, still practice ancestor worship rituals, albeit in a simplified form.

Another important component of Confucian ideology is its emphasis on children's education as the main channel for social mobility. Parents in South Korea make enormous sacrifices for children's education. To help their children get into prestigious universities, they spend a lot of money, time, and energy in their children's after-school programs. Many upper middle class parents now send their children to the United States and other English-speaking countries for formal education before college. Even well-educated women often sacrifice their careers to devote full time and energy to their children's education, and their achievements are evaluated mainly in terms of how well their children do in schools. Korean immigrants have transplanted the zeal for their children's education to this country. There are numerous after-school programs specializing in math, English, and other extracurricular studies in Flushing and other Korean enclaves in New York. The majority of Korean high school students have participated in one or more after-school programs at one time or another.[26]

Religion

Buddhism, Protestantism, and Roman Catholicism are three major religions in Korea, all transplanted from other countries. Missionaries from China and Central Asia brought Buddhism at the end of the fourth century, the progressive-minded Koreans who were critical of Confucianism adopted Roman Catholicism spontaneously in the 1760s, and American missionaries imported Protestantism in the 1880s. But none gained popularity among common people until the 1960s. In 1962, Buddhists made up only 2.6 percent of the population in Korea, Protestants 2.8 percent, and Catholics 2.2 percent.[27] This does not mean that Koreans were not religious before the 1960s. For centuries, they had practiced one of the two more traditional forms or a combination. One is ancestor worship related to Confucianism. The other is shamanism. Ancestor worship rituals are based on the belief in the existence of the soul after death, whereas shamanism, the oldest belief system in Korea and a folk religion, involves rituals performed for good luck for their jobs, good health, and family prosperity.

As South Korea rapidly urbanized, industrialized, and modernized from the early 1960s onward, its people have gradually adopted the three organized religions by incorporating the two traditional religious forms into each of them. The proportion of Buddhists increased from 2.6 percent

Table 2.5   Self-Reported Religions in Korea and New York, 2005

	In Korea		In New York (Now)	
	Number	Percentage	Number	Percentage
Protestantism	133	48.0	162	58.5
Catholicism	35	12.6	39	14.1
Buddhism	36	13.0	22	7.9
Other	1	0.4	2	0.7
None	72	26.0	52	18.8
Total	277	100.0	277	100.0

Source: Author's compilation.

in 1962 to 20 percent in 1985, to 28 percent in 1991 and then slightly decreased to 25 percent in 2003. Protestants and Catholics also each made up increasingly higher proportions of the population, from 2.8 percent and 2.2 percent in 1962 to 16 percent and 5 percent in 1985, to 19 percent and 6 percent in 1991, and to 20 percent and 7 percent in 2003. We may refer to this increase as a modernization of religion that followed the modernization of society. Because all three imported religions have incorporated elements of Confucianism and Shamanism and given that Confucianism constitutes the core of Korean culture, it is easy to change religions in Korea. In many cases, the same family practices two religions. For example, parents are often Buddhists and their children are Christians.

Table 2.5 shows the religious distribution among Korean immigrants in New York City's five boroughs at the time of the interview and in Korea before immigration based on results of my 2005 survey. Forty-eight percent and 13 percent of the respondents respectively chose Protestantism and Catholicism as their religion in Korea, and another 13 percent chose Buddhism. The findings indicate that among Korean immigrants in New York City, Christians predominate and Buddhists are underrepresented relative to the population in Korea. This is largely attributable to two factors. First, Christians—both Protestants and Catholics—are overrepresented in large cities and among the middle class in Korea, and immigrants have been drawn more from the urban middle class. Second, regardless of whether they are urban or rural, proportionally more Christians have chosen U.S.-bound immigration because the United States is known as a typical Christian country. Buddhists are underrepresented among Korean immigrants partly because they are underrepresented in the segments of the population prone to U.S. immigration and partly because they may be unwilling to emigrate to a predominantly Christian country.

The right panel of table 2.5 shows that the proportion of Protestants among Korean immigrants has increased from 48 percent in Korea to almost 60 percent in New York City, and the proportion of Buddhists has

Table 2.6   Comparative Educational Attainment of Adult Immigrants in New York–New Jersey, 2000

	High School	Four Year College	Advanced Degree
Korean immigrants	90.9%	49.9%	15.6%
Koreans in Korea	63.7	24.3	—
U.S.-born white	94.0	43.3	18.0
U.S.-born black	77.8	21.1	5.7
All immigrants	69.5	22.6	11.0
Chinese immigrants	60.5	31.3	17.1
Indian immigrants	87.9	65.4	32.8
Filipino immigrants	96.2	68.7	12.5
Taiwanese immigrants	92.2	67.1	37.6

Source: Author's compilation from 5% Public Use Microdata Sample (PUMS) of the 2000 U.S. Census for adults twenty-five to sixty-four years old.

decreased from 13 percent to 8 percent. This suggests that many Koreans have changed their religious affiliation since immigration to Protestantism. Korean Protestant churches have been able to absorb many Buddhist or atheist Korean immigrants partly because they provide all kinds of services, friendship networks, and ethnic education useful for Korean immigrants' successful adjustment to American society. Korean churches, in New York and other cities, serve a number of social functions for Korean immigrants— providing social services, preserving cultural traditions, maintaining ethnic networks, and providing social positions.[28] It is difficult for most Korean immigrants to live comfortably here without being affiliated with a Korean church.

Both Protestant and Catholic churches provide similar services and fellowship for all church members, but Protestant churches have absorbed the vast majority of Korean religious converts mainly because they have aggressively recruited them. They have done so partly for survival and partly because of their more evangelical orientation. Because there are so many Korean pastors in the United States, there are too many Korean churches for the population. In 2006, there were nearly 600 Korean Protestant churches in the New York–New Jersey Korean community in a population of approximately 200,000. For a church to survive, it must aggressively recruit members by creating numerous programs. By contrast, Korean Catholic churches in New York, about twenty-five, are established only by the local diocese. The vast majority of Korean immigrant Protestant churches emphasize evangelism as a central component of Christian life.[29]

Education

Table 2.6 shows the educational attainment of Korean immigrants in the New York–New Jersey area, compared with other groups, based on the 2000 census. In both high school and college graduate rates, immigrants have a much higher educational level than the general population in Korea. About half aged twenty-five to sixty four completed a college education, compared to only 24 percent of their counterparts in Korea. Because the Korean data include everyone age twenty-five and older, they slightly underestimate the educational level of the Korean population. Nevertheless, data in table 2.6 indicate that Korean immigrants were self-selected from the middle and upper middle class segments of the population in Korea. South Korea has seen a radical improvement in people's educational level over the past three decades. College graduation rates in 1965, 1975, and 1985 respectively were 3.2 percent, 5.8 percent, and 10.2 percent.[30] Thus, Korean immigrants who came to the United States in the earlier years were drawn from an even smaller group of highly educated people.

Korean immigrants have a slightly more education than the white population in New York and much more than all other immigrants. They do not, however, fare well compared to other Asian immigrant groups. It is not surprising that they are better educated than immigrants from mainland China, who include a large number of undocumented residents.[31] However, they are far behind Taiwanese, Indians, and Filipinos in college graduation rate. This is attributable partly to the fact that highly educated Indians and Filipinos have continued to immigrate to the United States in response to low standards of living in their home countries, and also partly to the fact, as mentioned earlier, that the significant improvements in the standard of living and quality of life in South Korea have moderated the outmigration of highly educated Koreans. It is also important to note that among Filipino immigrants, more highly educated professionals, especially medical professionals, have chosen to settle in the New York–New Jersey area.

═ Chapter 3 ═

Concentration in Retail and Service Businesses

ere I outline background information about Korean businesses in
New York, specifically, the high self-employment among immigrants, changes over time in that rate, the clustering of Korean
businesses in particular industrial categories, and those changes over time.
Both changes in self-employment and categories of industries are tied to
the theme of this book, the radical reductions in business-related intergroup conflicts and ethnic solidarity. The final section examines the effect
of concentration in the ethnic economy on ethnic attachment.

High Self-Employment Rate

Large Korean populations are settled in China, Japan, and the former Soviet
Union republics (especially Uzbekistan and Kazakhstan). None of these
groups, however, is active in entrepreneurship. Only post-1965 Korean
immigrants in the United States and Canada have shown a greater tendency
to start their own businesses.[1] Korean immigrants in New York, like those
in other cities, show a high self-employment rate in small businesses.

The New York–New Jersey area is the only metropolitan area that has
received large numbers of immigrants for all four major racial groups—
whites, Latinos, Caribbean blacks, and Asians—in the post-1965 era.[2]
Moreover, the city has several Asian immigrant populations, including
Chinese, Indians, and Filipinos. Thus we can effectively assess the self-
employment rate of New York's Korean immigrants by comparing Koreans
with other major immigrant groups, including other Asian groups, and
native-born whites. Table 3.1 shows the numbers of full-time workers
(those who worked for thirty-five or more hours per week and thirty-five or
more weeks in 1999) and their self-employment rates for twenty major
immigrant groups and non-Hispanic whites in the New York–New Jersey
metropolitan area (CMSA) based on Public Use Microdata Samples (PUMS)
of the 2000 census.

Table 3.1   Self-Employment Rates Among Immigrant Groups in New York–New Jersey Metropolitan Area in 1999

Major Immigrant Groups	Number of Workers[a] (Weighted)	Self-Employment Rate
Greek	21,864	27.0
Israeli and Palestinian	15,919	26.6
Korean	56,251	24.0
Italian	69,486	17.6
Pakistani	21,925	16.0
Russian	89,964	11.4
Non-Hispanic white	3,652,139	11.0
Taiwanese	22,877	11.0
Japanese	17,341	10.7
Cuban	35,017	10.0
Indian	109,751	9.9
Colombian	76,862	9.4
Chinese (mainland)	105,987	9.0
Dominican	169,179	8.2
Ecuadorian	81,335	7.2
Mexican	72,596	6.7
Jamaican	121,006	4.9
Haitian	72,969	4.7
Guyanese	74,368	4.6
Filipino	73,839	4.6

Source: Author's compilation from U.S. Census (2002).
[a] Immigrants twenty-five to sixty-four years old who worked thirty-five or more weeks and thirty-five or more hours per week in 1999.

Korean immigrants had the third highest self-employment rate with 24 percent in 2000 among major immigrant groups in New York, next to Greeks (27 percent) and Israelis-Palestinians (27 percent). The Korean work force, however, is much larger than that of either group. Thus, in sheer numbers, Korean businesses in New York are much more visible than Greek- or Israeli-Palestinian-owned businesses. The only immigrant group in the area with a comparable population and a higher self-employment rate than native-born whites is the Italian (18 percent). Korean immigrants are highly concentrated in several lines of retail and personal service business. Pakistanis are another Asian immigrant group with a higher self-employment rate than the native-born white population. Filipino immigrants, along with Guyanese, have the lowest rates.

I discuss changes in self-employment rate among Korean immigrants in New York City over time and sex differences based on data presented in table 3.2. Nationally, the self-employment of Korean immigrants increased significantly from 18 percent in 1980 to 27 percent in 1990, but slightly

Table 3.2   Changing Self-Employment Rates Among Korean Immigrant Full-Time Workers[a]

	Total	Men	Women
1980	27.3%	34.5%	15.0%
1990	30.5	33.6	25.6
2000	24.0	28.1	18.8

Source: Author's compilation from 5% Public Use Microdata Sample (PUMS) of the 1980, 1990 & 2000 U.S. Censuses.
[a] Immigrants twenty-five to sixty-four years old who worked thirty-five or more weeks and thirty-five or more hours per week in the previous years (1979, 1989, 1999).

dropped to 23 percent in 2000.[3] Surprisingly, though, the self-employment of Korean immigrants in New York in 1980 was significantly higher (27 percent) than in the United States as a whole (18 percent). It is only slightly lower than that in New York in 1990 (31 percent) and higher than even that in 2000 (24 percent). These figures partly indicate that Korean immigrants settled in New York in the late 1960s and 1970s were prepared to start their own businesses sooner than those settled in other areas. As pointed out in chapter 2, large numbers of Korean medical professionals, and Korean international students, moved to the area in the late 1960s and the 1970s. Both groups are more likely to have made their occupational adjustments in self-employment than in employment.

Nationally, the self-employment rate of Korean immigrants dropped slightly from 27 percent in 1990 to 23 percent in 2000.[4] The reduction in New York City during the same decade was greater (from 31 percent to 24 percent) than for the Korean population as a whole. I suggest that a big increase in the numbers of Korean nonimmigrant residents, such as international students, temporary workers, and visitors,[5] was the main cause of the decrease, because the nonresident populations are less likely to be self-employed.[6] The decline between 1990 and 2000 was more dramatic in New York City than in the United States as a whole because a larger proportion of Koreans in the city were these nonimmigrants. Moreover, even among Korean documented residents in New York City, there was a slight shift from self-employment to employment in Korean-owned stores. As will be discussed later in this chapter and in chapter 5, emergence of mega-stores and hikes in commercial rents forced many Korean retail stores in black and Latino neighborhoods to close beginning in the late 1990s. Those medium-sized Korean retail stores that have survived and a huge number of nail salons have offered jobs for more documented and undocumented Korean immigrants in 2000 and after.

Looking at changes over time in the gender difference in self-employment rate, there was a huge gender gap (about 20 percent) in the self-employment rate of Korean immigrants in New York in 1980 that narrowed significantly (8 percent) by 1990. Many Korean women nurses came to New York City as permanent residents before 1980, almost all of them employed by health care organizations. This is one of the main reasons that the self-employment rate for Korean immigrant women was much lower than for their male counterparts in 1980. The other important reason for the gender gap seems to be that many Korean immigrant women who worked for their family stores did not officially report themselves as self-employed business owners. In 1990, Korean women nurses comprised a much smaller proportion of Korean adult women in New York City, because the immigration of Korean medical professionals very nearly ended with the passage of the 1976 amendments to the Immigration and Nationality Act. Also, more Korean women had been able to start their independent businesses, especially nail salons, by 1990. These two factors explain the decline in the gender gap in self-employment rate between 1980 and 1990.

The census definition of self-employment is based on the respondents' selection of one of two categories (self-employed worker or employee of own corporation) out of seven categories regarding *class of work*. It significantly underestimates self-employment rate, especially for immigrant populations, for several reasons. First, when a person has two jobs, one through employment and the other through self-employment, he or she may not report the self-employed job.[7] Second, and more significant, the legal owner of a small business usually reports himself or herself as a self-employed worker and his or her unpaid family workers do not report themselves as self-employed or unpaid family workers. Census data thus significantly underestimated the self-employment rate of Korean immigrant women. According to the 2000 census, 28 percent of male Korean immigrant workers in the New York–New Jersey CMSA are self-employed, compared to 18 percent of their female counterparts. We all know that their rate is higher than women's, but not by 55 percent, as these census statistics suggest. When Korean immigrants have family businesses involving both partners, they more often register the businesses in the husbands' names than the other way around. Thus Korean immigrant women's self-employment rate seems to be underestimated to a greater extent than men's.

Third, census statistics on the foreign-born population significantly underestimate both male and female immigrant self-employment rates partly because the foreign-born include not only immigrants, but also the 1.5-generation, who were born in the home countries and immigrated at younger ages, accompanied by their parents. Because the 1.5-generation adults who came to the United States at the age of twelve or earlier have completed their high school and college education in the United States, they do not have a severe disadvantage for employment in the general labor market. They are thus more similar to the American-born second-generation than to the immigrant generation in their socioeconomic

Table 3.3   Occupation by Sex, 2005

	Self-Employed	Ethnic Economy	General Economy	Total
Men	56 (46%)	46 (38%)	20 (16%)	122 (100%)
Women	53 (34%)	71 (46%)	31 (20%)	155 (100%)
Total	109 (39%)	117 (42%)	51 (19%)	277 (100%)

Source: Author's compilation.

adjustment, including self-employment rate. When analyzing the self-employment rate by treating the two foreign-born groups separately, 28 percent of first-generation Korean immigrants in the New York–New Jersey area and only 7 percent of 1.5-generation Koreans are self-employed (see table 5.5). The 1.5-generation Koreans have a substantially lower self-employment rate than first-generation immigrants, partly because they have advantage over immigrants for employment in the general labor market and partly because they are much younger than immigrants. By lumping the 1.5 generation with the immigrant population, census data on the foreign born significantly underestimate the self-employment rate of Korean immigrants.

An independent survey can measure the self-employment rate of Korean immigrants more accurately. Moreover, an independent survey can also measure the concentration of Korean immigrants in the ethnic economy by asking employed workers whether they work in the general or in the ethnic economy.[8] Table 3.3 shows both the self-employment rate of Korean immigrants in the New York central city and their concentration in the Korean ethnic economy, based on results of the 2005 survey. Forty-six percent of Korean male immigrant workers and 34 percent of the female counterparts were self-employed in 2005. Thirty-nine percent of Korean immigrants as a whole were self-employed. This survey, however, underestimated the self-employment rate of the entire Korean work force in New York City because the sample included more women (56 percent of the total sample), who had a lower self-employment rate than men, although female immigrants who worked full-time made up only about 45 percent (N = 25,020) of the total Korean full-time work force (56,251). When we adjust the figure to increase the proportion of men, who had a higher self-employment rate, we estimate that about 41 percent of all Korean workers in New York City were self-employed.

The figures in the second and third columns of table 3.3 are as important for our purpose as those in the first column. We find that 42 percent of total Korean immigrant workers in New York City—38 percent of men and 46 percent of women—were employed in Korean-owned businesses. Altogether, 81 percent of total Korean workers were in the ethnic economy, with only 19 percent participating in the general economy. These figures suggest that Korean immigrants in New York City are economically highly segregated from the mainstream. Among contemporary immigrant groups, only Iranian immigrants in Los Angeles seem to have a similar concentration in the ethnic economy. Results of a 1986 survey showed that 57 percent of Iranian immigrants in Los Angeles were self-employed and that Iranian employees made up 58 percent of all employees of Iranian-owned businesses.[9]

Disadvantages in the General Labor Market

That Koreans in other countries do not concentrate in small businesses means that the high self-employment rate of Korean immigrants cannot be attributed to cultural traditions. Those with heavily middle class backgrounds turned to small businesses mainly because they could not find jobs commensurate with their educational levels because of language barriers and other disadvantages.[10]

As noted in chapter 2, approximately half of adult Korean immigrants in New York completed college, nearly two-thirds of male immigrants receiving a college degree. Koreans, however, have a more severe language barrier than other Asian immigrant groups, especially Asian Indians and Filipinos. For example, in the 2000 census (analysis of PUMS) 41 percent of foreign-born Koreans between twenty-five and sixty-four years old reported that they spoke English not well or not at all, compared to 3 percent of Filipinos, 10 percent of Asian Indians, and 17 percent of Taiwanese immigrants. When 1.5-generation Koreans are isolated from the equation, the majority of Korean immigrants have language barriers.

In the late 1960s and early 1970s, many well-educated Korean immigrants worked as janitors, gas station attendants, waiters or waitresses, seamstresses in garment factories, and truck drivers because they could not find meaningful white collar occupations. They began to launch labor-intensive small businesses, such as wig stores, grocery and produce shops, and garment factories, as alternatives to blue collar occupations. For example, Gene Kim arrived in Baltimore, Maryland, age thirty-two, with his wife, in 1974. Although he had worked as an assistant musical program director for the Korean Broadcasting Station in Korea after completing college, he could not find a meaningful job in the United States. He worked odd jobs, such as truck driving and carpentering, for three years before he established a carry-out sandwich shop. Moving to New York City in 1980, he opened a deli in Manhattan with his wife and ran it for twenty years before starting a construction business. Seung Chin Kim, who held a managerial job in a company in Korea, came to New York City with a visitor's visa in 1969 at the age of twenty-nine. He promptly enrolled in a two-year vocational school for dental assistants. To get a green card for permanent residence in the United States, he worked as a dental assistant for two years. After receiving his green card, he quit the job and opened a clothing store in a black neighborhood in Brooklyn in 1974.

The language barrier and other disadvantages in the general labor market became the main motivational factor for Korean immigrants to move into small businesses. Not everyone, however, can start a business. To establish and operate small businesses successfully, one needs start-up capital, business training, and information. Researchers have emphasized class and ethnic resources as two major contributing factors to immigrants' successfully establishing and operating businesses.[11] Korean immigrants are well represented in entrepreneurship in part because they have these advantages.

Korean immigrants have two particular class-related advantages for establishing and operating businesses in the United States. First, many were engaged in businesses or jobs related to businesses in Korea. Results of Yoon's survey study conducted in Chicago and Los Angeles reveal that approximately 25 percent of Korean immigrant merchants were owners of their own businesses before emigrating and that another significant proportion worked in management and sales.[12] Results of my survey study of Korean immigrant merchants in Atlanta also show that 23 percent of the 159 respondents engaged in various businesses in Korea and that many other respondents had managerial, sales and administrative occupations that could be helpful to business operations.[13] It is also important to note that Korean immigrants in the 1980s and after left a society that was undergoing a rapid economic development made possible by an export-oriented economic policy. Compared to Filipino or Indian immigrants, who came from far more underdeveloped countries, Korean immigrants brought with them capitalist values that proved especially useful in starting and running small businesses.[14]

Korean immigrants with heavily middle class backgrounds brought with them not only business skills and values, but also capital. Few who arrived in the United States in the 1960s and 1970s expected to start their businesses here. Few had large sums of money for business capitalization. Furthermore, the government did not allow emigrants to take any large sums out of the country. Those who arrived in the late 1980s and after, however, were better prepared to start their own businesses here because through immigrants' transnational networks prospective immigrants were well informed in Korea of self-employment in small business as the only viable option for most Korean immigrants in the United States. For example, in one pre-departure survey study, conducted in Seoul in 1986, 61 percent of all respondents and 71 percent of male respondents reported that they would go into business when they came to the United States.[15] Moreover, since 1989, in light of improved economic conditions in South Korea, the government has allowed emigrants to take larger and larger amounts of money with them when leaving the country.

Korean immigrants also have advantages for establishing and operating small businesses because of their strong family ties and ethnic networks. Most usually apply for naturalization as soon as they are eligible, after five years of residence, mainly to invite their parents and siblings. When their siblings arrive, naturalized Koreans help them not only with overall immigration orientations, but also, and more important, with their jobs.[16] If they have their own businesses, they train their siblings by employing them. They also help their siblings find business locations and lend them money for start-up capital to start their own businesses. Thus, Korean immigrants who arrived in the United States in the 1980s and after were able to start their own businesses faster than the earlier immigrants.

The following stories surrounding Chong Won Lee's siblings and siblings-in-law vividly illustrate how strong sibling ties helped new Korean immigrants establish their own businesses quickly. At twenty-seven, Lee came to New York City in 1970 as an occupational immigrant. After working for a jewelry company in Manhattan for three years, he started his own business, a beauty supply store selling wigs, braids, and other hair-care items, in a black-Latino neighborhood in the Bronx. The same year, he visited Korea and invited his wife, Chae Ok Lee, the next year. In 1975, he purchased another beauty supply store only five or six blocks away from his first store. After becoming a naturalized citizen, he filed petitions for his brother and two sisters, all married, for permanent residence in the United States. All of them immigrated here in 1978. His wife, Chae Ok, also invited all her married siblings—a sister and three brothers and their family members—who immigrated in 1984 and 1987. Chae Ok Lee, related to my wife, told me that she and her husband trained all seven families in their two stores to run the same type of business. They also offered private loans to all of their siblings' families for start-up capital. In fact, they gave one of two stores to Chae Ok's elder brother with no business capital whatsoever, but instead with an agreement that the latter would pay them monthly. As a result, all her brothers and sisters established beauty supply or similar businesses within six months of their arrival.

Now in their early sixties, Chae Ok and her husband have no children. Their nephews and nieces, the children of the seven brothers and sisters they had helped establish their businesses, serve them nicely, buying them gifts for their birthdays, in appreciation. In 2003, I attended a party celebrating Lee's sixtieth birthday, held in a large reception hall in Flushing. I learned that the expenses of the party, amounting to more than $10,000, were covered entirely by the first son of Chae Ok's oldest brother and an MIT-graduate daughter of her third brother. Although this is an unusually salient case, Korean immigrants usually maintain closer sibling ties than Americans[17] and thus many other Korean immigrants are likely to have received business training and private loans from their relatives. In fact, my survey study in Atlanta revealed that 72 percent of the interviewed

Korean business owners received help from family members in business capitalization in the form of private loan or credit of owner's financing, and that 40 percent of the respondents received business information or legal advice for establishing a business.[18] By contrast, according to data based on the native-born U.S. sample at that time, only 26 percent of the respondents used private loans from their relatives and friends for portions of their business capital, and 47 percent depended on institutional lenders.[19]

The ethnic resources of Korean immigrant entrepreneurship also include ethnic friendship networks. Although alumni and other pre-migrant ties contribute to these networks, churches also play a central role. As noted earlier, nearly 80 percent of Korean immigrants are affiliated with Korean immigrant churches (see chapter 2). Victoria Kwon has shown that Korean immigrant churches play an important role in helping immigrants start and operate businesses by providing social networks for business information, private loans, and a source of employees.[20] New immigrants often find their first jobs through businesses owned by church members and get private loans from church members when starting their own businesses. They often get useful information from the main pastor and other church staff members about what types of businesses are suitable for them. Korean immigrants' professional businesses—such as law, accounting and medical firms—and semiprofessional businesses—such as travel, real estate and insurance agencies—depend on Korean customers.[21] There are many other nonprofessional service and retail businesses, such as Korean restaurants, boutiques, beauty salons and barber shops, that cater mainly to Korean customers. Immigrants who are engaged in these businesses are usually active participants in immigrant churches, which partly serve as the customer basis of business owners.

Concentration in Labor-Intensive Service and Retail Businesses

Table 3.4 presents an analysis of the businesses owned by full-time self-employed Korean immigrants in the New York–New Jersey area by industry, compared to native-born white Americans and other Asian immigrant groups based on the 5 percent PUMS of the 2000 census. More than 60 percent of Korean business owners are concentrated in two industry categories: businesses classified as retail trade and personal services. By contrast, only 13 percent of the native-born white self-employed are. Other Asian immigrant groups have much lower representations in the two industries, though Asian Indian immigrants are also highly concentrated (24 percent) in retail trade (most likely convenience stores and card shops).

Business owners who offer personal services account for 31 percent (4,177) of all full-time self-employed Korean immigrants. As shown in table 3.5, these businesses increased from 7 percent in 1980 to 19 percent

Table 3.4   **Comparative Self-Employment in New York–New Jersey Area by Industry, 2000**

Industry	Immigrant Group				
	Korean	Chinese	Taiwanese	Indian	Native White
Agriculture, mining, forestry	0.3	0.2	0.0	0.0	3.1
Arts, entertainments, accommodations, food services	0.9	0.0	0.0	0.7	1.5
Business and repair services	4.5	7.5	11.5	2.9	12.1
Construction	2.4	5.3	8.5	3.1	16.1
Finance, insurance, real estate, rental and leasing	2.3	3.9	6.3	4.9	8.9
Manufacturing	4.7	9.3	5.0	4.1	5.4
Personal services	30.8	9.2	6.6	3.9	3.4
Eating and drinking establishments	4.4	17.9	9.7	3.1	2.7
Professional, science, management, administrative, waste management	9.8	14.2	19.2	20.7	29.3
Retail trade	30.8	14.2	11.7	24.4	9.8
Transportation and warehousing	4.0	10.1	4.3	14.8	3.4
Wholesale trade	5.1	9.4	17.3	11.7	4.2
Total	100.0	100.0	100.0	100.0	100.0

Source: Author's compilation from 5% Public Use Microdata Sample (PUMS) of the 2000 U.S. Census.
Note: The total number of workers for each group is the same as that in table 3.1.

in 1990, and to 31 percent in 2000. The vast majority of these business owners are likely to be engaged in dry cleaning shops and nail salons. Because in some cases each business owner has two or more shops, the total number of personal-service businesses owned by Korean immigrants in 1999 should have been more than 4,177—around 4,500. Both business types are labor-intensive, involve little English, and need less capital to establish. According to interviews with two Korean dry cleaners' associations in New York State and New Jersey, there were approximately 3,000 Korean-owned dry cleaners in the New York–New Jersey metropolitan area in 2006, accounting for about half of all such establishments in the area. This number is a huge increase from the 1,600 in 1991 that association leaders reported during my interviews with them.

Table 3.5   **Businesses Owned by Full-Time Self-Employed Korean Immigrants in New York–New Jersey**

Industry	1980	1990	2000
Retail trade	1,820 (59%)	4,943 (44%)	4,176 (31%)
Wholesale trade	280 (9%)	795 (7%)	688 (5%)
Personal services	220 (7%)	2,151 (19%)	4,177 (31%)
Eating and drinking establishments	60 (2%)	561 (5%)	595 (4%)
Professional and related services	300 (10%)	980 (9%)	1,321 (10%)
Manufacturing	240 (8%)	785 (7%)	638 (5%)
All others	160 (5%)	1,194 (10%)	1,947 (14%)
Total	3,080 (100%)	11,373 (100%)	13,543 (100%)

Source: Author's compilation from 5% Public Use Microdata Sample (PUMS) of the 1980, 1990 and 2000 U.S. Censuses.

The astronomical increase in the number of Korean-owned dry cleaners in those fifteen years indicates the change in American consumption culture toward greater dependency on commercial dry cleaning. In the early 1990s and before, Korean-owned dry cleaners were concentrated in white middle class neighborhoods. Now, however, many are in lower-income black and Latino neighborhoods as well. The dry-cleaning business is dominant in all major Korean communities. Before 1965, Chinese immigrants in New York concentrated in the hand laundry business, but Koreans have replaced them. About 40 percent of Korean-owned dry cleaners are family businesses run by a husband-wife team. These dry cleaners are usually drop shops with no washing machine in their shops. The others have one or two paid employees. Most have their own washing machines and four to six employees, mostly Latino.

The Korean Nail Salon Associations of New York and New Jersey estimate that there are approximately 4,000 Korean-owned nail salons in the New York–New Jersey area as of 2006, comprising the vast majority in the area. This number was a three-fold increase from about 1,400 in 1991.[22] In terms of simple numbers, and reflected in the 2005 survey, the nail business is the largest Korean business line in the New York–New Jersey area.[23] According to Chu Suk Pang, a former president of the Korean Nail Salon Association of New York, women alone own about 30 percent of Korean nail salons, husband and wife teams co-run about 60 percent, and male owners with women managers make up the remainder. A nail salon usually has five to six paid employees, the vast majority Korean women and the rest Latino women. The nail salon business is thus significant in New York in that it provides many jobs for approximately 20,000 Korean women, including temporary visitors, wives of international students, and Korean women from China.

Little theoretical attention has been paid to innovation as a major factor for the development of immigrant entrepreneurship. But the development of the nail business by Korean immigrants in New York City was made possible mainly because of their business innovations, responding to the increasing consumer demand for body-related services. Korean immigrants began to move into the nail business in the late 1970s after Korean women had learned those skills in their employment in Russian-origin Jewish immigrant salons, which usually provided manicure and pedicure services. Korean salons have innovated manicure and pedicure services by replacing the traditional acrylic gluing with linen or silk wrapping. Moreover, they have added two other important body-related services—spas and skin care. Most recently, they have added other massage services—eye, shoulder, and whole-body treatment. As they have added such services, they have attracted male clients as well. According to president of the Korean Nail Salon Association of New York, about 15 percent of clients for Korean nail salons are men. He optimistically predicts that male customers will continue to increase in the future and that therefore the market in the nail business is unlimited. Approximately 500 Korean-owned nail salons in Manhattan do better than those in other areas of the city because they can serve not only local residents, but also professional and managerial employees of corporations and tourists.

Major Korean retail businesses in New York include grocery and liquor, produce, and fish retail stores, and retail stores selling Asian-imported manufactured goods. As shown in table 3.5, in 1980 Korean merchants in New York were heavily concentrated in retail trade (59 percent). The proportion of Korean merchants engaged in retail dropped to 44 percent in 1990 and to 31 percent in 2000. Significantly, the Korean merchants engaged in various types of retail trade in the New York–New Jersey area declined in absolute numbers from 5,504 in 1990 to 4,772 in 2000, though the number of full-time self-employed Korean immigrants increased by more than 2,000. The decline in the number of retail businesses since 1980 has been the general trend across the American economy, caused by the emergence of mega-stores. White Americans in New York City also show a steady decline in the proportion of retail businesses from 21 percent in 1980, to 15 percent in 1990, and to 12 percent in 2000.

Korean-owned retail stores in New York City were overrepresented in lower-income black and Latino neighborhoods in the 1980s and 1990s, and dry cleaners and nail salons overrepresented in middle class white neighborhoods. The decline in retail stores and the increase in dry cleaners and salons is a major factor in the reduction of Korean-owned businesses in black and Latino neighborhoods (see chapter 5).

Garment manufacturing, along with wholesale and retail sale of wigs and other manufactured goods imported from Korea, is one of the earliest Korean business types in New York City. In the late 1960s and early 1970s, as Kyeyoung Park pointed out, among recent Korean immigrants, many women found their first jobs in Korean-owned garment factories.[24] My interviews in 1991 revealed about 350 Korean-owned garment factories in New York City, but the number has been reduced to about 150 as of 2006, mainly due to the manufacturers' relocation of garment production to Mexico and other third world countries. Table 3.5 shows that the number of full-time Korean immigrant workers engaged in manufacturing decreased slightly between 1990 and 2000. Korean-owned garment factories were concentrated in the midtown Garment District, a rectangle area covering 34th and 42nd Street and 9th Avenue and 6th Avenue.[25] But many Korean garment factories have moved in recent years to New Jersey and Long Island City to escape high rents and interventions of local labor unions in Manhattan. More than 90 percent of Korean-owned garment factories subcontracted work from white-owned, predominantly Jewish manufacturers. Woo Chun Kwak, president of the Korean Apparel Contractors Association of Greater New York, told me that Korean garment subcontractors had difficulty in competing with Chinese subcontractors who operated factories in two shifts using cheap Chinese workers. Korean garment subcontractors depend heavily on Latino workers. To compete with Chinese subcontractors, he said, Korean garment factories focus on making high-quality garment products. Now many Korean garment owners sell their products directly to department stores with their own brand names.

It is also important to note that self-employed Korean immigrants in New York are underrepresented in two categories: first, professional services and, second, finance, insurance, and real estate. Self-employed Taiwanese and Indian immigrants with substantially higher educational levels than Koreans are much more highly represented in these two high-paying industrial categories. My 2006 interviews with leaders of Korean professional organizations in New York City, however, revealed a substantial increase in the numbers of Korean-owned finance, insurance, mortgage, and real estate businesses in the 2000s.

Another industry that involves large-scale businesses is wholesale trade. Again, those engaged in wholesale trade account for a much smaller proportion of Korean business owners than their Chinese, Taiwanese, and Indian counterparts. Korean immigrants began to establish import and wholesale stores on Broadway in the 1970s, taking advantage of expanded Korean exports of manufactured goods. In the early 1990s, the Broadway Korean Businessmen's Association (which changed its name to the New York Society of Korean Businessmen in 2005) reported that about 400 Korean wholesale stores dealing in manufactured Asian goods were located in the Broadway Korean Business District.[26] Byungkwan Chun, president of the association, informed me that, as of December 2006, the number had decreased to about 250, and that many Indian and Chinese immigrants had established wholesale businesses there as well. Chinese and Indian

Table 3.6   Korean Businesses Catering to Korean Customers, 2007

Types of Businesses	Queens		Manhattan	
	All	Flushing-Bayside Enclave	All	Broadway Business District
Korean restaurants	145	120 (83%)	77	50 (65%)
Korean grocery stores and supermarkets	15	7 (47%)	4	1 (25%)
Drinking places	63	58 (92%)	23	21 (91%)
Korean bakeries	21	17 (81%)	2	2 (100%)
Beauty salons	110	80 (73%)	15	14 (93%)
Video rentals	26	21 (81%)	4	4 (100%)
Real estates agents	238	178 (75%)	67	43 (64%)
Travel agencies	43	38 (88%)	47	40 (85%)
Insurance agents	115	106 (92%)	39	23 (59%)
Acupuncture/ acupressure/ Oriental medicine	103	96 (93%)	26	19 (73%)
Accounting firms	50	46 (92%)	57	52 (91%)
Medical firms	233	175 (75%)	54	17 (31%)
Dental firms	75	56 (75%)	26	19 (73%)
Law firms	52	49 (94%)	77	50 (65%)

Source: Author's compilation from the 2007 Korean Directory by *Korea Central Daily.*

immigrants have a competitive advantage in running the wholesaler business selling imported Asian goods, partly because they can get merchandise more cheaply from their home countries and partly because, as new or recent immigrants from countries with lower standards of living than South Korea, they can work with lower profit margins.

According to Byungkwan Chun, in addition to difficulty in competing with Chinese and Indians in the area, Korean importers and wholesalers encountered hikes in commercial rents on the basis of urban renovation activities in the area. As a result, several members of the New York Society of Korean Businessmen purchased a lot in Jamaica, a middle class multi-ethnic neighborhood in Queens, to build a wholesale complex, International Merchandise Mart. Korean wholesalers in Broadway will move to Jamaica when the commercial building is completed in 2009.[27] The 400 stores within the complex will be rented not only to Korean wholesalers but also to non-Koreans, mostly Chinese, Indian, and Jewish.

In the 2005 survey, 23 percent of self-employed respondents reported that Korean customers comprised 50 percent or more of their customers. Nearly all businesses that cater largely to co-ethnic customers are located in Queens and Manhattan, where nearly 85 percent of Korean Americans in New York City reside. Moreover, as shown in table 3.6, these businesses in Queens are heavily concentrated in the Flushing-Bayside Korean enclave, and those in Manhattan in the Broadway Korean business district. For example, 83 percent of the 120 Korean restaurants in Queens are located in Flushing and Bayside, and 65 percent of the seventy-seven Korean restaurants in Manhattan are concentrated in the Broadway Korean business district. Semi-professional (real estate, travel, and insurance agencies) and professional (medical, dental, accounting, and law firms) businesses are also heavily concentrated in the Korean enclave or business district. Because of the language barrier and ethnic trust, Korean immigrants prefer Korean to non-Korean professionals for these services. Because of racism and cultural differences, most Korean immigrant professionals are also at a disadvantage in serving non-Korean clients. It is thus not surprising that the vast majority of Korean semi-professional and professional businesses are located in the Flushing-Bayside enclave and the Broadway Korean business district.

Korean-owned professional businesses in the Broadway Korean business district serve mainly Korean wholesalers and importers who have shops there. It is interesting to note that more Korean law firms are located in Manhattan than in Queens, and that the majority of the Manhattan-based Korean law firms are in the Broadway Korean business district, a relatively small area. These firms mainly serve other Korean professionals, as well as wholesalers and importers, who have businesses there. Korean businesses catering mainly to Korean customers with culturally distinctive retail items or services in New Jersey's Bergen County are also heavily concentrated in two Korean enclaves in Fort Lee and the Palisades Park.[28]

The Effect of Concentration in the Ethnic Economy on Ethnic Attachment

In the introductory chapter, I made a distinction between ethnic attachment as cultural, social, and psychological attachments to the immigrant-ethnic community and ethnic solidarity as use of ethnic collective action. As already cited, several researchers have shown the positive effects of immigrants' business involvement on ethnic attachment.[29] This book focuses on Korean greengrocers' solidarity. As such, several chapters of this volume document how Korean greengrocers used ethnic collective action through the KPA to neutralize external threats to their commercial activities (see chapters 4, 5, 6, and 7). Although doing so is not one of the major objectives of this book, it may be useful for readers to document how Korean immigrant concentration in the Korean ethnic economy strengthens their ethnic attachment.

We noted earlier in this chapter that Korean immigrants are highly concentrated in the ethnic economy (81 percent) either as business owners or as employees of co-ethnic businesses. Table 3.7 compares self-employed

Table 3.7   Cultural Ethnic Attachment by Class of Work

Attachment Variables	Self-Employed		Ethnic Firm		General Economy		Level of Significance (Chi-Square Test)
	Number	Percentage	Number	Percentage	Number	Percentage	
Frequency of speaking Korean at home[a]—Korean almost always	91/107	85	101/111	91	29/42	70	p < 0.005
Frequency of reading Korean newspapers & magazines[b]—Korean newspapers almost always	51/105	49	73/110	66	12/46	26	p < 0.0001
Frequency of watching Korean TV programs[c]—Korean TV more often or almost always	65/111	59	49/106	46	16/47	34	p < 0.05
Frequency of eating Korean food for dinner[d]—Korean food almost always	89/109	82	103/117	88	32/51	63	p < 0.001
Frequency of using Korean name[e]—Korean name more often or almost always	67/109	61	80/117	68	35/51	69	p > 0.1

Source: Author's compilation.

[a] How often do you speak Korean, compared to English, at home with your spouse and other family members?

[b] How often do you read Korean newspapers and magazines, compared to American newspapers and magazines?

[c] How often do you watch Korean TV and video programs, compared to American programs?

[d] How often do you eat Korean food, compared to American food, for dinner?

[e] How often do you use your Korean name, compared to the American name?

Korean respondents, employees of Korean stores, and respondents in the general economy in the cultural ethnic attachment variables. All questions measuring cultural ethnic attachment were ordinal variables with four or five response categories. Responses were recorded into two-category nominal variables to present the group differences in a way that lay readers can easily understand.

As expected, with the exception of one variable, two groups of respondents in the ethnic economy show higher levels of cultural ethnic attachment than those in the general economy. That is, they speak Korean and eat Korean food more often at home, and read and watch Korean news media more frequently. These findings are not surprising, considering that Korean immigrants in the ethnic economy do not have active social interactions with non-Koreans at workplace. Of course, most Koreans in the ethnic economy serve non-Korean customers and work with Latino employees, given that only 23 percent of Korean businesses have Koreans as the majority of their customers. But both Korean shop owners and their Korean employees run businesses with limited English and limited interactions with non-Korean customers. Korean immigrants working in the general economy use English and eat non-Korean food more often at home and depend on American media more often for news and recreational activities because they are more integrated in American society.

Comparing two groups in the ethnic economy, I found that the respondents working as employees of Korean-owned businesses have a slightly higher level of cultural ethnic attachment than self-employed respondents. This difference is not difficult to explain. Korean business owners have more work-related active interactions with non-Korean suppliers, employees, customers, and landlords than their Korean employees. As a result, they are more culturally integrated in the mainstream society. Results of my survey of Korean immigrants in Los Angeles show the same pattern.[30]

I expected the respondents in the general economy to use their Korean names less frequently than those in the Korean ethnic economy. Results of the survey do not support this expectation. This finding suggests one thing: by virtue of the multicultural environment, contemporary immigrants are not pressured to change their ethnic names into American names to work in American firms. Instead, the self-employed respondents are found to use their ethnic names less frequently than the other two employed groups, but the difference is not statistically significant, though it might be in a larger sample. Although unexpected, this finding may not be surprising, given that Korean business owners often need to use their American names for business purposes. Korean merchants involved in service businesses, such as nail salons and dry cleaning shops, in particular need American names to serve their regular customers effectively because their service delivery involves significant personal interaction. I have found out that most Korean women employees of Korean nail salons, who make up a significant proportion of the Korean immigrant female work force, go with their American names to serve their non-Korean regular customers effectively.[31] Considering it, the unexpected finding in table 3.7 that even Korean employees of Korean-owned businesses use American names as frequently as those in the general labor market is not surprising. As a result of the change from retail to service businesses during recent years, both Korean business owners and their employees have more opportunities for personal interactions with white and other nonethnic clients.

Table 3.8 compares the three occupational groups in the social ethnic attachment variables. The findings support my expectation about the advantages in social ethnic attachment of the respondents in the ethnic economy over those in the general economy. In two—affiliation with ethnic organizations and having three or more Koreans among five best friends— of the four given variables, the two groups in the ethnic economy have significantly higher levels of social ethnic attachment than those in the general economy.

In particular, there is a huge difference in the proportion of the respondents with three or more Koreans among five best friends. Although Korean immigrants in the general economy have the opportunity to make friends with their nonethnic co-workers, Koreans working in Korean stores have difficulty in making friends with their white suppliers or Latino employees because of their class and racial differences. Even in the other two variables, frequency of participation in ethnic organizations and frequency of eating dinner with friends, the two ethnic-economy groups have higher levels of social ethnic attachment. Although the three-group comparison does not show a statistically significant difference, the comparison between the two ethnic economy groups as a whole and the general economy group does show one.

We have noted that, overall, Korean immigrants in the ethnic economy have more cultural and social ethnic attachments than those in the general economy. Because of their heavy concentration in the ethnic economy, Korean immigrants as a whole have a greater ethnic attachment. The economic basis of Korean immigrants' ethnic attachment becomes clearer when we compare them with other Asian immigrant groups.[32] For example, earlier in this chapter, we noted that Filipino immigrants in New York City have an exceptionally low self-employment rate (see table 3.1), the lowest among all immigrant groups in the city. Given their heavy concentration in the general economy, Filipino immigrants need to speak English with Americans at the workplace regularly. They also have far more opportunities to make friends with nonethnic coworkers. They are thus likely to have much lower levels of cultural and social ethnic attachment than Korean immigrants, because they are culturally and socially far more integrated in American society.

Table 3.8 Social Ethnic Attachment by Class of Work

Variables	Self-Employed		Korean Firms		Non-Korean Firm		Level of Significance (Chi-Square Test)
	Number	Percentage	Number	Percentage	Number	Percentage	
Affiliation with one or more Korean organizations[a]	96/109	88	93/117	79	36/51	71	p < 0.05
Frequency of participation in Korean organizations[b]— Once or more often per week	73/109	67	78/117	67	30/51	59	p > 0.1
Frequency of eating dinner with ethnic friends[c]—Once every two week or more often	50/109	46	46/117	39	17/51	33	p > 0.1
How many Koreans among five best friends[d]— Three or more Koreans	103/109	95	109/117	93	32/51	63	p < 0.0001

Source: Author's compilation.
[a] How many Korean organizations are you affiliated with and what are they?
[b] How often do you participate in meetings of Korean organizations?
[c] How often do you eat Korean food with your Korean friends?
[d] What are racial, ethnic (Korean), and subethnic (member of the same Korean church) categories of your five best friends?

The concentration of Korean immigrants in the ethnic economy increases their ethnic attachment, but it also culturally and socially segregates them from the mainstream. Their high affiliation with Korean immigrant churches and their dependency on Korean-language media[33] are also factors.[34] Again, when comparing Korean adaptation with Filipino, we see the radical differences. Filipino immigrants have not merely not developed an ethnic economy. Despite the fact that about 80 percent of Filipino immigrants are Christian, predominantly Catholic, to my knowledge there is no Filipino ethnic church, Catholic or Protestant, in New York, though there are about 600 Korean. Similarly, where there are three Korean-language dailies, three television stations, and two radio stations in the New York–New Jersey area, there is no Filipino-language ethnic media.

= Chapter 4 =

Conflicts and Ethnic Collective Action

Korean-owned produce stores are similar to Korean-owned grocery
stores in that both sell food-related items. Korean greengrocers,
however, were subject to more discrimination and greater physical
violence by suppliers because of the different ways the two groups purchase retail items. Greengrocers need to visit HPM and other produce
wholesale markets a few times a week, whereas grocers get merchandise
delivered by suppliers. The Korean produce business is sociologically
interesting mainly because Korean greengrocers used ethnic collective
action in reaction to many conflicts with their white suppliers.

The Cultural Division of Labor Theory

Host hostility and intergroup conflicts as a causal factor for ethnic solidarity is consistent with the general proposition deriving from conflict
theory associated with Georg Simmel and Lewis Coser.[1] These theorists
posited that intergroup conflicts enhance internal solidarity. Acting on
the insight of classical conflict theorists, many researchers have tried to
demonstrate the positive effects of intergroup conflicts and host hostility
on ethnic immigrant groups solidarity. For example, Alejandro Portes
suggested that host hostility in the form of antirefugee campaigns and the
antibilingual referendum in Florida contributed to growing awareness
among Cuban immigrants.[2] Susan Olzak and Elizabeth West showed that
hostility and anti-immigrant violence encouraged white immigrants to
establish ethnic newspapers.[3] Yen Espiritu elaborated on how the increase
in anti-Asian violence in the 1980s contributed to pan-Asian solidarity.[4]
Recently, in the wake of discriminatory and violent anti-Muslim reactions
to the 9/11 terrorist event, Middle Eastern and Muslim Americans have
mobilized themselves in self-defense.[5]

Middleman minority theory is relevant in that Korean greengrocers are
typical middleman merchants that connect white produce suppliers and

lower-income minority customers. However, the cultural division of labor theory is most relevant to explaining Korean greengrocer conflicts with white suppliers and their use of ethnic collective action in self-defense. Middleman minority theory is most useful in explaining black boycotts of Korean retail stores and Koreans' reactive solidarity (see chapter 5).

The cultural division of labor theory, also known as the internal colonialism theory, and associated with Michael Hechter and his associates, emphasizes the ethnic division of labor as the major cause of ethnic solidarity. According to Hechter, when members of an ethnic group occupy a distinctive position, especially a disadvantaged position, in the class-occupational structure or in the labor market, they are likely to use ethnic collective action to protect their economic interest.[6] An occupationally specialized ethnic group is more likely to develop solidarity than one not specialized, partly because the members' occupational activities facilitate their intra-ethnic social interactions. But ethnic specialization in a particular occupation contributes to ethnic solidarity mainly because the members of the group share common material interests to the extent that they concentrate in the occupation.[7] In his earlier works, Hechter considered the position of the group in the stratification system as a major factor affecting the strength of group solidarity: "In general, the lower the position, the greater the probability that its members will come to think of themselves as sharing a community of fate."[8]

Later, Hechter and his associates revised the cultural division of labor theory by emphasizing the rational choice of individual members in participating in collective action and the critical role of ethnic organizations in the mobilization of group members for such acts.[9] In their view, because members of a group as rational actors determine whether to participate in collection action based primarily on their assessment of its costs and benefits, many members are likely to seek benefits as free riders, that is, without participating. Thus, ethnic stratification itself has an indirect effect on members' participation in ethnic collective action. It was in this context that Hechter and his associates stressed the role of one or more ethnic organizations as critical to promoting collective action by preventing free riding.[10] In their view, an ethnic organization can facilitate ethnic collective action partly by providing its members with rewards and punishments for participating or not and partly by controlling information about the success or failure of the contemplated collective action. In this way, it can prevent or at least reduce free riding from taking place.

The cultural division of labor theory is most relevant to understanding the use of ethnic collective action by members of an economically subordinate group, such as British colonies and internal colonies (low-income African American neighborhoods) in the United States. But it also provides us with an important insight for understanding the ethnic solidarity among occupationally segregated contemporary immigrant groups, such as Korean greengrocers in New York. In particular, the emphasis on the critical role of an ethnic organization in mobilizing ethnic collective action is useful in explaining Korean greengrocers' use of ethnic collective action. I have some reservation, however, about Hechter's overemphasis on the rational aspect of ethnic collective action being similar to class solidarity. As I will show, Korean greengrocer solidarity involved numerous irrational elements.

Development and Evolution of Korean Produce Retail Stores

Historically, the produce retail business is the third major Korean immigrant business to have emerged in the early 1970s, after wholesale and retail businesses in wigs and other Korean-manufactured goods, and garment subcontracting, both of which started in the late 1960s. Do Sup Kwack established the second Korean produce store in New York City:

> In 1973 I purchased from a retiring elderly Jewish owner a produce store in a black neighborhood in Brooklyn's Church Avenue area. At that time there was only one other Korean-owned produce store in Brooklyn. The other Korean owner purchased his store from an Italian owner. He soon sold it and began to work as a manager for my store.

According to Kwack and other interviewees, some Korean immigrants purchased greengrocery stores in minority neighborhoods from retiring white owners in the 1970s, but more of them established new stores in minority neighborhoods by leasing buildings vacated by white business owners. Because there was at the time one produce store in every ten or fifteen blocks in minority neighborhoods, Korean immigrants could establish their own, often not far from white-owned produce stores. Unable to compete with Korean-owned stores, some white-owned stores were forced to close.

As noted, in the 1970s Korean produce stores largely served minority customers, Caribbean black immigrants and African American customers in many neighborhoods in Brooklyn and Jamaica in Queens, and Puerto Ricans and African Americans in the Bronx. Minority neighborhoods needed produce retail stores because few supermarkets there sold fruits and vegetables. As Jewish and Italian American storeowners retired from the business in minority neighborhoods, a small business niche for the produce retail in these minority neighborhoods developed.[11] In the 1970s and early 1980s, some Korean immigrants also established produce stores in low-income neighborhoods in Manhattan where there was no supermarket. For example, arriving in New York City, Su Geun Lee bought a chicken restaurant and converted it into a produce store on the Westside of Midtown in 1978. He said that the rent was very reasonable in the lower-class neighborhood with many homeless people moving around every day.

Korean immigrants in New York were attracted to the produce retail business partly because they could open it with little capital and partly because they could use their family members and other Korean immigrants as cheap labor sources in labor-intensive business.[12] In this connection, it is important to note that running a produce store needs more workers than running a dry cleaning shop or a grocery-liquor store. They also preferred it because they could operate it with little English. For example, Sung Youn Kang, who came to New York in 1978, initially worked in a Korean-owned produce store in the Bronx. In less than a year and a half of employment in the Korean store, he, along with his two brothers, opened a produce store in Harlem with $30,000 in start-up capital. The savings from the store and private loans from their friends were enough to start the business. At the time, he said, there were four other Korean-owned produce stores in Harlem.

Korean immigrants' readiness to work long hours for social mobility helped them specialize in greengrocery businesses. Small Korean-owned produce shops are usually open from 7:30 a.m. to 11 p.m. seven days a week. The majority of Manhattan-based Korean produce stores, however, are open twenty-four hours a day, in large part because of exceptionally high rents. In addition, many owners get up around 3 a.m. to visit HPM to buy produce three or four times a week. Because Korean-owned produce stores are open for long hours, they can compete with supermarkets that usually close after 7 p.m. Moreover, in the 1980s and before, when there was no big demand for produce items, supermarkets sold dried fruits and vegetables because they could not purchase produce regularly from HPM. Therefore, according to a Korean pioneer of the greengrocery business, even Korean produce stores located close to supermarkets were able to do well. But since many supermarkets have begun extending their opening hours, small-scale Korean produce stores have run into difficulties in dealing with the competition. Because Korean owners of produce stores keep their shops open day and night for seven days a week, they have few opportunities to see their children. Some see only sleeping children at midnight. Another problem is the danger of armed robbery. Several Korean produce store owners and employees have been murdered during robberies in New York City.

Although Korean immigrants in other cities share the readiness to work long hours and the access to cheap labor, they have not developed the produce business as a major ethnic enterprise.[13] This suggests that the unique aspects of urban patterns in New York City have contributed to the development of the greengrocery business there. Two unique attributes of New York City's urban structure are especially significant. First, residential and commercial zones are adjacent to one another and sometimes overlap. Second, closely related to the dense population, complex subway and other mass transportation systems reach most neighborhoods. Many residents in New York City do not have a car and depend on mass transit. They buy fruits and vegetables on their way home from bus stops and subway stations. In fact, in the 1970s and early 1980s, most Korean produce stores were located close to subway stations expressly to serve the passengers. By contrast, in other cities, because suburban residents live so far away from commercial zones that it is not convenient for them to drop by a greengrocery store on their way home. Instead, they drive from home to a market or supermarkets.

Beginning in the early 1980s, Korean immigrants in New York began to establish produce stores in middle class neighborhoods in Manhattan and Queens, and suburban areas in Upstate New York and Long Island. In middle and upper middle class white neighborhoods, they paid higher rents and needed more start-up capital. They also encountered competition with supermarkets that carried fruits and vegetables. They were able to successfully compete, however, because they cleaned and displayed fruits and vegetables much better than the supermarkets did. For example, Sung Youn Kang, who established a produce store in Harlem in 1979, sold it in 1982 and purchased another in an upscale neighborhood in Westchester County. I asked him how he could compete with supermarkets in an upper middle class white neighborhood.

> Supermarkets in the neighborhoods also sold fruits and vegetables. But they could not clean and display greengrocery items as well as my store did. Also, they could not provide as fresh greengrocery items as my store did. While my brothers were running the store, I picked up greengrocery items almost every day from Hunts Point Market. So, we were able to display fresh fruits and vegetables every day. The business was so good at one time that we had as many as fifteen employees, all Koreans.

Man Sik Nam, a Korean immigrant who had run a produce store in a Queens neighborhood for twenty-eight years explained his long success this way:

> There is a supermarket two blocks from my produce store. But I have been able to successfully compete. Why? Because I go to Hunts Point Market four times a week and choose fresh produce items I like. But since the supermarket gets produce items delivered by trucks, it has little choice of items. My store can also compete with the supermarket in prices of items because each day I select produce items on special sales at Hunts Point Market.

It is very difficult to estimate the total number of Korean-owned produce stores in the New York–New Jersey area, in part because many

Korean-owned stores sell one or more of the following three types of items together: produce, grocery, and deli items. When I conducted research on major Korean businesses in New York in 1991, the executive director of the KPA estimated approximately 1,800 Korean-owned stores in the New York–New Jersey metropolitan area.[14] Chang Il Kim, a former president of the KPA, estimated that the number increased to about 2,500 around 1995, the peak year, but that it may have declined to approximately 2,000 as of 2005. As noted in chapter 3, the number of Korean-owned retail stores decreased from 4,943 in 1990 to 4,176 in 2000, though the total number of Korean-owned stores increased by about 20 percent during the period. Given this, the actual number of Korean produce stores in the New York–New Jersey area in 2005 may have been less than 1,800.[15] As will be discussed in more detail in chapter 5, urban renovations in minority neighborhoods have impacted Korean produce stores and other types of businesses by bringing many mega stores (supermarkets) to minority neighborhoods and raising commercial rents. Only medium-sized produce stores in minority neighborhoods have survived.

When I conducted research in the early 1990s, I found many Korean greengrocers complaining about excessive competition with other Korean-owned produce stores in the same block. As of November 2005, Korean greengrocers in white and multiethnic neighborhoods are involved in more intragroup competition because many stores in minority neighborhoods have closed. A Korean immigrant sometimes starts a produce store next to a well-established, successful Korean-owned produce store, which leads to strained relationships between the owners. For example, Sung Youn Kang had to close his produce store in a white neighborhood in Westchester when another Korean opened a store across the street. At the time of the interview, he was running a Korean restaurant in an upscale white neighborhood. Some Korean immigrants each own several big produce stores. Others operate supermarkets with their green-grocery sections enhanced. Small Korean-owned produce stores have a hard time surviving. Do Sup Kwack, one of the pioneers of the produce retail business in New York, commented about the difficulty:

> At that time [in the early 1970s], in Brooklyn a competing produce store was located ten or fifteen blocks away from my store. So I could make lots of money. On weekends, we had too many customers, so we could not serve them effectively. Now there are Korean-owned produce stores in almost every block there. Now most supermarket owners in Brooklyn are Koreans. Taking advantage of their previous skills of running produce stores, they sell fresh fruits and vegetables, cleaning and arranging them nicely. Therefore, small produce stores cannot compete with them. Some Koreans own three or four supermarkets. They make a lot of money. Koreans have changed everything.

New York City has not established a law that regulates commercial rents. Thus landlords, many of whom are Jewish, have continuously raised commercial rents. To cope, beginning in the mid-1980s, Korean greengrocers began to open their stores for twenty-four hours. Many Korean produce stores, especially those in Manhattan, do as well. These services are convenient for shoppers, but owners and employees have faced armed robbery, with some killed. According to Sung Youn Kang, who operated a produce store in Harlem and Westchester, many Korean owners, including Kang, have not reported their robberies in fear that the news may make selling the stores more difficult.

To maximize benefits from their limited space, Korean greengrocers throughout the New York–New Jersey metropolitan area also sell flowers, usually displayed on sidewalk tables, as well as fruits and vegetables. Before this, New Yorkers had to find a flower-shop to buy flowers. Now they have the convenience of buying flowers every two or three blocks for reasonable prices. In addition, Korean produce stores in Manhattan have added delis, soft drink and beer sections, and salad bars. Deli food was popular in the late 1980s and early 1990s, and salad bars since the mid-1990s. All Korean-owned produce stores in Manhattan currently include one or more of these additional food-service components. Some have been converted into deli-grocery stores, and thus the owners join the Korean-American Grocers Association of New York rather than the KPA. Commercial rent hikes in Manhattan have forced Korean greengrocers to add these ready-made food services. The demand, however, by virtue of the presence of a huge number of workers and single residents in Manhattan, has also contributed to addition of these services.

Another factor that has contributed to the phenomenal increase in the number and spread of Korean-owned produce stores throughout the New York–New Jersey area has been the gradual cultural change in American dietary habits to include more fruits and vegetables over the last three decades, especially among middle-aged and elderly whites. Although researchers have emphasized the supply-side, we need to pay attention to the demand-side. The great demand has led supermarkets to expand the produce and seafood sections. As mentioned, however, Korean produce stores in suburban areas have been able to meet the demand more efficiently than local supermarkets by cleaning, trimming, and cutting fruits and vegetables and displaying them more advantageously.

In this connection, I also like to point out that Korean and Chinese supermarkets do better than their mainstream counterparts by expanding the produce and seafood sections. There are five large Korean supermarkets in Flushing and one each in Fort Lee, New Jersey, and Long Island. In the 1970s and early 1980s, Korean grocery stores offered only Korean items. Korean immigrants thus shopped at both Korean and American grocery stores. By providing both ethnic and mainstream items, Korean grocery stores have attracted more ethnic customers than before. They have also attracted many nonethnic customers, because they provide better and fresher vegetables, fruits, and seafood for lower prices. Because they buy directly from large farms, large Korean supermarkets can offer major fruit and vegetable items for almost half the price American supermarkets offer.

I have closely observed changes in the ethnic composition of customers in Han Areum, the largest Korean supermarket, located in the Korean business district in Flushing where I regularly do grocery shopping. As of February 2007, approximately 35 percent of the customers are non-Korean customers: whites, Chinese or Indians, and Latinos or blacks. White customers, mainly middle aged and elderly, are the largest non-Korean group. I talked with several white elderly customers who regularly visited the supermarket. They told me they like it because it carries all kinds of fresh vegetables and fruits. One woman said, "Americans have health problems because they eat too much meat, but Asians remain skinny because they eat a lot of vegetables." Indeed, not only this Korean, but also other Korean and Chinese supermarkets in the area have huge vegetable and fruit sections. They also have big fish sections where two or three employees wait to cut fish for customers. American supermarkets not only in Flushing but also in other neighborhoods in Queens therefore have difficulty competing. In an interesting corollary, because of the same health consciousness and health messages, American fast food franchises in South Korea have lost more and more customers in recent years.

Retailer Dependence on HPM Distributors

There were for some time three major produce wholesale markets in New York City: Hunts Point Market, the Brooklyn Terminal Market, and the Bronx Terminal Market (closed in 2005). Hunts Point Market (HPM) is the largest of the three and the largest fruit and vegetable distribution market in the United States. Because Caribbean immigrants are heavily concentrated in Brooklyn, the Brooklyn Terminal Market has many wholesale produce stores that specialize in Caribbean fruits and vegetables. Thus Korean greengrocers with stores in black neighborhoods in Brooklyn need to visit the Brooklyn Terminal Market to buy Caribbean fruits, such as plantains, green bananas, yuccas, and coconuts. They also need to visit HPM for the standard American produce items, such as oranges, tomatoes, strawberries, and broccoli, because produce wholesale companies in Brooklyn usually order these from HPM. Korean greengrocers who had stores close to the Bronx Terminal Market often visited that market for small quantities of fruits and vegetables until it closed, but they too needed to use HPM for major orders of fruits and vegetables. Korean greengrocers had conflicts with produce suppliers in all three markets, once boycotting a company in the Bronx Market and another in Brooklyn. For the most part, however, their encounters, and ethnic collective action, focused on white produce suppliers at HPM, where the KPA was located.

According to a booklet published by Hunts Point Terminal Produce Cooperative Association, HPM in the Bronx, which opened in 1967, is America's largest fresh fruit and vegetable distribution market. The site was chosen because it was "both removed from traffic-dense Manhattan and close enough to the economic center of metropolitan New York for ready radial access to the food consumer."[16] Its 125 acres feed 22 million people in the tri-state area and many additional tourists in New York City.

For not quite twenty years, HPM was operated by the city, but in 1986 became a cooperative governed by a board of directors with sixteen distributor members. Each company pays a ground rent to the city for the land and has its own employees for handling sales. All distributors pay for security, maintenance, and sanitation together. Distributing companies are usually open twelve hours a day to customers, from 10 p.m. to 10 a.m. About seventy distributors receive fresh fruits and vegetables from all over the United States and more than twenty other countries. Jewish and Italian Americans, the two major white ethnic entrepreneurial groups in the city, owned almost all distributing companies at HPM. Their employees used to be predominantly white, but now are Latinos with some blacks.

In 2005, some 60 to 65 percent of HPM customers were the approximately 2,000 Korean-owned greengrocers in the New York–New Jersey area. Earlier, Koreans had gone to HPM with trucks three or four times a week. Most visited early, before dawn. Many of them, however, had difficulty visiting HPM regularly, in part because of their need to stay in their stores all the time and in part because of the language barrier. As a result, a growing number of Korean produce delivery drivers have started to deliver produce for Korean retailers. According to Young Tea Kim, KPA president, there were approximately 250 Korean produce drivers as of November 2005 providing delivery services for Korean greengrocers. About 40 percent of Korean greengrocers continued to visit HPM regularly, three or four times a week.

According to pioneering Korean owners of produce stores, perhaps a dozen retailers have started wholesale stores, but most have failed, partly because of preventive measures taken by Jewish and Italian distributors at HPM and partly because of capital shortage. Only three are inside HPM as of 2005. Five others are outside. These five still serve Korean produce retail customers who visit HPM, but are outside because the cooperative association has not approved their entry into the market. In addition, there are four Korean-owned produce and grocery wholesale stores, all small-scale, in the Brooklyn Terminal Market. The number is very small, given that Korean greengrocers make up approximately 60 to 65 percent of HPM customers. Hahn-gyoung Jo, executive director of the KPA, said that it is difficult for Korean immigrants to establish wholesale businesses within HPM partly because Jewish and Italian distributors are reluctant to allow them to do so.[17] White distributors have tried to control, in particular, American-brand fruits and vegetables. According to a long-time Korean greengrocer, white distributors put pressure on farms not to sell key American-brand fruit and vegetable items to Korean owners. Thus, Korean wholesale stores generally import tropical produce items and grocery and health food items from South American and Caribbean countries on a small scale, though some buy limited quantities from white distributors at HPM.

Korean produce wholesalers cannot compete with white distributors in terms of prices because they run businesses with much smaller capital scales. I asked Joo Tae Yoo, another Korean old-timer who was active in the KPA, why Korean wholesalers could not compete with white suppliers. He explained it this way:

> Some white distributors have operated their wholesale companies over generations. They maintain their own farms to reduce costs for products. So, they can offer products for lower prices than Korean wholesalers. They have the capital large enough to sell their items for wholesale prices for a few months to kill Korean-owned wholesale stores. No Korean produce wholesaler possesses such a large capital.

Korean produce owners who purchase produce items in small quantities at HPM prefer to do so from Korean wholesalers to avoid the language barrier. But Korean wholesalers provide only limited items of merchandise. Moreover, Korean supermarket owners who purchase them in large quantity depend upon large white distributors for major produce items because of the better prices.

A few others mentioned that the mafias that controlled HPM in the 1970s and 1980s had used threats and intimidations against Korean greengrocers and the KPA to block Koreans from establishing wholesale stores. Young Il Kim recounted one episode that occurred in the late 1980s:

> It seems to have occurred about fifteen to eighteen years ago. A Korean used a trailer to purchase grapes directly from a farm in California and sell them to Korean greengrocers at his office building across from Hunts Point Market. The mafia traced his business activities with farm. One day, on his way home from California, he was stopped on the highway by mafia members wielding machine guns. They warned him if he continued his business they would kill him and all of his family. He ran away, leaving his trailer. Later, they called him and let him know where he could pick up the trailer. They had taken all of the grapes.
>
> The mafia still controls Hunts Point Market and the Fulton Fish Market. White distributors use it to protect their business interests, though they try to hide the existence of the mafia from the public.

Based on statements alone, however, I cannot determine whether the mafia had a significant influence on Hunts Point Market operations in the 1980s, or do even now. New York City Mayor Giuliani's 1996 proposal to eliminate the influence of organized criminal groups from HPM suggests, however, that the mafia had exercised some degree of influence in HPM up to that time.[18]

Robberies and Conflicts with HPM Distributors

From the beginning, Korean greengrocers and truck drivers were discriminated against and threatened with physical violence, by both managers and employees of HPM distributors. According to interviews with KPA leaders and Korean produce store owners, discriminatory treatment includes higher prices for the same produce items, no exchanges for rotten items included in fruit boxes, refusal to sell hot items after receiving orders, false accusations of theft, discrimination in parking allocations, unreasonably high penalties for parking tickets, and vehicle towing.

Before discussing Korean greengrocer experiences with discrimination, I first need to touch on the frequency of robberies, which is attributable to inadequate security measures at HPM in the earlier years. Since March 1982, HPM has issued decals to buyers who regularly visit the market. Since the cooperative association began to operate HPM in 1986, it has used several patrols to maintain security in the market. These changes have significantly reduced, but not stopped, robberies of Korean produce store owners who visited HPM. Because before 1982 anyone could visit HPM and because until 1986 there was no security patrol, HPM had many cases of armed robberies every week. Many of the Korean greengrocers who visited the market early in the day experienced physically dangerous robberies. Most Korean greengrocers visit HPM around four o'clock in the morning, which increases their chances of being robbed. In this connection, remember that armed robberies in Korean grocery stores is also commonplace, given their extended operating hours. In a September 1986 survey of 236 Korean greengrocers, 40 percent reported that they experienced one or more assaults related to robbery or theft.[19]

Hung Sik Nam, who started his produce retail business in 1980, described the danger of robbery at HPM:

In the early 1980s there was no security system at HPM. When it was dark early in the morning, robbers with knives or pistols came in. Many Koreans were robbed and injured. Robbery occurred most frequently when we moved from one building to another. From behind, robbers choked our necks. Some Koreans got their teeth broken. Because we were scared of robbery, we tried to move in groups of four or five.

Records from the KPA show that several Korean greengrocers suffered serious injuries in the course of robbery. For example, on July 8, 1981, Jae Moon Kim suffered an armed robbery while looking for a parking lot at HPM. Two robbers—one threatening with a gun and the other hitting him with a steel pipe—asked for money. He was robbed of $3,000 and required several stitches in his head. On April 11, 1984, when Sung Soo Kim, then executive director of the KPA, was notified of the robbery, he called the police and described the two suspects and their vehicles. Then, using his own car, he helped the police chase and arrest the suspects. These two robbers were found responsible for five or six previous similar robberies targeting Korean greengrocers at HPM. According to the police officers, Kim volunteered to pursue the suspects despite being told that the police and the holdup men "might become involved in dangerous combat."[20] Sung Soo Kim's heroic actions won him the $1,000 Daily News Crimefighter of the Week Award.[21] In February 1987, Joo Tae Yoo, who had a store in Manhattan, fought against two robbers after he had been robbed of $2,000 near an HPM coffee shop. He suffered a head wound, but was able to help a dispatched police officer catch one of the robbers.[22] Yoo decided to fight because he had been a judo and tae kwon do champion in Korea. He told me, however, that he realized he had taken a considerable risk after hearing from the police officer that the robber had a pistol and a knife in his pocket. Both stories illustrate Korean greengrocers' frequent victimization through robbery and their unflinching responses to it.

Without fail, the KPA recognized local Bronx police officers who provided security for Korean greengrocers at HPM. In April 1984, for example, the KPA held an awards ceremony, at which they rewarded ten police officers who had shown dedication and exceptional kindness in protecting Korean merchants at HPM from robbery. Many other police officers, the deputy chief of the New York City Police Department, the Bronx Borough president, a few New York City Council members, and about eighty KPA members participated.[23] It was the largest awards ceremony by a Korean organization in New York to recognize police contributions to the security of Korean merchants. In the years that followed, the KPA frequently gave its annual appreciation awards to officers at the 42nd Precinct, which was responsible for policing HPM.

All former and current staff members of the KPA and Korean produce owners interviewed agreed that they experienced different forms of discriminatory treatment by the owners and employees of white produce suppliers, especially in the early years. According to one individual, in the 1970s, when the number of Korean produce store owners was very small, employees of wholesale stores often even did not answer when Koreans asked questions about prices. The most common form of damaging discrimination is not giving ordered items in the event of shortage of merchandise. Do Sup Kwack, one of the pioneers of the Korean produce business, described it this way:

> We usually ordered all needed produce items and paid for them, and then picked up merchandise with our vans at the end. We often found distributors posting a "Sold Out" sign in case of shortage of merchandise for a particular item. When we ordered it, they had merchandise. But they sold it to white greengrocers and supermarkets first, even if we had paid for it in advance. When they gave money back to us, we tried to argue it's not fair. But they did not listen.

This is a major problem for businesses because failure to get merchandise means a great loss of daily sales.

Regarding discrimination in parking allocations, distributors gave trailers from supermarkets a priority over Korean produce owners or truck drivers, often keeping Koreans waiting more than half an hour in front of the wholesale store. The following complaint by a Korean greengrocer, Sang Sung Lee, submitted to the Korean Produce Association on October 21, 1992, illustrates this form of discrimination:

> I was moving my car to park after a trailer had moved out. But a foreman of A & J told me to wait for another trailer. I waited half an hour in front of the store, but no trailer came. I asked the foreman why I could not park there when no trailer was coming. Cursing me, he pulled out his pistol and shouted at me, "I will shoot at your tires and puncture them." I waited. But he cursed me and told me to get out. It was early in the morning and I could not see anyone else around there. I was scared and left without buying any merchandise.

Korean greengrocers and truck drivers also had numerous conflicts with white truck and trailer drivers at parking lots, some of them turning into physical confrontations. Korean immigrants, who were usually physically weaker than whites, were often beaten.

Among the more serious problems were frequent beatings, other physical violence, and verbal threats and intimidation. Some Korean greengrocers were beaten by employees of distributors when they pointed out the poor quality of produce. For example, on April 12, 1982, when Jae Moon Choi complained about a box of rotten plantains, the manager (a son of the owner) of a white wholesale store punched him—a regular customer of the company—in the face. When the Korean victim tried to push back, four other employees joined the manager in beating and choking him.[24] Choi tried to run away, but a security guard chased and beat him. In another instance, a Korean greengrocer, Shin, was beaten in April 1986 by three employees of a produce wholesale company who chased after him screaming "Kill Koreans."[25] In a third case, a Korean truck driver, Jong Sun

Won, was beaten on October 27, 1995, by several Hispanic employees of K & H, a distributor at HPM. Won was hospitalized for three days with head injuries.

Most interviewees agreed that the language barrier, the failure of Korean greengrocers and truck drivers to follow regulations, and their hot tempers contributed significantly to their experiences with various discriminatory treatments and beatings. Especially in the 1970s and early 1980s, most Korean immigrants had severe language barriers, to the extent that they dealt with employees of distributors and security guards at HPM with only limited English phrases, such as "give me this" and "how much?" To make matters worse, Korean immigrants tend to have hot tempers and attitudes. These cultural factors, along with the language barrier, mean frequent altercations with distributor employees. One interviewee observed that both Korean greengrocers and Italian managers have hot tempers, which contributes to the conflicts between them. Some Korean greengrocers failed to pay after receiving produce items on credit several times, often leading to the middleman's bankruptcy and protests by distributors.[26] Interviewees also agreed that distributors charged higher prices to Korean greengrocers mainly because Koreans ordered in smaller quantities.

However, it is also true that many disputes and beatings arose from racial prejudice on the part of whites, both owners and employees, against Koreans. Moreover, that HPM is run by the cooperative association to protect the distributor interests and security needs rather than buyers is a major factor in the problems and inconveniences Korean visitors to the market encounter. The cooperative association charged extremely high penalties for parking violations to maximize their parking space and thus their business. Koreans paying parking penalties were often forced to pay two or three times because of clerical errors. Many Korean had their cars towed. It is one of many problems caused by the market structure. For this reason, in 1996 when the mayor proposed a new bill to eliminate the influence of organized criminal groups from HPM,[27] the KPA lobbied the Giuliani administration to demand that New York City rather than the distributors' association operate the market.[28]

Ethnic Collective Action and the KPA

Initially, Korean produce owners at HPM felt powerless because they more or less depended on white distributors for merchandise. Over time, however, they organized themselves to protect their interests and ensure their safety from distributors and the cooperative association through their trade organization, the Korean Produce Association. When the number of Korean greengrocers reached a critical point in the early 1980s, they were able to use their number power in collective action against suppliers. As we will see, greengrocers organized ten boycotts and demonstrations, nine of them against suppliers or the cooperative.

Informal meetings by a dozen Korean greengrocers at Korean restaurants for a few years led to the establishment of the KPA as a mutual aid and friendship association in 1974. Gradually, though, it evolved into an empowerment and service organization as Korean greengrocers encountered more and more conflicts with white suppliers and other interest groups. The association soon found its office at HPM and established a service center in 1980 to provide all kinds of services to Korean greengrocers and truck drivers. The KPA was formally registered as a nonprofit organization in New York State in 1982 and focused on helping Korean greengrocers and truck drivers at HPM with regard to their various problems in dealing with distributors and the cooperative association. As will be discussed in detail in chapter 7, these services also involve helping greengrocers in connection with various retail business issues, such as renewing building leases, disputes with customers, labor disputes, armed robberies, excessive competition among Korean business owners, violations of government measures, and administrative attendance for various ticket violations.

Most of the approximately 250 Korean truck drivers delivering produce items from Hunts Point Market to Korean retailers are one-truck independent business owners. Many of them, though, are employees of Korean trucking companies with two or more delivery trucks. Korean truck drivers maintain stronger social interactions and solidarity than Korean greengrocers because they meet with one another almost every day at Hunts Point Market and other wholesale produce markets. In 1990, they established the Korean Truck Drivers' Association to strengthen friendship and protect common interests. In 2002, it merged with the KPA. I asked Se Mok Lee, who had served as president of the Korean Truck Drivers' Association twice and as president of the KPA from 2003 to 2005, why the two organizations merged so late, given their common interest in fighting white produce suppliers at wholesale markets. He explained it this way:

> Korean truck drivers and greengrocers met at Hunts Point Market and other terminal markets every day, but they did not maintain close relations. There are two reasons. One was the tendency of some Korean greengrocers to look down on truck drivers. The other reason was the deliberate effort of produce suppliers to make the two Korean groups split so that we could not take the united front against them.

The KPA mobilized greengrocers effectively to take collective action against white suppliers' unfair treatment. To protect the retailers from higher prices charged by the suppliers, the KPA tried to establish a group purchase (gongdong gumae) system. Group purchase allows the trade association to buy large quantities of selected items for distributors' prices directly from farms and food-processing companies. The KPA staff had discussed the group purchase since the beginning and the issue arose regularly during board and executive meetings over the years. They visited farms in California, New York, and other states several times to explore the possibility of purchasing directly from producers.[29]

According to KPA annual reports and Korean newspaper articles, the trade association initiated group purchases of several produce items several times, in the late 1970s, in the late 1980s, and in the mid-1990s.[30] At no time, though, was it successful in continuing the group-purchase system, partly because Jewish and Italian wholesalers tried to destroy it and partly because KPA leaders did not have enough capital to compete with major HPM produce suppliers. Chang Il Kim, a greengrocer who had been deeply involved in the KPA activities in its early years, wrote a series of essays in *Korea Times New York* between March and June 1996. According to him, KPA leaders collected about $60,000 in 1978 to initiate a group purchase of selected produce items. When they purchased 500 boxes of one item (it did not specify what) to distribute to greengrocers for lower prices, he said, Jewish-owned wholesale companies sold the same items for farm prices to kill the group purchase system. Other interviewees also indicated that white suppliers put pressure on farms to not sell directly to KPA or Korean wholesalers.

Although KPA has not been successful in maintaining the group purchase system, it has been very effective in protecting Korean greengrocers and truck drivers from discrimination, mistreatment, and physical violence by suppliers at HPM. The KPA encouraged Korean visitors to report any mistreatment, dispute, or beating to its office. In the 1980s and early 1990s, staff members even regularly patrolled the HPM to ensure the security of all Korean visitors. Many disputes between Korean greengrocers and distributor employees, partly derived from language barriers, were resolved by the KPA. In the early 1980s, the KPA even held discussions with the cooperative association to work out Korean-language instructions for employees of produce suppliers to facilitate their communications with Korean clients, but the plan never materialized. KPA staff members also had regular (quarterly or monthly) meetings with representatives of the cooperative association to discuss the areas in which distributors needed to improve services to Korean merchants. Based on its members' complaints, the KPA also sent letters of protest and visited those distributors who treated Korean greengrocers unfairly in parking allocations and in other ways, warning them they would encounter more serious responses if they continued.

If a Korean visitor suffered physical violence or intimidation by a distributor employee or foreman, the KPA quickly reported the case to the

local police to arrest the perpetrator. The KPA then warned the distributors that if they did not accept its demands for an apology and other
requirements, they would face boycotts or demonstrations rather than
peaceful settlements. With a Korean victim's approval, they usually tried
to settle the matter before taking the case to the court or staging a boycott
or picketing. The KPA were successful several times before they took
collective action. In the case of Jae Moon Choi's beating by distributor
employees and foreman in April 1982, for example, the KPA made the
two perpetrators visit its office and make a formal apology.[31]

When distributors did not accept the KPA's proposal for peaceful
settlements, it organized demonstrations or boycotts against them. As
shown in table 4.1, between 1977 and 1995, it organized seven protests
against distributors and one against the cooperative association. One
boycott held in 1991 was organized by the Bronx Korean Merchants
Association against a produce distributor at the Bronx Terminal Market
after its member had been beaten by a white employee.[32] The 1995 demonstration was directed at the cooperative association as a protest against
the association's unfair treatment of Korean greengrocers and truck drivers
who visited HPM.[33] I have found that most protests occurred after physical violence against a Korean greengrocer by one or more distributor
employees.

The 1982 demonstration was the only mass KPA mobilization against an
organization other than produce suppliers; it targeted the *Daily News* that
had run Owen Moritz's "Point of View" column, charging Korean produce
store owners with being financially supported by the Unification Church.[34]
After three days of demonstrations in front of its building,[35] the *Daily News*
sent an apology and published a letter of protest sent by the Korean Association of New York.[36] The *Daily News* later carried two articles, one by its
staff member and the other by a reader, that described Korean greengrocers
as hard-working merchants and disputed their Moonie connection.[37] The
KPA's demonstrations against the *Daily News* and exchanges of articles in
the daily helped publicize the organization and greengrocers to New
Yorkers. Despite their initial bad relations and probably because of this
initial connection, the KPA and the *Daily News* collaborated on a few projects
in later years. For example, in 1987 and 1988, when Ki Jung Kim served
as president, the KPA and the *Daily News* co-sponsored City Harvest, a
nonprofit agency that helps feed the homeless in the New York area.[38] It
donated 10,000 pounds of onions and potatoes in 1987 and 13,000 pounds
in 1988. In 1987 the KPA and the *Daily News* also co-sponsored the Korean-
American amateur boxing match (see chapter 7).

In April 1986, the KPA organized a large-scale picket and boycott
against a produce supplier, deciding to boycott the wholesale produce
store after store employees severely beat two greengrocers in one month
on separate occasions, resulting in injuries in both cases.[39] As mentioned

Table 4.1   Demonstrations and Boycotts Against Produce Suppliers

Date	Issue or Immediate Cause	Demonstration Participants	Boycott— Duration
6/13/1977	Labeling Korean green-grocers as Moonies by white employee of Korean distributor	100	—
2/28–3/6/1980	Discrimination against Korean greengrocer by white employee of distributor	—	1 week
8/4–11/1981	A Korean greengrocer beaten, bleeding and unconscious, by several employees of a dis-tributor	250	1 week
8/2–5/1982	*New York Daily News* article charging Korean produce store owner with being financially supported by Unification Church	500	—
5/26–6/2/1985	Korean produce retailer falsely accused of stealing and detained	60	1 week
3/13–19/1986	Two Korean produce retailers beaten by employees of same dis-tributor at one week interval	200	1 week
7/4–8/20/1991	Korean produce store owner beaten by white employee of distributor	—	7 weeks
7/25–8/3/1991	A Korean produce store-owner at Bronx Terminal Market beaten by white employee of distributor[a]	—	1 week
2/18–21/1995	Protesting against vari-ous unfair measures of the Cooperative	30	—
11/8–17/1995	Korean greengrocer beaten by employees of distributor	200 300	10 days

Source: Author's compilation.

[a] The Bronx Terminal Market is another produce wholesale market, smaller than Hunts Point Market, located in the Bronx. The Bronx Korean Merchants Association organized the boycott.

earlier, in the second case, the foreman of a wholesale produce store and two employees beat a retailer, detaining and intimidating him for some time before releasing him. When the KPA notified the distributor of its decision to picket against and boycott the supplier, the owner responded by saying: "I am not concerned, because you Koreans easily fight amongst yourselves. Since you lack the spirit of ethnic unity, your boycott will end within a few days."[40]

Korean media reported on the physical violence and boycott with a headline of "Stop Racial Discrimination and Physical Violence."[41] In his announcement of the plan, which was posted on the wall of its office, Sung Hwan Kim, president of the KPA appealed to its members:

> [The supplier] still continues its racist and barbarian conducts against Koreans. . . . This is a god-given opportunity we Koreans can show up to those who look down upon us how strongly we can be united as a nation. With you members' full agreement we are starting a boycott against [the supplier] today. Every one of you should participate in the picketing this morning so that we can show our unity strong enough to break a rock with our individual minds and announce Korean ethnic pride to the whole world.

About 200 participants in the morning picketing on the first day of the boycott included ten Korean fish retailers.[42] After picketing for an hour and a half, a few KPA staff members distributed fliers about the boycott to Korean visitors and persuaded them not to purchase from the company. They also called all KPA members to let them know about the KPA's decision to boycott the company and asked them not to buy from it. The KPA made five demands as conditions for stopping the boycott, including the company's printing an apology in English-language dailies and firing the main perpetrator of the beating. When the boycott had been in force for several days, the HPM cooperative association and the produce distributors' association, at the request of the produce company, intervened to negotiate with the KPA. The New York City mayor's office also put pressure on both parties to settle the conflict quickly. On April 18, the produce company delivered a written letter to the KPA, accepting all but one demand. Its representative explained it could not fire the foreman because doing so would violate a labor law. With significant pressure from the mayor's office and the Justice Department, the KPA decided to end the boycott the following day.

All boycotts ended when the distributors accepted most of the KPA demands. With one exception, the boycotts lasted a week or a little longer. The distributors were forced to accept the KPA's demands because a boycott by greengrocers, who already made up about half of their customer base, would be a significant financial blow to any of them. The KPA leaders were well aware of their financial clout. The distributors also realized that if they did not treat the Korean merchants fairly, they would face more boycotts. They therefore made efforts to satisfy Korean merchants.

Since the latter half of the 1990s, the distributors have responded quickly to complaints and requests and boycotts are no longer necessary. The distributor attitudes toward Korean merchants have changed radically since the mid-1990s. In response to increasing health consciousness among consumers, supermarkets have begun to carry larger quantities of fruits and vegetables in recent years. The increasing tendency of supermarkets to buy produce items directly from farms since the early 1990s has contributed to greater distributor dependency on Korean greengrocers. White-owned distributors and Korean-owned greengrocers have in recent years grown mutually dependent, whereas Korean merchants more or less depended on distributors before 1990.

By organizing Korean greengrocers, the KPA has also been able to secure huge donations from produce suppliers. Its annual budget in 1991 was $650,000, larger than that of any other Korean business association at the time. Donations from produce suppliers comprised a signification proportion of the revenue, the rest being membership dues and profits from events. The KPA has asked produce suppliers to support its major annual activities: golf tournaments, the year-ending party held in a hotel ball room, and the Korean Harvest and Folklore Festival (the Korean version of Thanksgiving). It has also received monies from produce distributors for advertising in its monthly newsletters. Because it represented greengrocers, who were in the early 1980s already a significant proportion of produce supplier customers, the KPA had no difficulty in persuading produce suppliers to support its official activities. The KPA has spent some of the donations on scholarships and special donations to particular ethnic organizations.

= Chapter 5 =

Black Boycotts and Reactive Solidarity

The Korean Produce Association (KPA) was more concerned with black boycotts than any other Korean trade association in New York City, primarily because produce stores were targets of five of the seven long-term boycotts of Korean stores. However, when any boycott occurred, all Korean stores in the same neighborhood were affected. Moreover, not only the KPA but many other Korean ethnic organizations and individuals also participated in collective action to terminate the boycotts.

Korean-black conflict is probably the most hotly pursued topic relating to Korean immigrants' adjustment to American society; scholars have focused on the topic from different theoretical angles.[1] For example, Nancy Abelmann and John Lie use racial discourse theories to explain Korean-black conflicts. In their view, American racial ideologies, especially through mass media, depict Korean immigrants as a hardworking, model minority and African Americans as a lazy urban underclass, thus pitting them against each other.[2] Similarly, Claire Kim emphasizes the American racial order as generating Korean-black conflicts: "The differential positioning of blacks and Asian Americans (including Korean Americans) in the American racial order and their physical juxtaposition in the urban economy creates an immanent tendency for conflict between the two groups."[3] As we will see, Korean-black conflicts, which peaked in the later 1980s and early 1990s, have almost disappeared since the mid-1990s. Racial discourse theories or the racial order theory cannot explain the drastic change from the peak of the intergroup conflicts to their near-disappearance within the fifteen year period, because American racial ideologies and the racial order have not changed much since the mid-1990s.

The advantage of middleman minority theory in explaining black boycotts and other Korean-black conflicts is that it helps us understand both the causes of the middleman role in low-income black neighborhoods and its consequences (boycotts and other forms of rejection). Although many Korean immigrants still run businesses in black neighborhoods, Korean merchants there no longer encounter boycotts because they are no longer perceived as prominent middleman merchants. Thus the theory also helps us understand how and why Korean-black conflicts, which had been prevalent in the 1980s and early 1990s, have almost disappeared.

Middleman Minority Theory

Middleman minorities concentrate in trading and usually distribute merchandise produced by members of the dominant group to minority customers.[4] Jews in medieval Europe, the Chinese in Southeast Asia,[5] and Asian Indians in Africa[6] are prominent examples of middleman minorities. Middleman minorities existed in Third World pre-industrial, agrarian societies, such as in medieval Europe and pre-war Poland, or colonized societies, such as pre-war Philippines and pre-1994 South Africa. Both types needed an alien middleman minority because, as extremely polarized societies, they did not have a middle group to bridge the status gap, that is, to distribute merchandise produced by the ruling group to the consuming masses.

Several researchers have loosely used middleman minorities to refer to immigrant and ethnic groups with high concentrations in commercial occupations.[7] However, I believe the term *trading minorities* should be used to refer to immigrant and minority groups that concentrate in commercial occupations in various societies. In my view, as the classical theorists used it, middleman minorities should be reserved for the immigrant and ethnic minority groups that played or play an intermediary economic role in extremely stratified societies.

Middleman minority theory posits triadic causal relations among a middleman group's ethnic solidarity, its intermediary economic role, and its subjection to host hostility.[8] Ethnic solidarity contributes to a middleman minority's commercial activities, which generate host hostility. Host hostility further enhances the middleman minority's ethnic solidarity. Nevertheless, the literature on middleman minorities has focused on documenting host hostility encountered by middleman minorities and the various stereotypical characterizations of middleman merchants.[9] Middleman minority studies have neglected to empirically examine the effects of business-related intergroup conflicts and host hostility on ethnic solidarity on the part of middleman minorities.

A middleman minority is unlikely to develop in a contemporary postindustrial society with a large middle class segment such as the United States. Light and Bonacich pointed out that because of this they did not use middleman minority theory as a framework for examining

Korean immigrant entrepreneurship in Los Angeles.[10] However, in his article, Irwin Rinder suggested that the United States might need a middleman minority to bridge the huge white-black racial status gap.[11] Later, James Loewen tried to explain the concentration of Chinese immigrants in the Mississippi Delta in the black-oriented grocery business based on the white-black status gap.[12] He argued that, because of the racial status gap before 1960, few whites were willing to operate grocery stores in the black neighborhood and that this social structure provided Chinese immigrants with an opportunity for the grocery business in the black community.

In their 1980 book, *The Economic Basis of Ethnic Solidarity*, Bonacich and Modell treated Japanese farmers in California in the first half of the twentieth century as a middleman minority. The farmers, however, never played a middleman role in that they neither depended on white suppliers nor served predominantly minority customers. Moreover, notwithstanding its title, the book showed the positive effects of participation in the ethnic economy on ethnic attachment, not on ethnic solidarity. In my 1996 book, I used largely middleman minority theory to explain Korean merchants' multifaceted intergroup conflicts and their reactive solidarity in New York and Los Angeles. However, to consider all Korean merchants as middlemen is to overgeneralize their commercial activities because Korean service-oriented businesses neither depend on white suppliers nor serve primarily minority customers. Korean-owned retail businesses, such as grocery and liquor stores and produce stores, depend on white suppliers. Many are located in minority neighborhoods and thus have had numerous conflicts with both white suppliers and black customers.[13] Accordingly, only businesses in minority neighborhoods should be considered middleman minority businesses.

Typical middleman minorities, such as the Chinese in the Philippines and Indians in South Africa, maintained their middleman economic role over generations, because the ruling groups in these societies brought them there to play only that role, but did not allow for their intergenerational social mobility. However, social mobility is open at least to voluntary migrant groups in the United States. Before Korean immigrants moved into low-income black neighborhoods for business ventures in large numbers, beginning in the 1970s, Jews and Italians concentrated in black-oriented grocery and other retail businesses.[14] The race riots that had swept American cities in the 1960s, however, pushed them out of those neighborhoods. Third- and fourth-generation Jewish and Italian Americans could find more meaningful occupations in the general labor market. Korean immigrants, who were well educated but seriously handicapped in the general labor market because of the language barrier, replaced Jewish, Italian, and other white merchants in minority neighborhoods. But, as will be discussed later, newer immigrant groups—Indians, Pakistanis, and Arabs—have gradually been replacing Korean merchants in black neighborhoods since the early 1990s. This means new immigrant groups with disadvantages in the general labor market now play the middleman merchant role. Thus, I propose that the serial middleman minority thesis is useful in understanding the intermediary economic role of a new immigrant group in low-income minority neighborhoods in the United States. Light and Bonacich commented that because "a plurality of immigrant and ethnic minorities occupied fragmentary niches" in Los Angeles, their occupation of these business niches should be considered "middleman minority economic function."[15]

Some researchers referred to the phenomenon of newer immigrant groups replacing the earlier groups in retail businesses in minority neighborhoods as "ethnic succession."[16] But the ethnic succession thesis can be incorporated into the serial middleman minority thesis in that a series of new immigrant groups with disadvantages in the general labor market succeed the earlier groups in undertaking middleman businesses that bridge white corporations and low-income minority customers. The serial middleman minority thesis seems more useful than the ethnic succession thesis because the ongoing white-black racial inequality in the United States has helped new immigrant groups find small business niches in low-income minority neighborhoods.

Middleman minority theory posits that triadic causal relations among a middleman group's ethnic solidarity, its intermediary economic role, and its subjection to host hostility in the form of prejudice and physical violence.[17] Ethnic solidarity contributes to a middleman minority's commercial activities, which generate host hostility. Host hostility further enhances the middleman minority's ethnic solidarity. Because of their vulnerable economic position, along with their visibility, cohesion, and alien status, middlemen merchants were subjected to prejudice, hostility, and scapegoating by both the ruling group and subordinate groups in host societies. Minority customers blamed middleman merchants for their economic problems because they, having no political power, became easy targets. Thus, middleman merchants in different societies encountered boycotts, riots, and stereotypical prejudice.[18] Moreover, the government controlled by the dominant group can also use middleman merchants as scapegoats to protect itself from possible violence by members of a minority group in time of economic or political distress.[19]

Several studies have documented the boycotts and riots that victimized Jewish and other white merchants in African American neighborhoods.[20] Also, a number of studies pointed out that African Americans' economic contacts with Jews as landlords, merchants and employers greatly contributed to the development of anti-Semitism among African Americans.[21] Loewen also documented that Chinese grocers in the Mississippi Delta, as middleman merchants, were singled out for attack by black rioters in the

1960s. He suggested that Chinese grocers became easy targets because of their lack of power and scant police protection:

> A first consideration is that the Chinese stores are located directly in black areas. White-owned stores are mostly downtown, in the central business district. Rioters usually stay in their own neighborhood, where they know the turf and can remain more anonymous than if they venture outside. In addition, because whites, too, are still prejudiced against the Chinese, Chinese are perhaps a safer target than businesses owned by Caucasians. The Chinese cannot mobilize the police or other forces of repression against vandals as effectively as white merchants could.[22]

Is serving as a middleman merchant on its own a condition for antagonism? Many middleman theorists, including Bonacich,[23] would say yes. A few scholars, though, provided an additional condition. In response to Bonacich's 1973 article that emphasized the inevitability of victimization of middleman merchants, Sheldon Stryker pointed out that middleman merchants in some societies did not encounter hostility.[24] In his view, antagonism developed in a particular political context. He emphasized that they were subjected to rejection and hostility in societies in which ideologies associated with "emergent nationalism" developed. In his book focusing on middleman minorities, Walter Zenner similarly argued that antimiddleman ideologies played a critical role: "Anti-Semitism fits the nationalist conception that the nation must control its own economy and sees the danger in letting important sections fall under the control of strangers such as Jews."[25]

We can find similar anti-middleman tones in the Black Nationalist ideology in the United States. Founders of Black Nationalism—Marcus Garvey, Malcolm X,[26] and Stokely Carmichael and Charles Hamilton[27]—viewed the condition of black Americans as a colonized people within the United States. As internal colonies, black neighborhoods were politically, economically, socially, and educationally controlled by white society. The founders of the Black Nationalist ideology emphasized the economic, educational, and political autonomy of the black community as the central goal of the movement. In their view, the liberation of black neighborhoods from economic control by Jewish, Italian, and other white business owners was essential. We will see later that many boycotts of Korean stores were organized by Sonny Carson, a long-time Black Nationalist leader in New York City, and his associates, and that the Black Nationalist ideology was often used to criticize Korean commercial activities in black neighborhoods.

As noted, studies of middleman minorities have documented the victimization of middleman merchants by customers and the ruling group in the forms of boycotts, riots, and expulsion. They have neglected, however, to examine how middleman merchant experiences with boycotts and other forms of rejection solidified them. They have not said much about reactive solidarity against host hostility, because merchants had little power to react. They were almost completely government controlled. They maintained solidarity for protection and welfare, but a kind of internal solidarity focusing on mutual aid and cultural retention.[28]

Unlike the middlemen in aristocratic or colonial societies, in the United States middleman merchants are not subordinate to the dominant group. They can thus use ethnic collective action in response to both minority customer hostility toward their commercial activities, white supplier discrimination against them, and government agency measures to restrict their commercial activities. Korean immigrant merchants have used different forms of ethnic collective action to protect their business interests against all three groups.

Korean Stores in Black and Latino Neighborhoods

Korean immigrants' prevalence in business in lower-income black neighborhoods in New York and other cities was made possible by the influx of Korean immigrants and changes in American urban structure in the 1960s and 1970s. Based on his ethnographic research conducted in the late 1970s, Illsoo Kim published the first study on Korean immigrants in New York City. In it, he described how the retirement of Jewish and other white merchants from businesses in black and Puerto Rican minority neighborhoods helped Korean immigrants find small business niches there in the 1970s. As he put it, "Korean immigrants are able to buy shops from white minority shopkeepers, especially Jews, because the second- or third-generation children of these older immigrants have already entered the mainstream of the American occupational structure, and so they are reluctant to take over their parents' businesses."[29]

Nearly thirty years later, in 2006, I interviewed several elderly Koreans who had run businesses in minority neighborhoods in the 1970s. They told me similar stories about how retirement of white business owners encouraged Korean immigrants to move into black-oriented businesses at the time. As mentioned earlier, an elderly Korean produce wholesaler gave me a vivid story of how he and other Korean immigrants succeeded Jewish and other white ethnic members in the black-oriented produce retail business in Brooklyn. Won Duk Kim, who had opened a clothing store in Harlem in 1972, also said that he had found many empty buildings in Harlem in the early 1970s. An article in *New York Amsterdam News* supports his statement: "On 125th Street, between 1972 and 1978 there were about 29 vacant stores between Fifth Avenue and St. Nicholas Street."[30]

My fieldwork and personal interviews conducted in 1991 and 2006 indicate that Korean-owned stores located in minority neighborhoods offer produce, grocery and liquor, seafood, and manufactured goods imported from Korea and other Asian countries, such as clothing, handbags, hair-care items, and costume jewelry. The first three businesses depend entirely on white suppliers, whereas clothing and fashion stores depend largely on Korean wholesalers and importers. We can thus consider only produce, grocery, and seafood stores to be typical middleman businesses connecting white suppliers and minority customers. By contrast, Korean-owned dry cleaners and nail salons, two major service-related Korean businesses in New York City, have been highly concentrated in middle class white neighborhoods, although some of them are now visible in working class minority and multiethnic neighborhoods as well.

In addition to the retirement of white store owners, another important factor enabled Korean immigrants to run these retail businesses in minority neighborhoods in the 1970s and after. This was the withdrawal of supermarkets and department stores from minority neighborhoods and their reluctance to invest there on the basis of the low spending capacity of residents, high crime rates, and vandalism.[31] Many of these neighborhoods were transitional areas in the 1950s and 1960s, from which white residents were moving to suburban areas, and African Americans, Caribbean black immigrants, and Puerto Ricans were moving in.[32] As a result, until recently supermarkets and department stores were almost invisible in these minority neighborhoods but highly concentrated in white middle class neighborhoods.

For example, a survey conducted by the New York City Consumer Affairs Department in 1990 revealed that in Manhattan's Upper East Side, a predominantly white upper middle class neighborhood, there was one supermarket for every 5,762 persons, whereas in the Williamsburg area of Brooklyn, a poor black area, there was one for every 63,818 persons.[33] The withdrawal of supermarkets from lower-income black neighborhoods, or their unwillingness to invest there, helped immigrants establish grocery, produce, and seafood retail stores there. Similarly, the unwillingness of department stores to move into lower-income black neighborhoods enabled immigrants to run clothing and other types of fashion stores there. Korean immigrants, well educated but unable to find professional occupations in the United States because of the language barriers and other disadvantages, seized the opportunity in the small business vacuum. They began to move their retail businesses in these four sectors into black neighborhoods in the 1960s and 1970s.

By the mid-1980s, Korean-owned stores had become very visible to local residents in many black neighborhoods in New York City and made up a significant proportion of all stores located there. For example, when the boycott of Korean-owned grocery stores in Harlem occurred in October 1984, about forty of the 160 storefront businesses between Fifth and St. Nicholas Avenues on Harlem's main commercial strip (125th Street) were owned by Korean immigrants.[34] Almost all Korean-owned businesses there were retail shops that sold clothing, general merchandise, hair care, fruits and vegetables, grocery or seafood items.[35] Jewish and Italian merchants owned larger retail businesses, including furniture shops. African Americans owned most service-related businesses, such as barber shops, beauty parlors, and restaurants.[36] In 1991, the Korean Merchants Association in Harlem counted fifty-five Korean-owned stores in the same area of Harlem.

In April 1990, when the widely publicized boycott of two Korean produce stores in Brooklyn were in progress, the Church Avenue Merchants Block Association surveyed the ethnic background of store owners within six blocks between Flatbush Avenue and Buckingham Road on Church Avenue. According to the survey, Korean immigrants owned twenty-three of sixty-seven small businesses, blacks owned thirteen, and Jews owned eight.[37] Heon Chol Lee reported that all except three Korean stores there were retail, including four produce stores, and that they were very visible because of what they sold and what the owners looked like. Black-owned stores, on the other hand, were not easily visible to the casual observer. Many were located on the second story of buildings and were heavily service-related businesses, such as beauty parlors. Many Korean-owned retail stores were visible not only in that neighborhood, but also in many other black neighborhoods in Brooklyn in the early 1990s. In 1991, the president of the Jamaica Korean Merchants Association informed me that there were approximately 180 Korean-owned stores in Jamaica, a heavily black neighborhood in Queens.

Illsoo Kim reported that Korean immigrants in New York City preferred to establish their small businesses, not only in lower-income black neighborhoods, but also in lower-income Puerto Rican and Puerto Rican–black mixed neighborhoods in the Bronx in the 1970s.[38] He pointed to wig and fashion stores and produce-grocery stores as typical examples of major Korean retail stores in these neighborhoods at the time. Like Harlem and many other black neighborhoods in Brooklyn, these Latino or Latino-black mixed neighborhoods were racially transitional areas where Jewish, Italian and Irish storeowners were retiring. Dominican, Mexican, and African immigrants moved into various neighborhoods in the Bronx in the 1980s and 1990s. The number of Korean-owned stores in the Bronx that served mainly Latino and black customers continued to increase up to the early 1990s, reaching about 2,000 in 1991, according to the president of the Korean Merchants Association in the Bronx. Korean-owned stores in the Bronx included not only retail businesses, but also many dry cleaners and nail salons.

Prevalence and Process of Black Boycotts

As indicated in chapter 2, middleman merchants in other societies encountered boycotts, physical violence, prejudice, and even expulsion. Korean merchants in black neighborhoods in the United States experienced similar

Table 5.1   Black Boycotts of Korean-Owned Stores in New York City

Store Type	Location	Starting Date	Duration
Two produce	Jamaica	June 1981	35 days
Produce	Flatbush	February 1982	1 month
Grocery	Harlem	October 1984	6 months
Seafood	Jamaica	1986	not known
Produce	Bedford Stuyvesant, Brooklyn	August 1988	4 months
Produce	Harlem	September 1988	13 months
Two produce	Church Avenue, Flatbush, Brooklyn	January 1990	17 months
Fried fish	Nostrand Avenue, Brooklyn	March 1990	not known
Produce	Rockaway, Brooklyn	August 1990	12 days
Grocery	Lafrak City, Queens	February 1991	4 days
Toys	Brooklyn	May 1991	10 days
Grocery	Nostrand Avenue, Brooklyn	January 1992	3 days
All nonblack stores	Harlem	October 1994	11 days
Hats	Greenwich Village	1995	3 months
Bank	Broadway Manhattan	February 1995	7 days

Sources: Author's compilation based on Korean and English newspaper articles.

forms of rejection: verbal threats, physical violence, boycotts, arson, and the 1992 Los Angeles riots.[39] As Patrick Joyce pointed out, Korean merchants in black neighborhoods in New York City suffered far more long-term boycotts than those in Los Angeles, who suffered more violent forms of damage, such as shootings and firebombing of stores.[40] But nonviolent long-term boycotts, which Joyce characterizes as "heat without fire," are in a sense more threatening to Korean immigrants' economic survival than shootings and firebombing because they are direct and formal challenges to Koreans' commercial activities in black neighborhoods. Unlike shootings or arson, boycotts were organized in advance by black leaders and involved chanting "All Korean Merchants, Get Out of Black Neighborhoods."

As shown in table 5.1, between 1981 and 1995, Korean merchants in New York City encountered fifteen boycotts organized by blacks, six of which were long-term, that is, four weeks long or longer.[41] Korean produce stores became the main targets. Four of the six long-term boycotts occurred against Korean produce stores in black neighborhoods (two in Brooklyn, one in Jamaica, Queens, and one in Harlem), and another against a Korean-owned grocery-produce store in Harlem.[42] The last occurred in 1995 against a Korean-owned hat store in Greenwich Village, Manhattan, not a black neighborhood but nonetheless organized by black customers. The picketing against a Korean bank branch in Manhattan in February 1995 was organized by the African American Coalition against Racism, complaining about discrimination against blacks in mortgage and business loans and not hiring black employees.[43]

Some scholars have criticized Korean American researchers for exaggerating Korean-black conflicts. For example, Nancy Abelmann and John Lie and Sumi Cho argue that Korean-black conflicts were reifications of media stereotypes deeply rooted in American racial discourses.[44] Data presented in table 5.1 and results of Joyce's comprehensive survey of cases of Korean-black conflicts in many other cities, however, cast no doubt about the seriousness of these conflicts at least in the 1980s and early 1990s.[45] Jennifer Lee says: "By focusing only on the structural context, past researchers have allowed few options beyond conflict, and, in essence, overpredicted the level of conflict between merchants and customers in urban neighborhoods."[46] But what she calls "past researchers" have focused on collective conflicts, such as boycotts and demonstrations, rather than individual disputes involved in social interactions between Korean store owners-employees and black customers.[47] That Korean merchants in New York City faced fourteen boycotts in black neighborhoods, six of them long-term, during the fifteen years, but none in white neighborhoods,[48] is an important social issue that needs to be explained. However, in reporting numerous black boycotts of Korean stores, no one intends to suggest that a majority of black customers do not like Korean stores in their neighborhoods. As will be shown in the following paragraphs, according to a survey of residents in black neighborhoods, only a small proportion, but still a substantially higher proportion of them than white residents, supported the 1990 and 1991 boycott.

I summarize two of the six long-term black boycotts that occurred in New York City, the Harlem boycott of 1984 and 1985 and Church Avenue boycott of 1990 and 1991, and analyze Korean greengrocers' and other Korean merchants' responses to them. The Harlem boycott occurred on October 12, 1984, against two Korean retail stores on 125th Street, adjacent to each other and owned by I-Chul Shin. The boycott began after the police arrested an African American male customer, identified as Mark Jinks, who had allegedly beaten the female manager of Ike's Grocery and two white female police officers were called to the store to evict him.[49] The customer reportedly attacked the police officers by throwing a stool.

The boycott was organized by the Concerned People of Harlem Committee, represented by Juliet Hogan, a female black pastor. Hogan claimed that the customer had been tackled and attacked by five employees of the store and the police officer before he took action to defend himself.[50] She emphasized the lack of respect given to other black customers in the store as a justification for organizing the boycott: "I am just demanding a little respect to my brothers and sisters. I have watched a senior citizen— an elderly lady—mistreated by the merchants and I am tired of it."[51] When the grocery store was closed the next day, the boycott expanded to a produce store next door, which was owned by the same Korean. According to the daily reports of pickets prepared by the Korean Association of New York, several picketers picketed in front of the two stores, distributing fliers for the Buy-Black campaign to passers-by and blocking customers from getting into the stores.

On November 3, 1984, during the long-term picket, one of the picketers knocked down the fifty-four-year-old mother of a Korean seafood store owner to the pavement and struck her in the head, inducing a coma.[52] The seafood store was located on 125th Street, a few blocks from the two picketed stores. The picketers distributed fliers, urging blacks to boycott all Korean stores in Harlem. In fact, most Korean-owned stores on West 125th Street were closed during most of the boycott period. Some of the anti-Korean posters read "Get out of Harlem, Go back Home."[53] The picketers also made four requests, which included termination of the four designated Korean-owned stores in Harlem and the end of all Korean produce retail business in Harlem. The boycott ended in February 1985 when several Harlem black community leaders criticized it and news came that the Federal Bureau of Investigation was about to intervene.

The Church Avenue boycott in the Flatbush section of Brooklyn, beginning in January 1990 and ending in April 1991, is the longest boycott of Korean stores that has ever occurred in the United States. It received international media coverage and a great deal of scholarly attention.[54] It began after a dispute between Bong Ok Jang, the manager of the Family Red Apple, a Korean-owned produce store, and Giselaine Felissainte, a middle-aged female Haitian immigrant customer. She claimed that she had been falsely accused of shoplifting and slapped on the face several times by the owner of the store before she fell on the floor.[55] According to Bong Ok Jang, however, she had paid $2 for $3 worth of plantains and peppers and responded to the request for another dollar by hurling peppers to the cashier, who threw them back to her. Jang said that when the woman spat at the cashier and began interfering with the register displays, he put his hands on her shoulders to restrain her, but that she intentionally fell on the floor, screaming.

When the residents saw the woman being carried out of the store on a stretcher, they quickly gathered in front of the store and began picketing. The owner of the Church Fruits, a nearby produce store owned by Koreans, hid an employee of the Family Red Apple in his store, when the latter missed a van ride home and was chased by angry picketers.[56] Picketers therefore began to boycott the store a few days later. In the first week of the boycott, approximately 150 blacks participated, which led many Korean-owned stores in the neighborhood to close. Boycott organizers demanded that the two stores be closed as a precondition for further negotiations.

In 1990, white and black residents respectively made up 41 percent and 39 percent of the population of Flatbush.[57] Caribbean immigrants, most of whom were Haitian, accounted for the vast majority of residents in the business districts. Whites were concentrated in residential areas. The Flatbush Coalition for Economic Empowerment, a local Haitian empowerment activist group, initially organized the boycott.[58] Later Black Nationalist president Sonny Carson and his associates made it a long-term boycott by putting a dozen demonstrators on the street almost every day. Their leaflets exhorted residents to "boycott all Korean stores" and to avoid shopping "with people who do not look like us."[59] By emphasizing "people who do not look like us," boycott leaders tried to "racialize the issues and (people)" to get support from Haitian immigrants.[60] In fact, all Korean stores in the Flatbush area suffered a significant reduction of sales during most of the boycott period.

A Brooklyn District judge gave the temporary restraining order requiring boycotters to stay fifty feet away from the boycotted stores. The police did not enforce the order, however, for which New York City Mayor David Dinkins was severely criticized by the mainstream media, politicians, and citizens. Bona Jae Jang, one of the owners of the boycotted stores, along with five police officers, was beaten by picketers and residents, and Eun Ha Park, the pregnant wife of the other storeowner, Man Ho Park, was beaten by a picketer and because of it forced to have an abortion.[61] A boycott is typically a nonviolent technique, but this one and the one that occurred in Harlem in 1984 involved considerable violence. Mayor Dinkins's lukewarm effort led the Korean community to organize a major demonstration against the mayor in front of City Hall in September 1990. More than 7,000 Koreans participated.

Dinkins made a symbolic visit to the two boycotted stores and purchased fruits and vegetables a few days afterward.[62] His visit encouraged black residents to visit the boycotted stores. Additionally, in January 1991, a Brooklyn grand jury declared the store manager, who had been charged with a third-degree assault on the female Haitian customer, innocent. These two events seriously weakened the effort of the boycott organizers. The boycott ended in May 1991, after the owner of the store where the altercation had occurred sold the store to another Korean.[63] The Justice Department helped him get a $500,000 loan from the Small Business Administration to buy a new business in a white neighborhood.[64] The Brooklyn borough president, the New York City government, the FBI, the Justice Department, and numerous New York politicians were involved in resolving what was called one of the "most serious racial crises" in New York City.

As shown in table 5.1, four short-term boycotts of Korean stores in black neighborhoods occurred during the Church Avenue boycott. One, which focused on the R. & N. Fruit and Vegetable Market, was terminated sooner than expected, after twelve days, because Mayor Dinkins intervened quickly, attacking the legitimacy of continuing it after a change in ownership.[65] Also during the period, several Korean business owners and employees in black neighborhoods in Brooklyn and other parts of the city were the targets of harassment and physical violence by young blacks[66] and several other Korean stores were threatened with boycotts.[67] Korean merchants usually tried not to let their troubles with black customers be known publicly for fear of difficulty in selling their stores to other Koreans. In addition, several cases of altercations between Korean business owners or employees and black customers and physical violence against the former were reported during the same period.[68] It is also noteworthy that black boycotts in New York City in the early 1990s spread to other eastern cities, such as Philadelphia, Washington, and Atlanta.[69] It seems that the publicity and length of the Church Avenue boycott encouraged boycotts elsewhere.

A few cases of arson against Korean stores in black neighborhoods also occurred. The most prominent case involved Tong Kwang Kim and his wife, who purchased a grocery-produce store on Nostrand Avenue in Brooklyn in October 1990. After altercations with the owner of a neighboring black-owned store, Kim faced a boycott in January 1991 (see table 5.1) and a demand to hire a black worker.[70] The boycott ended after three days (see table 5.1) when he hired a black employee. Later, in August 1991, their neighbors told the Kims that two black men had attempted to break into the store at night and that one appeared to be a friend of their black employee. In response, they fired the employee. In December, about ten masked black men burst into their store and indiscriminately attacked them, leaving the wife severely injured. The police considered the attack a racial-ethnic bias incident and began round-the-clock surveillance. In February 1992, shortly after the surveillance ended, a fire broke out, destroying Kim's and several other stores. They had no fire insurance and thus lost their business. They strongly believed the fire was arson.[71] The Korean Association of New York, the Korean Small Business Service Center, and other organizations put pressure on the police to investigate the incident as a hate crime. The police, however, made no serious effort to arrest the suspect.

Explanations for the Boycotts

Other black boycotts of Korean stores started with similar confrontations between Korean store owners or employees and black customers. Generally, there were two different versions of how the confrontation had arisen. Disputes between owners or employees and customers became cause for immediate boycotts. Such sociopsychological factors as mutual prejudice, language barriers, and cultural differences as well as frequent shoplifting contributed to individual disputes in the stores. Given the nature of their business structures, Korean produce stores in black neighborhoods were more vulnerable to disputes with customers than other types of Korean retail businesses. Korean produce owners or employees often had conflicts with customers over which part of yams to cut, customers tasting fruits displayed on sidewalk tables, and customers' price bargaining.[72]

Even grocery stores have conflicts with customers over these issues less frequently than produce stores because grocery items are usually sealed with price marks. Korean service businesses in black neighborhoods, such as dry cleaners and nail salons, typically did not have disputes with customers, partly because of the nature of interactions between customers and owners or employees, and partly because of the class backgrounds of customers. As Jennifer Lee pointed out, Korean nail salon owners have better relations with their black customers than their co-ethnics in the grocery business do because "manicures require both extended physical contact and one-to-one conversation in a more private social space."[73] Moreover, customers of Korean-owned nail salons and dry cleaners in black neighborhoods are either middle class or working class with steady jobs, whereas customers of Korean produce or grocery stores include many people with no regular jobs. In addition, shoplifting, which occurs frequently in these retail stores, is by definition impossible in nail salons or dry cleaners. Because shoplifting is so common, Korean merchants need to watch their customers more closely, which many black customers consider disrespectful.

The boycotts, however, were catalyzed by more fundamental issues, such as black residents' underrepresentation in retail businesses in their own neighborhoods and their perception of Korean merchants as exploiting blacks economically. In this connection, it is important to note that almost all major boycotts of Korean stores in black neighborhoods in New York City were organized by Black Nationalists such as George Edward Tait and Sonny Carson. In 1981, even before residents targeted a particular Korean store in Harlem, members of the Universal Negro Improvement Association, representing the remnants of Marcus Garvey's Black Nationalist movement of the early 1920s, posted the Buy Black and Boycott Korean Store signs (Rule 1982). In a special interview with the *New York Amsterdam News* in 1981, Malvin Locus, president of the 125 Business Association, expressed his opinion that "If they [the Black merchants] want to drive them [Korean merchants] out . . . the voice of the community will rule."[74] Tait, secretary of the African Pioneer Movement and a leader in organizing two major boycotts against Korean stores in Harlem, was an ardent supporter of the Buy Black campaign. He expressed the boycotts' major goal in economic terms: "There is only one uncompromising objective, the removal of non-Black businesses from the Black community; there is only one unequivocal goal, the economic control of the Black community by its Black resident majority."[75] The critical role of the Black Nationalist ideology and Black Nationalists in organizing boycotts of Korean produce stores in black neighborhoods is consistent with the propositions of middleman minority theory. Historically, nationalistic anti-middleman ideologies played a central role in rejecting middleman merchants.[76]

By presenting it as an anti-middleman ideology that challenged commercial activities of Korean and other immigrants in black neighborhoods, I seem to paint Black Nationalism in this chapter as a somewhat racist, dogmatic ideology. But I must point out that it has many positive elements essential to the empowerment and autonomy of the black community in the United States, a highly racist society. In this connection, we need to note that rejection of immigrant merchants in black neighborhoods by Black Nationalists beginning in the 1960s had intellectual root in the Double Duty Dollar doctrine preached by black pastors and writers in the 1940s. The doctrine emphasized the importance of black customers supporting black merchants by pointing out that a dollar spent in a black-owned store not only served the duty of buying merchandise for the black consumer but also contributed to the economic prosperity and economic autonomy of black neighborhoods.[77] As a Koran immigrant sociologist sympathetic to Korean immigrant merchants' difficulties, I use middleman minority theory to explain black boycotts of Korean stores. I also, however, believe it important that some scholars explain the same social phenomenon with the Black Nationalist perspective. For example, it is good that Claire Kim, a second-generation Korean scholar, interpreted the Church Avenue black boycott of two Korean stores from the Black Nationalist perspective, though I have found a number of problems in her results.[78]

By emphasizing the role of Black Nationalism, however, I do not intend to suggest that the majority of blacks embrace the emphasis of the ideology on economic autonomy. My 1992 survey of black and white residents in three black neighborhoods where Korean merchants encountered boycotts indicates that 27 percent of the ninety-eight black respondents endorsed the statement that "I supported the 1990–1991 boycott" and 14 percent agreed that "blacks should not buy from Korean stores." However, substantially more black respondents agreed to these two statements than white respondents who lived in the same neighborhoods. Only 8 percent of fifty white respondents supported the boycott and none endorsed the statement of not purchasing from Korean stores. Results of a Gallup Poll conducted in June 1990 showed similar findings about racial differences in supporting the boycott: 27 percent of black respondents, compared to 6 percent of white respondents and 8 percent of Latino respondents, supported the boycott.[79] Although relatively small proportions of black respondents supported the boycott and not purchasing from Korean merchants, their numbers were enough to challenge Korean merchants in black neighborhoods. The racial difference in the degree of supporting each statement helps us understand why Korean merchants

Table 5.2   Acceptance of Statements Stereotyping Korean Immigrants

Stereotypes	Black Respondents (Number = 97)	White Respondents (Number = 50)	Significance
Koreans are overly concerned with making money	45.4	26.0	$p < 0.05$
Koreans do not try to learn English and American customs	34.4	24.4	$p > 0.1$
Koreans care only about other Koreans	44.3	30.0	$p < 0.1$
Koreans are in general rude and nasty people	22.7	8.0	$p < 0.05$

Source: Author's compilation from the 1992 New York City Survey of Black and White Respondents.

in black neighborhoods encountered several boycotts and those in white and Latino neighborhoods encountered none.

My 1992 survey results also show that Korean merchants in black neighborhoods were subjected to stereotypes similar to those Jews and other middleman groups encountered (see table 5.2). There is a significant black-white racial differential in the degree of endorsing each stereotypical statement. For example, 45 percent of black respondents, compared with 26 percent of white respondents, accepted the statement that "Koreans are overly concerned with making money." Forty-four percent of black respondents, compared with 30 percent of white respondents, endorsed the statement that "Koreans care about only other Koreans." Both statements are typical stereotypes ascribed to middleman merchants in different societies. About 25 percent of black respondents also agreed to the statement that "Koreans are in general rude and nasty people," but only 8 percent of white respondents did.

As indicated, local residents accused minority middleman merchants of being aided by the dominant group to run businesses in their area, which partly contributed to antagonism toward the merchants. In much the same way, black boycott leaders often charged that the federal government, commercial banks, or even the Unification Church funded Korean businesses in black neighborhoods.[80] There is no evidence, however, that either the federal government or commercial banks did so. As indicated in chapter 4, survey studies of Korean immigrant merchants reveal that Korean immigrants used the savings brought from Korea and made in the United States as the major sources of capital for their initial businesses, and only a tiny fraction depended on commercial loans.[81]

I have pointed out that many Korean merchants ran similar types of retail businesses in Latino neighborhoods in the Bronx, but did not encounter any rejection by Latino residents or customers.[82] Latinos in the Bronx—not only Latino immigrants but also native-born Puerto Ricans—did not reject Korean merchants by using collective action because, unlike African Americans, they had not developed an ideology to emphasize their economic autonomy. Latino residents did not consider Korean immigrants' commercial activities in their neighborhoods as an economic invasion. In fact, as suggested by Lucie Cheng and Yen Le Espiritu[83] and documented by In-Jin Yoon,[84] and as will be discussed in chapter 7 in more detail, Latinos and Korean merchants share the immigrant dream ideology, that if they work hard they can make it in the United States. Latino residents do not seem to consider Korean merchants in their neighborhoods to be intruders, and thus seem more willing to accept them. In Yoon's survey, Korean merchants reported experiencing far less frequent clashes with Latino customers than with black customers.[85]

I have tried to show that Korean merchants experienced boycotts and other forms of rejection by black residents and customers mainly because of their middleman role. Nevertheless, I agree that language barriers, Korean prejudice, and cultural differences contributed to personal disputes between Korean merchants or employees and black customers. Although I do not consider that these are primarily responsible for black boycotts, I address them here to give readers a more balanced perspective on Korean-black conflicts. They are relevant because they determine the development of Korean-black relations at present and in the future, when Korean immigrants no longer run businesses in black neighborhoods in large numbers.

As noted, blacks have many misperceptions about Korean merchants. Koreans, however, seem to have more prejudice against blacks than the other way around, which negatively affects the way Korean merchants serve black customers. In the 1992 survey, even 23 percent of Korean merchant respondents agreed that Korean merchants' rudeness to black customers contributed to interracial tensions in Korean-owned stores in black neighborhoods. To examine this systematically, I provided four stereotypical statements in the 1992 survey and asked Korean merchants to report the degree of their agreement or disagreement to each statement using five categories. Table 5.3 offers percentages of the respondents who *strongly or moderately agreed* to the four statements regarding negative stereotypes of blacks. The majority of the ninety-three Korean merchant respondents accepted two stereotypical statements about blacks (being less intelligent or less honest than whites), and two-thirds of them accepted the view that blacks are more criminally oriented than whites. Results of Yoon's 1995 survey of Korean merchants in Los Angeles about diligence, self-supporting, intelligence, and violence also show similar findings about their unfavorable views of blacks, compared to whites, Asian and Latinos.[86]

Source: Photo by Dong Wan Joo, used with permission.
The main gate of Hunts Point Market (New York City Produce Market). Hundreds of Korean greengrocers pass this gate every day, mostly early in the morning, for purchase of fruits and vegetables.

Source: Photo by Dong Wan Joo, used with permission.
Approximately seventy produce wholesalers are located inside Hunts Point Market. In the 1970s and 1980s, many Korean greengrocers experienced physical violence and unfair treatment from wholesalers, which led them to boycott wholesalers several times.

Source: Photo by Dong Wan Joo, used with permission.
Photos of the Korean Produce Association's past and current presidents and proclamations and awards presented in various years by New York City and State governments and their legislative branches to recognize the trade association's achievements and services for the Korean community and New York City are hung on the wall of the KPA's main office.

Source: Photo by Dong Wan Joo, used with permission.
Since 1982, the Korean Produce Association has held the Korean Harvest and Folklore Festival at the Flushing-Meadow Park in October. This two-day festival has drawn more than 150,000 people annually during recent years. This photo captures a team of Korean experts performing samulnori, the most famous Korean traditional folk dance, at the 2006 festival.

Source: Photo by Dong Wan Joo, used with permission.
Hwang Chin Min came to New York City in 1986 and opened his produce store in 1990 in Jamaica. He established this one in 1997. He said that sales from the sidewalk table (jwadae) outside of the store comprise a significant proportion of total sales.

Source: Photo by Dong Wan Joo, used with permission.
Many trailers from supermarkets are parked in front of produce wholesalers at Hunts Point Market. In the 1970s and 1980s, Korean greengrocers had conflicts with trailer drivers over parking space, sometimes escalating into physical confrontations.

Source: Photo by Dong Wan Joo, used with permission.
Korean produce retail stores can successfully compete with supermarkets in selling fruits and vegetables because they can clean and display them nicely, as shown in this photo taken in a upper-middle class white neighborhood in Westchester County.

Source: Photo by Dong Wan Joo, used with permission.
The Korean Produce Association arranged the Korean Agricultural Cooperative to display and sell major Korean farm products at the annual Korean Harvest and Folklore Festival.

Table 5.3   Korean Merchants Stereotyping Blacks

Stereotypical Statements	Number of Respondents = 93
Black people are generally less intelligent than white people	61.3%
Black people are generally lazier than white people	45.2
Black people are generally less honest than white people	61.3
Black people are generally more criminally oriented than white people	69.9

Source: Author's compilation from the 1992 New City Survey of Korean Merchants in Black Neighborhoods.

Some researchers have pointed out that Korean immigrants had, for the most part, learned their negative views of African Americans in their home country before they immigrated through exposure to the American media.[87] No one would deny this effect. But attributing negative stereotypes to American cultural influence before immigration is as simplistic as the attempt to reduce all forms of racial conflicts in the United States to white racism. I also consider it somewhat irresponsible to blame white racism alone for Korean immigrants' prejudiced attitudes toward blacks without analyzing the complexity of its sources. Korean immigrants are far more strongly influenced by the mainstream media now than before. This interpretation suggests that Korean immigrants' prejudice will only deepen the longer they live in the United States.

I presume that Korean immigrants, especially those who came to the United States in the 1970s and early 1980s, had little knowledge of African Americans before their immigration. I believe that Korean merchants' prejudice against blacks, as well as black residents' prejudice against Korean merchants, developed mainly through their contact in Korean-owned stores. The merchant-customer relationship is by definition prone to conflict because each party has a different interest. In particular, the relationship between Korean merchants and black customers in a retail store in a lower-income black neighborhood maximizes this inherent stress.[88] Herbert Blumer's view of racial prejudice as "a sense of group position," rather than individual feelings, is useful in understanding mutual prejudice between Korean merchants and black customers.[89] As mentioned, in a 1995 survey of Korean merchants conducted in Los Angeles, 60 percent of the respondents reported that they had more clashes with black customers than with Latinos.[90] In responding to the follow-up question about the reasons for more clashes with blacks, the majority said that "blacks are more demanding and assertive" in terms of their requests for better prices, credit, and services. Another 34 percent reported that blacks are more likely to lie, shoplift, and use bad language.[91] These reports suggest that

Korean merchants' prejudice has developed very much in the process and context of business transactions in the stores.

Most Korean immigrants who run businesses in lower-income black neighborhoods are college-educated, middle class people, living in intact families. In sharp contrast, a large proportion of their customers are unemployed, often living in nontraditional family settings. Many of the neighborhoods where the Koreans operate their businesses are infested with crime, gang violence, and drugs and many merchants in black neighborhoods have been killed during armed robberies. Because Korean merchants have had little contact with middle class professional blacks, it is easy for them to generalize characteristics of their customers to the black population in general.

An important factor in the racial attitudes of Korean immigrants toward blacks is their Confucian cultural values, which emphasize hard work, frugality, strong family ties, and education as the main channel for social mobility.[92] Many other Asian, Latino, and Caribbean voluntary immigrant groups emphasized the same values.[93] As segmented assimilation theory suggests, these values help immigrants achieve social mobility in the United States.[94] However, these values, combined with the immigrants' lack of racial history in American society, also hinder immigrants from understanding social sources of class, racial, and gender issues.[95] In the 1992 survey, 40 percent of Korean merchant respondents *strongly agreed* to the statement: "In this country, anyone, regardless of race, sex, or national origin, can make it if he or she works hard." But only 20 percent of black and 14 percent of white resident respondents *strongly agreed* to it. The tendency of Korean merchants to embrace the American dream ideology—their strong cultural orientation to social issues—is a major source of their negative views of blacks, which are reflected in the results of my 1992 survey.

Effects of Boycotts on Ethnic Solidarity

Black boycotts of Korean produce and other types of stores were more threatening to Korean immigrants' economic survival than discrimination from white suppliers and thus contributed to stronger Korean ethnic solidarity. Moreover, whereas conflicts with white produce suppliers contributed primarily to class solidarity, black boycotts solidified the Korean immigrant community as a whole. Here we examine the positive effects of black boycotts on Korean ethnic solidarity with a focus on the two boycotts of Korean stores reviewed earlier.

When the 1984 boycott started in Harlem, the executive director of the KPA, Sung Soo Kim, took a leading role in the effort to end it, working closely with both the president of the Korean Merchants Association in Harlem (KMAH), Won Duk Kim, and the president of the Korean Association of New York (KANY), Ik Jo Kang. Kim took the leading role partly because he was able to communicate with boycott organizers, politicians, and American media effectively, and partly because the owner of the boycotted stores was a KPA member. This shows the importance of the involved business association's leadership and its political skills in dealing with black boycotts. Kim has been involved in resolving not only the 1984 Harlem boycott, but also all other subsequent major black boycotts of Korean stores. Moreover, later, as president of the Korean Small Business Service Center and the Small Business Congress, he has fought passionately to protect Korean and other small business owners from white suppliers and government agencies. Fluent in English, with degrees from Seoul National University and the University of Virginia and graduate work at Columbia University, he has been tough in negotiations with government officials about various regulations of small business activities.

To terminate the boycott, Kim, along with his KANY and KMAH colleagues, had meetings with New York City Mayor Koch, several black city council members, and the local police, a few times. Kim also organized several rounds of meetings between Korean leaders and leaders of the Uptown Chamber of Commerce (a Harlem-based black merchants association) to ask them to intervene to stop the boycott.[96]

The Uptown Chamber of Commerce (UCC), however, was unwilling to intervene before it reached a set of agreements with the Korean representatives to make Korean merchants hire more black employees, donate to the Harlem neighborhood, and participate in coinvestment and vocational training programs as a long-term solution. Korean representatives insisted on ending the boycott as a precondition for working out these agreements. Thus Korean leaders gave up negotiating with the UCC and focused on influencing the city government and politicians to condemn the boycott. After several meetings, Kim persuaded several New York State legislators and New York City councilmen to hold a press conference to express their criticism of the boycott.[97] As a result, the political leaders read the following statement on January 20, 1985:

> We firmly believe that shopkeepers are entitled to locate anywhere in the city without regard to race, religion, country of origin, or sex. We deplore picketing shopkeepers if the aim is to prevent them from carrying on a lawful business. We believe that the picketing of certain Korean green grocers on 125th Street is not a proper way to deal with the various problems that have arisen.

All this seriously weakened the will of the boycott leaders to continue. The lawyer of one Harlem business owner asked the FBI to investigate. That news persuaded the organizers to stop the boycott in the mid-February.

The Church Avenue boycott occurred about a year after a Brooklyn boycott organized by Sonny Carson and his associates had forced three Korean stores to shut down.[98] Korean leaders believed that if the two boycotted stores were closed, more stores would be targeted. Thus they made all efforts not to allow the two stores to be closed. In the early stages, the KPA and the Korean Merchants Association in Brooklyn raised donations, mostly from their members, to help the victims of the boycott keep their stores open without sales. The Korean Association of New York and other business associations followed them in collecting donations. *Korea Times New York,* the largest Korean ethnic daily in the area, and other ethnic media joined the fundraising and buy-merchandise campaigns, receiving monies from Korean immigrants in other cities as well as in the New York area. Some Korean church members handed the owners of the boycotted stores envelopes with a few hundred dollars collected through special donations in Sunday mornings. The donations collected in the first year of the boycott (approximately $150,000) helped each of the two owners of the boycotted stores receive $7,000 each month for ten months.[99]

The donations given by greengrocers made up the bulk of the $150,000. The KPA established the ad hoc committee (the Church Avenue Boycott Resolution Committee) in early February 1990 to deal with the boycott. It put priority on donations so that the stores could survive.[100] It then collected more than $10,000 within a few days from staff members of the KPA and other Korean greengrocers who visited HPM and the Brooklyn Terminal Market.[101] Bo Young Jung, president of the KPA during the Church Avenue boycott, said that produce retailers were very generous in donations, several staff members each donating $500 per month. Beginning in April 1990, the owners of the two boycotted stores kept their businesses open for twenty-four hours each day, taking advantage of the fact that there would be no picketers early in the morning and late in the evening.[102] Some greengrocers also took turns in working at the boycotted stores at night to relieve the store owners. According to the president of the Flatbush Korean Merchants Association in an interview conducted in 1991, before the boycott, the two store owners were not on speaking terms.[103] Their common experience with the boycott, however, united them solidly.

Korean business and community leaders met many politicians in the New York area, some of them several times, and pressured them to take action. The politicians they contacted included the Brooklyn borough president, the mayor, and members of the city council and of the state legislature. Sung Soo Kim, who served as KPA executive director during the 1984 to 1985 Harlem boycott, established the Korean Small Business Service Center in April 1985 to help to protect Korean merchants from outside interest groups and government agencies.[104] Both Kim and Michael Kang, the new executive director of the KPA, were involved in lobbying politicians in the early stage of the boycott, often competing with each other for the initiative. By virtue of his experiences with previous black boycotts in Harlem and Brooklyn, however, Kim gradually took the initiative in dealing with government agencies and politicians, and Kang focused on negotiating with black community leaders and black organizations. Kim's aggressive but effective publicizing efforts to frame the black boycott as the racist attempt to scapegoat innocent victims contributed to severe criticisms of Sonny Carson and other boycott organizers by political leaders and the media in the New York area. A group of Korean community leaders also visited the White House to ask President Bush to help terminate the boycott.[105] That meeting prompted the Justice Department to intervene.

The prolonged boycott prompted the Korean community to organize the Korean-American Civil Rights Committee (KACRC) within the Korean Association of New York to protect Korean Americans' civil rights and racial justice.[106] In September, the newly established KACRC organized the mass rally, mentioned earlier, to put pressure on Mayor Dinkins to take quick action against the boycott. In the rally, not only Korean community leaders but also many white and black community leaders and politicians went to the podium to condemn Dinkins for having not personally intervened. Two of the major demands were that the boycott be immediately terminated and that Dinkins enforce the court order that picketers stay fifty feet away from the stores.[107] Dinkins accepted the demands quickly and enforced the court order the same day.

No More Middleman Role
and No More Boycott

The Church Avenue boycott is the last long-term black boycott of Korean stores in a black neighborhood in New York City,[108] and the number of boycotts and other forms of rejection of Korean stores in black neighborhoods in other cities has dropped dramatically,[109] to the extent that Korean-black conflict is no longer an important research issue. Black boycotts of Korean stores have disappeared. What factors have contributed to this? The increasing sensitivity of Korean merchants to black customers and the strengthening of ties between Korean-black communities[110] have of course played a minor role. The movement of mega-stores and many non-Korean immigrants into black neighborhoods for business ventures and the gradual change in racial composition in black neighborhoods are the two most important reasons for the decline.

Results of my ethnographic research conducted in the three major black areas in 1991 and 2006 support this interpretation. According to my interview with president of the Korean Merchants Association in Harlem in 1991, there were fifty-five Korean-owned stores in the heart of Harlem (on 125th Street between St. Nicholas Avenue and Madison Avenue). In

2006, I counted only fourteen in the same area. Ten of the fourteen were beauty supply, clothing, and shoe stores. In 1991, ten of the fifty-five were middleman businesses, three grocery, four produce, and three seafood. In 2006, only one produce store and one seafood store survived. The three blocks between St. Nicholas Avenue and Lenox Avenue on 125th Street were filled with more than thirty chain mega-stores, among them, Modell's Sporting Goods, Pathmark, Old Navy, Duane Reade, and Foot Locker.

This change is a specific result of the change in the zoning laws in the late 1990s. In 1996, Mayor Rudolph Giuliani made a proposal to make it easier for mega-stores to open in city neighborhoods.[111] Sung Soo Kim, president of the Small Business Congress of New York City and director of the Korean Small Business Service Center, led many Korean and non-Korean small business organizations in lobbying City Council members and holding a major demonstration to oppose the proposal.[112] Many other community groups were also concerned about increased traffic near residential areas.[113] Despite their combined lobbying efforts, the New York City Council passed a revised version of his proposal in 1997.

I asked a few Korean business owners who had shops on 125th Street about the reduction of Korean-owned stores in Harlem. All emphasized rent hikes as the main reason for the drop. Sang Hwa Lee, who owned a clothing store on the busiest part of 125th Street, described what had happened:

> Since mega-stores moved into this area in the late 1990s, landlords have raised commercial rents ruinously. Especially after former president Bill Clinton opened his office in this area in the early 2000, rents jumped. When I renewed my lease two years ago, my landlord doubled the rent. So I pay $13,000 per month for this little space. Former Mayor Giuliani emphasized the benefits to black residents when he tried to invite mega-stores to Harlem. But it has helped only Jewish landlords and developers at the expense of small business owners. The only positive change for us is a more security due to the increase in the police force.

I talked with another Korean immigrant who had a beauty supply store that sold wigs, braids, and other hair-care items in the heart of Harlem and paid nearly $20,000 in monthly rent. According to him, Korean immigrants can compete with mega-stores and other independent business owners carrying beauty-supply items because they get merchandise from Korean wholesalers for special prices.[114] He was concerned, however, that another rent hike in two years might prevent him from continuing his business at the same location. My interviews with Korean business owners in Harlem indicate that white landlords and developers may have benefited far

Table 5.4   Racial Composition of Central Harlem

Race	Year		
	1980	1990	2000
Non-Hispanic black	101,830 (94.1%)	88,760 (88.1%)	84,224 (76.9%)
Native-Born black	—	—	74,643 (68.2%)
Foreign-Born black (predominantly Caribbean and African-born)	—	—	9,581 (8.7%)
Non-Hispanic white	1,058 (1.0%)	1,367 (1.4%)	2,399 (2.2%)
Non-Hispanic Asian and Native American	575 (0.5%)	624 (0.6%)	1,205 (1.1%)
Hispanic	4,540 (4.2%)	9,778 (9.7%)	18,450 (16.8%)
Other	157 (0.2%)	163 (0.2%)	3,256 (3.0%)
Total	108,160 (100.0%)	100,692 (100.0%)	109,534 (100.0)

Source: Infoshare (1980, 1990, 2000).

more than residents in low-income minority neighborhoods from zoning changes.

The movement of mega-stores into Harlem hurts Korean and other small business owners in terms of retail prices as well. Pathmark grocery stores carry grocery, produce, and seafood items. Two such stores less than ten blocks apart have killed all but two similar Korean-owned enterprises. These have survived mainly because, as medium-sized stores, they were able to offer items for reasonable prices.

Another factor was the emergence of many other non-Korean immigrant business owners. Indian, Pakistani, Middle Eastern, and African immigrants have moved into Harlem for commercial activities since around 1995. They own retail stores selling clothing items, hats, bags, costume jewelry, and convenience items. Chinese immigrants also run restaurants, nail salons, and dry cleaners in Harlem. Korean store owners complain that these other immigrants run businesses with tiny profit margins. A positive aspect of the change is that the ethnicity among business owners is now so diverse that Korean merchants there are no longer perceived unfavorably. Neither Koreans nor any other group in Harlem are perceived as middleman merchants, although they still do serve that function.

Finally, the change in the racial composition of residents in Central Harlem over the years seems to have seriously weakened the African American sense of territory. As shown in table 5.4, the proportion of non-Hispanic black residents in Central Harlem decreased from 94 percent in

1980 to 77 percent in 2000. The Hispanic population, on the other hand, increased from 4 percent in 1980 to 17 percent in 2000. The movement of many Dominican immigrants into Central Harlem contributed to this increase. In 2000, about 9 percent of black residents in Harlem were Caribbean and African immigrants. African Americans, who might have considered Harlem their territory in 1980, made up less than 68 percent of its population in 2000.[115] By 2007, the Hispanic and black immigrant populations in Central Harlem are likely to comprise even larger proportions than in 2000. Moreover, under the impact of the government-initiated gentrification plan, many middle class white and black Americans have moved into Harlem in recent years, further contributing to the racial and class diversity. In short, Harlem has changed from a predominantly lower-class African American neighborhood to a multiracial neighborhood.

In the Church Avenue–Flatbush Avenue area, I found that similar changes had pushed out Korean immigrant merchants. As noted earlier, Korean immigrants owned twenty-three of the sixty-seven stores within six blocks between Flatbush Avenue and Buckingham Avenue on Church Avenue in Brooklyn in 1990. In the summer of 2006, I counted only twelve Korean-owned stores in the same area, though the total number of stores appeared to have increased well beyond sixty-seven. The five Korean-owned produce stores were reduced to two. Interestingly, these two were those that had been the targets of the Church Avenue black boycott in 1990 and 1991. I noticed Dominican, black, South Asian, Middle Eastern, and Chinese store owners as well as eleven mega-stores, including a mini department store, two dollar stores, a pharmacy, and a jewelry shop. The two Korean produce stores could offer produce items more cheaply than their competitors because they purchased directly from farms in large quantities.

I talked with Young-Sik Kim, former president of the Flatbush Korean Merchants Association, who owned a supermarket and a large produce store on Flatbush Avenue about seven blocks from the Church Avenue's main shopping strip. He had started his produce business in 1989. According to him, the numbers of Korean-owned stores in Brooklyn generally have been substantially reduced since the mid-1990s. He explained it this way:

> Dominicans, Indian, Pakistani and Arab immigrants have also moved into this area for business ventures. As young and new immigrants, they can run businesses with lower margins. Therefore, Koreans cannot compete with them in small grocery, clothing and general merchandise businesses. They own even large stores. Dominicans control four or five C-Town chains in this area. Pakistani, Indian and Arab immigrants own some Key Food chains.

Kim explained that this diversity had nearly eliminated the major source of Korean-black conflicts. As he put it:

Earlier, some black residents came to my produce store and said, "Why do you Koreans control businesses in my territory?" They can no longer ask that question. Should they ask that question, I can say, "What about the Dominicans, Indians, and Arabs who have their shops here?"

Young-Sik Kim also mentioned about the change in the ethnic and racial composition of the residents in the neighborhood. According to him, the ethnic composition of customers of two stores of his in the Flatbush area has changed significantly from predominantly Caribbean black immigrants (largely Haitian and Jamaican) in the early 1990s to black-Latino immigrants. He said that Latino immigrants (largely Mexican and Dominican) comprise a significant proportion of customers of his supermarket and produce store. Census data indicate that the number of Hispanics in Flatbush increased moderately, from 16,577 in 1980 to 21,385 in 2000, whereas the number of Asians and Native Americans increased significantly, from 7,067 to 13,451. The Hispanic population may have increased significantly since 2000, however. He reported that the mixing of black and Latino customers reduced disputes between his employees and customers because it seriously weakened black residents' sense of territory.

In Jamaica, I also witnessed similar changes in the ethnic diversity of business owners and residents, the increase in mega-stores, and the decrease in Korean-owned stores. In 1991, the president of the Korean Merchants Association of Jamaica told me that there were approximately 180 Korean-owned stores there. The business association was no longer functioning when I conducted fieldwork in 2006 and I could not accurately count the total number of Korean-owned stores to determine the change between 1991 and 2006. According to my conversations with several Korean business owners there, however, the number dropped to less than half. First, the emergence of mega-stores, the construction of the air terminal connecting Jamaica and JFK International, renovations of Long Island Railroad and subway stations, and the establishment of several retail bank branches have led to escalating commercial rent hikes in Jamaica over the last fifteen years or so. The New York City Department of City Planning is primarily responsible for these changes. The Greater Jamaica Development Corporation, however, which represents landlords, real estate companies and developers, and even the owners of mega-stores, have worked very hard to bring about the changes.

Joon Choi, a shoe store owner in a mall located in the middle of the downtown Jamaica shopping area along Jamaica Avenue, explained how the changes have pushed Korean merchants out of the Jamaica neighborhood.

Over the last several years, the total number of businesses in Jamaica has greatly increased. But numbers of Korean-owned and Jewish-owned businesses have decreased significantly with a big increase in Indian, Chinese, Guyanese and other immigrant-owned businesses. When landlords have raised monthly rents to $20,000 or more for retail spaces, Koreans cannot continue businesses. But Indian, Chinese, Guyanese and other immigrants accept the rents. Because they have come from countries with much lower standards of living, they are ready to run businesses with exceptionally low profit margins. But we cannot do that.

When I asked him why the number of Jewish-owned stores had decreased, he explained it this way:

Jews control commercial buildings in Jamaica. Some Jewish store owners have sold their businesses and focus on renting commercial buildings. They make a lot more money from commercial renting than from their retail stores. So they do not have to work for their businesses. Jews have recently purchased some buildings in Jamaica and turned them into shopping malls. There is a rumor that the landlord will renovate this mall and raise rents. Then, I may not be able to continue my business here.

In 1980, native-born white and blacks were the overwhelming majority in Jamaica. However, the influx of Caribbean (Guyanese, Haitian and Jamaican), Latino (Dominican and Guatemalan) and Asian (Indian, Filipino and Chinese) immigrants between 1980 and 2000 converted the neighborhood into a multiracial one, with whites constituting only 18 percent in 2000 (Infoshare). In the early 1980s, when black customers organized a boycott of a Korean produce store in Jamaica, many Korean retail stores there served exclusively African American customers. Since then, increasing numbers of Indian, Chinese, Guyanese, and Arab immigrants have established businesses there. In addition, recently, with the construction of several apartment complexes a fair number of whites have moved into the neighborhood, adding to its racial diversity. In Jamaica as in Harlem and Flatbush, racial and ethnic diversity of both residents and business owners has almost eliminated rejection of immigrant-owned businesses by black customers.

The changes in structure of traditional black neighborhoods are not limited to New York City. In Chul Choi also reports similar trends in the South Side of Chicago.[116] The trend of Latino immigrants to move into traditionally black neighborhoods in large numbers is also not unique to New York City. Already in 1990, Latinos, mostly documented and undocumented immigrants, made up 44 percent of the population in south central Los Angeles, the major black concentration in that metropolitan area.[117]

Table 5.5   Self-Employment Among Korean American Full-Time Workers[a] in New York–New Jersey, 1999

	Rate (%)
First generation (immigrated after age twelve)	27.7
1.5 generation (immigrated at twelve or before)	7.0
American-born (second generation)	5.1
American-born white (multigeneration)	10.9

Source: Author's compilation from 5% Public Use Microdata Sample (PUMS) of the 2000 U.S. Census.
[a] Full-time workers are defined as those who worked for thirty-five weeks or more in 1999 and for thirty-five hours or more per week and are between twenty-five and sixty-five years old.

The dramatic reduction of the number of Korean-owned stores in black neighborhoods in these and presumably other cities has also been affected by the significant reduction of Korean immigrants to the United States[118] and by the participation of the vast majority of 1.5- and second-generation Korean American adults in the mainstream economy. By contrast, the increasing presence of businesses owned by South Asian and Arab immigrants in black neighborhoods is largely attributable to the escalation of Koreans leaving these areas in recent years.[119] As noted, many middle-aged and elderly Korean merchants complain that they cannot compete with young South Asian and Arab merchants who operate businesses with exceptionally low margins. In the late 1960s and early 1970s, Jewish and other white merchants made similar complaints when new Korean immigrants were opening stores.

As shown in table 5.5, 1.5-generation and native-born Korean American adult workers in the New York–New Jersey area have much lower self-employment rates than first-generation Koreans. They have lower rates than even native-born whites, who are for the most part third generation or more. Because 1.5-generation and native-born Korean workers are much younger than native-born white Americans, their self-employment rates are likely to increase as they grow older. Even with age controlled, however, younger-generation Koreans may not show a greater tendency to start their own businesses than whites.

The radical intergenerational reduction in the tendency to start one's own businesses among Korean Americans sharply contrasts with Jewish Americans, who have transmitted entrepreneurialism over numerous generations.[120] For example, the Ivan Light and Elizabeth Roach analysis of PUMS of the 1990 census[121] revealed that native-born whites of Russian ancestry, who were presumed to be mostly multigeneration Jewish Americans, in the Los Angeles–Riverside–Orange Counties CMSA, had a much higher self-employment rate (25 percent) than other native-born white Americans in the area (13 percent).

The Korean-Jewish differential in the level of intergenerational transmission of entrepreneurship seems to be an important, but neglected, research issue. I like to point out here two major factors that seem to have contributed to the intergroup differential, though it is beyond the scope of this book. First, under the impact of Confucian cultural traditions, Korean immigrants push their children to pursue high-status, high-paying professional and managerial occupations in medical, law, engineering, and managerial fields.[122] Thus they do not want their children to run businesses.[123] For example, results of a survey of business owners in New York City in the late 1980s show that only 3.4 percent of Korean respondents wanted their children to go into business, versus 20 percent of white and 22 percent of Hispanic respondents.[124] By contrast, a number of studies have documented that many contemporary Jewish émigrés from Russia want to pass on their entrepreneurship to their children.[125] In his book on contemporary Soviet Jewish immigrants, for example, Steven Gold made the following assessment: "By passing on a business, they hope to ensure financial independence for their children. For example, Sophia's wedding present from her father was a guaranteed income in the form of three taxis along with the medallions required for their operation."[126]

Second, and more importantly, by virtue of many high-paying, high-status professional and managerial occupations created by the contemporary postindustrial economy in the United States, second-generation Korean and other Asian Americans with high education levels do exceptionally well socioeconomically, the vast majority of them holding professional and managerial occupations in the mainstream economy.[127] Given that many of them can secure six-digit earnings with a master's degree from decent universities, they have little incentive for getting into business. However, highly educated second- and third-generation Jewish and other white Americans did not have the same opportunity in the first half of the twentieth century due to the differences in the industrial structure. Moreover, up to 1950, Jewish Americans had encountered employment and occupational discrimination, more than second-generation Asian Americans at present.[128] To avoid discrimination, even highly educated professionals chose to be self-employed. More significantly, the long Jewish experience with formal occupational discrimination in Eastern European countries encouraged their children to go into business for themselves.

= Chapter 6 =

Latino Conflicts and Reactive Solidarity

Korean immigrant merchants have depended heavily on Latino employees and prefer them, both documented and undocumented, to African American workers mainly because they are cheap and reliable. This means that, like other business owners, many Korean merchants exploit Latino employees by not paying minimum wage and overtime. In response, helped by local labor unions and encouraged by government labor agencies, Latino employees in many cities have picketed against Korean stores. Although all types of Korean businesses in New York City have depended on Latino employees, retail produce stores in Manhattan have become the primary targets of the picketing. The Korean Produce Association of New York (KPA) and other Korean organizations have responded in self-defense to labor unions, Latino employees, and government labor organizations, by using ethnic collective actions.

Painting Korean-Latino relations mainly as owner-employee exploitation, however, is one-sided and distorts the reality. Korean business owners and Latino employees often maintain and benefit from strong personal ties. Here I try to provide a more balanced picture of Korean-Latino relations in New York City by looking at both sides of the relationship. However, where many books and articles have been published on Korean-black relations, few have examined Korean-Latino relations.[1] Almost all these focus on Los Angeles. I focus on New York City.

The Literature

The contemporary period of post-industrial international migration, which got underway in the early 1960s under the impact of globalization, is characterized by the outflows of people from densely settled countries at the earliest stage of industrialization to densely settled, economically mature, postindustrial societies.[2] Immigrants from less developed countries to postindustrial countries usually fill lower-level, menial service-related and manufacturing occupations unattractive to native workers. Immigrants in contemporary postindustrial America are socioeconomically polarized to fill both ends of the service-related spectrum. Whereas Asian and Middle Eastern immigrants meet the demand for professional and managerial occupations in the United States, Latin American and Caribbean immigrants meet that for bottom-level jobs. In particular, recent immigrants from Mexico, El Salvador, Guatemala, Dominican Republic, and Haiti, many of whom are undocumented, have extremely low levels of education and are concentrated in low-wage unskilled jobs.[3]

With these disadvantages and a huge standard of living gap, Latino American and Caribbean immigrants are ready to take any menial job and to work for long hours. They are less likely to complain about violations of labor regulations involving overtime pay and minimum wage than native-born workers. A number of studies have documented the preference of business owners and managers for Latino and Caribbean workers, for example, Roger Waldinger and Michael Lichter in Los Angeles[4] and Mary Waters in New York City,[5] Lawrence Bobo and his associates.[6]

Dependency on Latino Employees

Los Angeles is the largest Korean population center in the United States. It is also the major destination of documented and undocumented Mexican immigrants. A number of studies document Korean garment subcontractors' heavy dependency, especially in Los Angeles in the late 1960s, on Mexican workers.[7] Ivan Light and his colleagues have referred to the Korean garment business in Los Angeles as the immigrant business, in that Korean immigrants provide the capital and Latino immigrants provide the labor. This is a good contrast to the ethnic economy, where a single ethnic group provides both capital and labor. The tendency of Korean merchants to hire Mexican and other Latino employees in Los Angeles was gradually extended to other types of Korean businesses and other cities, as Mexican documented and undocumented immigrants became more and more dispersed.[8] The dependency of Korean merchants on Latino employees is thus a prominent feature throughout the United States.

According to my 1986 survey, Mexicans made up 48 percent of all employees in Korean-owned stores in the Los Angeles–Orange County area, and Koreans and blacks for 31 percent and 5 percent respectively.[9] The black employees were largely limited to south central Los Angeles. Businesses in that area, however, were found to depend far more on Latinos (54 percent) than blacks (16 percent).[10] Results of my 1992 survey indicate that Korean merchants in three black neighborhoods in New York City hired more Latino employees (44 percent) than black (32 percent) or Korean (23 percent).[11] In New York, not only Korean-owned garment factories, but also produce and grocery stores, dry cleaners, restaurants, and other ethnic enclave businesses depend heavily on Latino employees.

Only the Korean-owned stores in black neighborhoods that sell clothing, costume jewelry, and beauty supply items have significant numbers of black employees, whom they hire primarily as salespersons and sometime as managers, because native-born blacks can more effectively communicate with black customers. I found two middle-aged black women working as managers in two Korean retail stores in Harlem, one a beauty supply store and the other a clothing store. The owners told me the employees had worked for them for more than twenty years.[12]

In his 1995 survey of Korean merchants in Los Angeles, Yoon asked whether they preferred blacks or Latinos as employees. Eighty percent preferred Latinos, and only 10 percent preferred blacks.[13] In responding to the open-ended question about the reasons for their preference, 50 percent emphasized "work ethic and personality traits" and 19 percent pointed to "cultural similarities."[14] Regarding cultural similarities, both Korean and Latino immigrants put emphasis on family and kin ties, children's respect for parents and other adults, and patriarchal values. Both groups like soccer games; I found in the early 1990s that the Korean Sewing Contractors Association of Los Angeles organized monthly soccer games between Korean merchants and Mexican employees to forge ties between the two groups.

Much of what Korean merchants consider work ethnic and personality traits, such as punctuality and dependability, are both cultural values and behavior patterns related to their immigrant status. This commonality is an important factor. As disadvantaged immigrants, they share the American dream ideology, the belief that if they work hard here they can make it. Results of my New York survey corroborated the preference for Latino employees. In the 1992 New York City survey of Korean merchants in black neighborhoods, I asked those with no black employees why they were not hiring blacks. Most said that black employees were not dependable, and that Latino employees are.[15] A Brooklyn store owner who had hired black workers explained it this way:

> Black employees are not responsible, not reliable. They often do not come to work without giving any notice. They have no motivation to continue working unless they need money immediately. Two years ago, my black employee asked for money for lunch. I gave him money, but he did not come back to work after lunch.[16]

In Yoon's survey of Korean merchants in Los Angeles, 10 percent indicated lower wages as an important reason for their preference.[17] I believe his survey underestimated the importance of lower wages and related factors (no overtime and no fringe benefits) that contribute to the preference

Table 6.1   Comparison of Businesses in Racial Composition of Employees in New York City, 2005

Ethnic Group	A	B	C	D Ethnic	Other Asian	Latino	Black	White
Korean	91/108	433	4.0	220 (51%)	25 (6%)	163 (38%)	15 (3%)	10 (2%)
Chinese	29/33	197	6.0	171 (86%)	5 (3%)	17 (9%)	2 (1%)	2 (1%)
Indian	26/37	113	3.1	66 (58%)	10 (9%)	17 (15%)	8 (7%)	12 (11%)

Source: Author's compilation from results of the 2005 telephone survey of Korean, Chinese, and Indian immigrants in New York City.
A = businesses with at least one paid employee/total main businesses
B = total number of paid employees
C = the mean number of paid employees per business
D = racial composition of employees

for Latino workers. Because wages below minimum wage, no overtime pay, and no fringe benefits are all labor law violations, many Korean merchants are unlikely to report any of these factors as their reason and prefer Latino workers because they are less likely to report violations.

Although almost all employers or managers tend to prefer Latino workers, not all immigrant groups depend on them equally for business operations. Currently, three immigrant groups in New York City—Korean, Chinese, and Indian—are most active in small businesses. Korean merchants depend more than either Chinese or Indian merchants on Latinos. Table 6.1 shows the ethnic composition of employees for Korean-, Indian- and Chinese-owned businesses in New York City based on telephone interviews conducted in 2005 and 2006.[18] Co-ethnics make up 51 percent of employees in all Korean-owned businesses, compared with 86 percent in Chinese-owned businesses and 58 percent in Indian-owned businesses. Co-ethnics include those of Korean ancestry from China. Most of the approximately 15,000 documented and undocumented Korean-Chinese immigrants in New York are employed in Korean-owned stores. Latinos make up 38 percent of employees of Korean-owned businesses, compared to 15 percent of Indian-owned and 9 percent of Chinese-owned. Korean immigrants proportionally own more businesses and depend on Latino workers far more than either Chinese or Indian immigrants. This is the main reason Korean-Latino relations, rather than Asian-Latino relations, are a sociologically important issue.

Dependency on Latino workers has decreased over time. For example, according to my survey conducted in 1997 and 1998 based on the same Kim sampling technique, Latino employees made up about 54 percent of total employees (N = 81) of Korean self-employed respondents (N = 53), and Korean employees 31 percent. Korean grocery, produce, and seafood retail businesses, especially those in minority neighborhoods, where they were overrepresented, depended heavily on Latino employees. As noted, their numbers in minority neighborhoods have dropped significantly. Instead, as discussed in chapter 3, the number of Korean-owned nail salons has increased dramatically, to approximately 4,000 in 2005 from about 1,400 in 1992. Korean nail salons, which have more employees per business than any other major Korean business line, depend almost exclusively on Korean women. This is the main reason that the proportion of Latino employees has decreased over the years and the proportion of Korean employees has increased. The drop in the number of Korean-owned garment factories, noted in chapter 3, has also been a factor.

Chinese immigrant businesses depend heavily on co-ethnic employees mainly because large numbers of lower-class immigrants, many undocumented, have recently arrived in New York City.[19] New Chinese immigrants are as hardworking and as inexpensive as Latino. Thus Chinese businesses do not have the same need as their Korean counterparts to hire many Latinos who do not speak Chinese. However, the reduced Korean immigration since the early 1990s, the relatively higher socioeconomic class background of new Korean immigrants, and the overabundance of small businesses in the Korean immigrant community have made it difficult for Korean business owners to find Korean workers for low-level jobs and turned them toward Latino employees.[20] Korean business owners usually depend on co-ethnic workers for managerial and cashier positions, and use Latino workers for more menial jobs, such as dishwashing, helping to cook, ironing, garment-manufacturing, and moving and stocking retail items.

Latino employees in Korean-owned businesses are paid less than Korean immigrant employees holding higher-level jobs.[21] Korean Chinese immigrants, fluent in Korean, also usually find higher status jobs—female employees often working as cashiers—in Korean stores than Latino employees. Korean and Korean Chinese immigrants holding higher status jobs and getting paid more than Latino employees in Korean-owned stores is not an issue, however, in light of their having advantages in terms of education or fluency in Korean, or perhaps both.

The main issue is the extent to which Latino employees are subjected to exploitation, whether labor law violations or rude treatment by Korean business owners. We need more systematic research to answer this question. But newspaper articles and my conversations with Korean immigrants suggest that until recently many Korean merchants in the New York–New Jersey area had paid Latino workers less than minimum wages and failed to pay overtime wages, let alone cover sick days or holiday pay. Piecemeal information also suggests that some Korean merchants and managers have treated Latino workers badly in personal interactions, often shouting and cursing at them. In a few isolated cases, some have even treated Latino workers inhumanly. About three years ago, to take one example, Korean dailies in New York reported that a large Korean ethnic grocery store often did not give Mexican employees time to eat lunch when business in the store was very busy.

Picketing in New York City

Most Latinos working in Korean-owned businesses in New York are Mexicans, followed, at a considerable distance, by Ecuadorians. The immigration of Mexicans to New York City began to explode in the late 1980s.[22] Latino employees in Korean-owned stores, especially in restaurants, were visible in the early 1980s. Their numbers rapidly increased in the late 1980s and early 1990s. As Latino workers in Korean produce stores in Manhattan became visible, local labor organizations began to organize them to picket against the shops in the early 1990s.

Before 1998

Small short-term pickets by labor union members and Latino workers against one or two Korean stores did not, in comparison to the black boycotts, attract much Korean attention. Thus, staff members of Korean business associations do not remember when and how many times Korean stores were picketed. Korean ethnic media, however, hungry for news about the Korean immigrant community, seem to have covered almost every case of picketing, where mainstream media covered only long-term efforts. It is therefore the Korean ethnic media that provide the most accurate information.

In 1991, I asked a graduate student to review every issue of *Korea Times New York* published between 1970 and 1987 and to select all reports of business-related conflicts and ethnic collective actions. We found only two cases of picketing against Korean stores by staff members of labor unions, not by Latino workers, during the period. I did not address Korean-Latino conflicts in New York City in my 1996 study for two reasons. First, Latino workers did not organize any pickets. Second, local English-language newspapers did not carry any related articles.

In the late 1980s, a few incidents of labor-related picketing against Korean stores were documented in Korean dailies. In April 1989, the president and other staff members of the local 1500 of the United Food and Commercial Workers picketed against one Korean produce store in Manhattan and another in Queens, pushing all Korean merchants to join the union.[23] The target was J & S Produce, located in Midtown (53rd Street and Broadway) and owned by Bo Young Jung, president of the KPA at the time. The local union deliberately chose the store to put pressure on Jung to influence KPA members to join the union. They started the picket in April 1989, immediately after Jung had been elected president. When I asked Jung how he responded, he recounted his experience this way:

> When the picket lasted for two weeks, our sales volume was reduced to only one-fourth of the regular sales. Because we had a salad bar, we got a lot of foods, fruits and vegetables rotten every day. My wife and I could not sleep much, worrying about financial problems. In the third week, I, together with executive secretary of the KPA, visited the local union office to negotiate with them. When I asked them why they targeted my store, they told me to sign a letter, asking all Korean produce owners to join the labor union. They said, "the Korean produce store in Queens already signed to join the labor union. If you sign it, we will stop picketing against your store right away." I told them I cannot do it, pointing out that "if Korean stores pay union fees they cannot survive."

The boycott against Jung's store ended after a month. When the KPA rejected the request, the labor union tried to put pressure on Korean produce stores in Manhattan with several employees by distributing fliers indicating that employees of Korean stores were being exploited in regard to minimum wage and overtime pay.[24] The local union hired a Korean to translate a booklet containing labor regulations about minimum wage, overtime pay, paid holidays and health insurance coverage, and distributed copies of the translation to Korean employees.[25] Leaders of Korean produce stores told staff members of the union that family-based Korean mom and pop stores could not survive by paying legal wages and covering legal benefits. In its July 24 editorial, the *New York City Tribune* criticized the union, defending the position of Korean produce leaders that unionization was not applicable to "Korean family-oriented businesses."[26] However, because the majority of Korean-owned stores have at least one paid employee, the argument is not persuasive. Another article, published in *Korea Central Daily*, reported that employees of four Korean produce stores had joined the labor union.[27]

As noted, all pickets against Korean stores in 1989 were organized by the local 150 of the United Food and Commercial Workers, with no Latino employees participating. Pickets organized by Latinos, however, had occurred three times before 1999, and picketing accelerated thereafter. The first was in December 1995, against a produce store in downtown Manhattan.[28] The Latino Workers' Center organized the effort to help a Mexican employee recently fired by the store get back pay based on minimum wage and overtime pay. The picket organizers claimed that the employee was paid $180 a week for seventy-two hours of work in the first six months of employment and then $220 in the next year, but that he should have been paid $400 per week at minimum and $480 at maximum.[29] They threatened to take legal action if the owner of the store did not respond favorably to their demand. How the dispute was resolved does not seem to have been published. KPA files also show that three Mexican employees picketed against a Korean produce store in Brooklyn in December 1996, demanding back pay based on minimum wage and overtime.

In February 1997, another picket against a Korean store by Latino employees was reported.[30] In this case, the target was a large-scale Korean garment factory in Manhattan. On February 10, approximately 200 Latino employees picketed, demanding payment of back pay that had accumulated for six weeks. A Latino participant said that they had decided to picket against the garment factory because the owner tried to pay only $100 to each of the employees for six weeks of work before the factory closed. A local labor union reported the case to the New York State Department of Labor. Two days later the factory was shut down. The owner was not able to pay the wages for six weeks. Many garment factories closed during this period. The case, however, exposed the vulnerability of Latino undocumented employees to employer exploitation and abuse.

After 1998

As noted in chapters 4 and 5, Korean greengrocers came into numerous conflicts with white suppliers and black customers before 1998. They also had headaches in dealing with tough government regulations and heavy penalties for their violations (see chapter 7). Other Korean retailers—grocers, seafood vendors, and resellers of Asian-imported manufactured goods—experienced similar conflicts and government regulations, albeit to a lesser extent. Korean merchants did not feel threatened in dealing with labor issues before 1998, though apparently many of them failed to comply with labor laws, especially in regard to Latino workers. Nonetheless, attacks on Korean business owners by local labor unions, the state government, and Latino workers accelerated beginning in late 1998 and culminated between 2000 and 2002.

In early 1998, after hearing complaints about working conditions by employees of produce stores, the Association of Mexican Workers organized several boycotts and pickets against Korean produce stores in Brighton Beach.[31] Local 169 helped the association organize pickets in Brooklyn, though it later focused its efforts on Manhattan. In September 1998, the KPA received a letter from president of a local union, expressing its concern about abuses employees of Korean produce stores were suffering and hoping to find a solution beneficial to both employers and employees. I cite below one paragraph from the letter:

> Local 169 of the Union of Needletrades, Industrial, and Textile Employees has been active in signing workers in the Korean green grocery stores through-

out New York City. In the course of our organizing campaign we have uncovered numerous abuses that simply cannot be ignored. Among these abuses are wage and hour violations and minimum wage violations. In addition, workers have been threatened with firing and stores have threatened to close simply because the store workers have exercised their right to organize a labor union. This is a right protected by law.

Since many of the stores we are attempting to organize belong to your association, I would like to discuss the ways in which we can come to an equitable agreement with the owners of these stores and with the Korean Produce Association.[32]

The letter indicates that the union had already contacted the interviewed employees of numerous produce stores and wanted to negotiate with the KPA to influence owners to change abusive treatment of workers before picketing. In October, the president of the union sent a similar letter to the Korean Consulate of New York. In it, he reported that the labor organization visited a number of Korean greengrocery stores in New York City in the previous two months to help them become members of the union. He also protested against various labor-related abuses that Latino, especially Mexican, employees encountered at the hands of Korean business owners.

I asked the 1998 president of the KPA how the KPA had responded to the request. He said he did not respond quickly because there was no solution. He pointed out that most small stores could not pay union wages because they operated on narrow margins. Because the KPA did not take quick action, Local 169, staffed largely by Mexican employees, approached several Korean produce stores in Manhattan and asked the owners to allow their employees to join the union.

When the Korean owners refused, Local 169 organized Latino employees to picket in front of the stores beginning in May 1999. The Community Labor Coalition, based in Lower East Village, rendered its assistance. In June 2000, it sent letters to several Korean produce stores in the East Village, demanding meetings with the owners to discuss the workers' rights. This involvement influenced local residents to boycott the targeted Korean stores. Local 169 reported that it provided a $210 weekly stipend for the picketers to survive.[33]

At the end of 1999, the owners of the seven targeted stores agreed to allow their workers to join unions.[34] Pickets against eight other stores in the East Village continued through early 2001, with the student labor coalitions at New York University and Columbia University joining it on occasion.[35] Local 169 distributed leaflets saying "Your Boss May Owe You Thousands of Dollars In Back Pay" and "No Matter What Your Legal Status—You Are Entitled To Back Pay If You Have Been Cheated" to Latino workers and other rally participants. It mobilized about 100 demonstrators several times in the spring of 2001 to march around the eight targeted stores. The pickets led to a dramatic drop in sales for the targeted stores and led, ultimately, to the closure of a few of them.[36]

Korean retailers in Manhattan encountered threats not only from the local labor union and Latino workers, but from government agencies as well. Tipped off about the labor violations by Local 169, Eliot Spitzer, New York State attorney general at the time, investigated the stores targeted for boycotts from late 1999 forward. Latino workers in those stores, he found, were usually paid around $240 per week for seventy-two hours of work, twelve hours per day six days a week.[37] This pay grossly violated minimum wage and overtime laws. The workers should have been paid $463 per week. He also found that the stores' payroll records were not in compliance with standards. In early May 2001, he sued three Korean greengrocers for labor law violations, seeking penalties of approximately half million dollars for some thirty former and current employees.[38] He later reached a settlement of $315,000.[39] The attorney general threatened to investigate all Korean businesses and seek appropriate back pay for all minimum wage and overtime violations. His tough enforcement of labor laws prompted Korean business and community leaders to take action to educate business owners about labor laws and to negotiate with the attorney general to work out settlements acceptable to both workers and merchants.

The disputes, though bitter between 1999 and 2002, have never evolved into collective conflict. During the period, many Latino workers did picket the stores for which they had worked, but they made up only a tiny fraction of the whole. Moreover, as noted, in almost all cases it was the local union that organized the picketing. It may have done so to increase union dues through membership drives as much as to protect Latino workers. Its ulterior motive was revealed when several Latinos, who had been employed by the union to picket, exposed their story.

Business and Community Leader Reactions

Korean merchants were not able to use ethnic collective action as effectively in their conflicts with Latino employees as they had done with black customers a decade earlier. Their failure to comply with labor laws regarding minimum wage and overtime pay was and is neither legally nor morally justifiable. Nevertheless, they did use ethnic collective action to deal with the labor law problem. On the one hand, Korean business leaders emphasized their willingness to educate Korean merchants about details of labor laws, partly to stop further pickets and investigations and partly to repair their reputations. On the other, they collectively responded to local labor unions, which they claimed unjustifiably singled out Korean immigrant merchants even though most other small business owners violated labor regulations as well.

The Focus on Education

In September 2000, the KPA established the Korean Task Force for Resolution of Labor Disputes (KTF) to resolve pickets against Korean produce stores in the East Village. It quickly evolved into a community-wide organization to address Korean merchants' labor disputes with Mexican workers effectively. Among its ranks were leaders of several other Korean trade and local merchants associations. It held several meetings in the fall of 2000 to discuss how to deal with labor disputes, with the owners of the produce stores targeted for picketing in the East Village invited. By the time of its third meeting in October 2000, it had already established "a fund of about $50,000 to counteract the pickets."[40] The majority of donations were made by Korean greengrocers.

Task force leaders discussed more or less long-term solutions to labor disputes with Latino workers that applied to all Korean merchants. The participating East Village owners argued that the organization should take quick action to terminate the pickets, which they feared threatened their livelihood.[41] The victims of the pickets, like the victims of black boycotts, may have wanted to get more concrete community support, such as donations to cover lost sales during the picketing period. As pointed out earlier, however, pickets against Korean stores for violations of labor laws were different from black boycotts of Korean stores, and thus neither the Korean Task Force nor any other community organization could engage in the donation campaign to help the owners.

To educate Korean merchants about labor regulations, the task force hurriedly organized a seminar about labor laws for October 10. Ironically, it invited Soon Young Hong, director of the Korean Immigrant Workers Advocate (KIWA) in Los Angeles, who was considered the arch-enemy of Korean merchants in the area, to speak about labor disputes. Under his leadership, KIWA organized numerous pickets against branches of Korean firms and Korean immigrant stores in Los Angeles to help Latino and Korean workers. After the seminar, the task force produced a pamphlet summarizing labor regulations and distributed it to Korean merchants. In the following position statement, the Korean Task Force explained the importance of complying with the regulations:

> Not long ago, the American mainstream media widely exposed Korean merchants' illegal labor practices. Only when we Korean merchants show that we do comply with labor laws can we fight effectively against the local labor union's unreasonable targeting of Korean merchants alone.[42]

Many Korean merchants considered it unreasonable for the attorney general, under the influence of the local labor union, to target Korean merchants for labor investigations. To express their concern and to moderate tough enforcement of labor laws, members of the task force visited the attorney general's office at Albany on December 20, 2000, and discussed how to resolve Korean-Latino labor disputes without further investigations of Korean stores. Spitzer promised not to target Korean merchants and to coordinate with the task force in resolving any Korean labor law violations.

About 250 Korean merchants participated in a seminar held on February 20, 2001, in Flushing, at which Attorney General Spitzer and two other Justice Department officials lectured on labor laws.[43] Spitzer awarded certificates of education on minimum wage and overtime laws to all participants. These include the name of the owner, the name of the store and address, and the following statement:

> This certificate verifies that the owner of the foregoing green grocery retail establishment has attended an education seminar, conducted by the Office of the New York State Attorney General Eliot Spitzer, about basic minimum wage and overtime laws. The seminar, held in the Macedonia Church in Flushing, New York, addressed a variety of New York State labor law topics including the minimum wage, calculation of overtime, recordkeeping requirements, and required break times.

The KPA, the Korean Garment Apparel Contractors Association of New York, and other Korean trade associations had previously organized similar seminars at which labor-related government officials gave lectures. This, however, was the largest ever held in the Korean community in New York City in terms of the number of Korean participants and the prestige of the lecturers. At the end of the seminar, the Korean Task Force gave a plaque of appreciation to Attorney General Spitzer, apparently to strengthen ties with him. Despite all this, he never stopped investigating Korean produce stores and sued three Korean produce owners for violations of labor laws in May 2001.

In March 2001, the Department of Labor sent an investigator to the KANY office to educate association staff and publicize labor laws before beginning the investigations of Korean-owned stores. In response, KANY publicized the importance of complying with the regulations to the Korean community. In early April 2001, Andrew Sockchu Kim, the newly elected KANY president, along with two staff members, visited the East Natural Deli, which was the main target of the East Village picketing, and later the headquarters of Local 169 for negotiations.[44] As a disabled person sitting on a wheel chair, he "tried to stop Latino employees from cursing at their female owner in Korean." In his meetings with leaders of Local 169, Kim emphasized the economic interdependence between Korean merchants and Latino workers and the need for them to reach a mutually acceptable agreement through dialogue. Local 169 agreed to stop the picketing for ten days.

Although the task force tried to educate merchants about labor laws, it was powerless to end the long-term picketing in the East Village. The owners of the picket targets severely criticized the KTF for not taking any action to end the picketing.[45] Because it could not find a solution, it could not get financial support from Korean merchants. Because of this difficulty, the task force had become almost inactive by March 2001. Later, in May 2001, the newly elected president of the Korean Association of New York incorporated it as a committee under the umbrella organization.[46]

More Aggressive Reactions to Local 169

Whereas the KTF focused on protecting Korean merchants by educating them about labor regulations through seminars and booklets, two other organizations, established in reaction to long-term pickets against Korean stores, took more aggressive measures. These were the Korean Anti-Discrimination Association, which included the owners of the picketed stores, and the Committee for Protection of Merchant Rights. Both were ad hoc committees spontaneously created in spring 2001 partly because the members were terribly dissatisfied with the KTF's defensive measures.[47] The two organizations worked both together and separately. They engaged in solidarity activities for less than five months in 2001 but their activities are interesting enough to introduce.

The members of the two organizations felt that "Local 169 targeting only Korean merchants and Attorney General Spitzer investigating only Koreans were racist actions" because most other small business owners were also violating labor laws.[48] The two organizations thus organized picketing and demonstrations to "protest unjustifiable pressure on Korean merchants." The Korean Anti-Discrimination Association organized the first picket with about twenty participants on April 3, 2001, close to the Local 169 picket line in front of East Natural Market.[49] The next day, Koreans picketed in front of Valentino Market, a Korean produce store near to East Natural Market to protest its having joined Local 169 in July of the previous year.[50] Korean protests continued until the end of May 2001, and included several physical confrontations between Korean picketers and Local 169 members.[51]

The conflicts took an odd turn in the middle of May when Jorge Hernandez and fifteen other Latino workers picketed in front of the union building. They had been hired by Local 169 three years earlier to walk picket lines in front of Korean produce stores but had been dismissed about two weeks before "because of what Local 169 called downsizing."[52] Picketing against Local 169, they claimed that the union paid them "as little as $100 for 40-hour workweeks."[53] As Korean activists, merchants, and journalists watched nearby, the Latino picketers distributed leaflets to people entering the union building, one of which said: "Mexicans against

Local 169. You have put me and 100 of my brothers out of work by forcing East Natural, Jin Market, and Abbigail to close." Their protest seems to have been abetted by Korean activists, though the Koreans denied it. The exposure of the union's grave violation of the minimum-wage law proved a severe blow to the union's moral integrity. The picketing encouraged Korean business and community leaders to organize two large-scale demonstrations against Local 169.

On May 21, the Committee for Protection of Merchant Rights organized a demonstration in which about 130 Koreans participated in front of headquarters of Local 169.[54] This was a larger demonstration than any other organized by Local 169 in the previous two years. Attorney General Spitzer indicted three Korean produce stores, including East Natural Market, which had been targeted in early May. This contributed to a mobilization of a large number of Koreans. Korean business and community leaders believed that Local 169 had pressured Spitzer to investigate and indict the three Korean stores for violating labor laws. The participants shouted "Boycott Local 169," "Stop Attack Only Korean Stores," and "Attorney General, Stop Your Support of Local 169."

On June 1, the committee, along with the KANY, organized a much larger demonstration in front of union headquarters. The approximate 1,000 participants included many leaders of Korean ethnic organizations as well as owners and employees of Korean produce stores, including Latino employees.[55] After speeches by several Korean business and community leaders, Terrence Park, a Korean candidate for the City Council for the Flushing–College Point–Whitestone district in the Democratic Party's primary, led the chanting in the demonstration. The demonstrators also picketed in front of the Korean-owned Valentine Market on the grounds that it had helped Local 169 attack Korean produce stores in the East Village by joining the union.

As noted, Korean-union conflicts contributed to a minor divide among Korean merchants. Recall that Korean participants picketed not only Local 169 but also Valentine Market, one of the Korean stores in the East Village, for having joined the local union the previous year. Their justification for picketing the store was that the owner, by accepting the request to join the union, had weakened the united Korean front against the union's "intimidation."[56] But Valentine Market's proximity to East Natural Market and strong business competition with it may have been why it was the only store picketed even though several others had joined Local 169. In spring 2001, East Natural Market was suffering the union picketing and the attorney general's investigations. Meanwhile, Valentine Market was enjoying good business. The owner was angry about the unexpected and unexplained picket against his store by the organizations that had been established to protect Korean merchants' rights. He sent two handwritten letters, protesting what he called the "nonsense" picket against his store and clarifying his position, to Korean media and the KPA.

In 2002, Andrew Sockchu Kim, KANY president, tried to negotiate with the Attorney General's Office, the local labor union (AFL-CIO), and Casa de Mexico, a Mexican immigrant advocacy group, to work out a mutually agreeable settlement on Korean-Latino labor issues. He organized several rounds of meetings at the KANY office in Manhattan among the representatives of the four parties. According to him, Attorney General Spitzer, who presided over the meetings, tried to narrow the differences in opinions about labor disputes among the three parties. The Mexican representatives—unlike those from the union—did not consider Korean stores' joining the local union a major issue in settling labor disputes. Spitzer was able to broker into agreement on a code of conduct in September 2002 that did not focus on belonging to the union.[57]

Under the code, Korean business owners would pledge to pay the minimum wage and, for any overtime (more than forty hours a week), time and a half. They would also pledge to provide paid sick days and a week of paid vacation per year for employees, and to allow investigators to monitor firms to inspect their workplaces and financial records at least twice a year. In return, the attorney general would ignore past violations of labor regulations. Spitzer warned that he would enforce back pay penalties against Korean business owners who did not sign the code of conduct by December 31, 2002. To encourage customers to patronize stores that adopt the code of conduct, Spitzer designed an insignia that the greengrocers could display in their windows.[58] About 200 Korean produce owners, mostly in Manhattan, are known to have signed the code, and most have complied with minimum wage and overtime laws. Those whose stores are outside Manhattan generally have not signed. Most, however, have significantly raised wages for Latino workers, even if many others seem to still not observe labor regulations strictly. According to my interviews with a few Korean business leaders, to not violate the overtime pay regulation, most owners have arranged for Latino employees to work only forty hours a week instead of seventy-two.

This is one of the major changes in the pattern of hiring Latino workers after the aggressive investigations of labor practices between 1999 and 2002. The code of conduct agreement ended the picketing against Korean stores in New York City. As an article published in the *New York Times* pointed out,[59] Attorney General Spitzer's success in persuading the Korean association to accept the code is not only a political success, but also success for the Mexican workforce. Andrew Sockchu Kim said in an interview that the Korean representatives were also relieved, mainly because the union picketing would cease without Korean merchants having to join the union. According to him, the union threatened to extend picketing to

Queens, where many Korean produce and grocery stores and restaurants depend heavily on Latino workers.

New York Versus Los Angeles

As noted, picketing against Korean-owned stores for Latino employees in New York were organized mainly by local labor unions and few Latino employees participated in most pickets. In addition, many Latinos participated in the anti-union demonstrations organized by Korean business and community leaders. This suggests that labor-related conflicts between Korean merchants and Latino workers were not as serious as other business-related intergroup conflicts. It also suggests that, because of their common immigrant background, Latino workers could not fight against Korean merchants as strongly as native-born non-Korean workers might have.

The mobilization of Latino workers against Korean merchants was more successful in Los Angeles. This difference may have been caused partly by the greater vulnerability of Latinos to workplace exploitation in Los Angeles, especially those in Koreatown, given the overabundance of Latino workers there.[60] In 2000, Latinos made up 46 percent of the population in Los Angeles, compared with 28 percent in New York City.[61] Latinos also made up the majority of the population in Los Angeles' Koreatown, and Koreans only 20 percent.[62]

However, the significant difference seems to be in the type of labor organization that led the movement against Korean merchants. In New York, the union was local. In Los Angeles, it was a Korean-Latino bi-ethnic organization, the Korean Immigrant Workers Advocates, and both Latino and Korean workers were mobilized. The KIWA was originally created in 1992 to protect Korean immigrant workers from exploitation by Korean merchants. It has since then had to help Latino workers as well as Korean immigrant workers, however, because most Korean-owned stores in Los Angeles, especially those stores in Koreatown, have both Latino and Korean employees.

In the early years, the KIWA fought against two Korean hotels—the Wilshire Hyatt and the Los Angeles Hilton and Towers—in downtown Los Angeles to help the Latino employees exploited and ultimately fired by the hotels through letter writing, boycotts, and demonstrations.[63] Later, the KIWA, with its office in Koreatown, focused its efforts on helping Koreatown restaurant workers—heavily Korean and partly Latino, documented and undocumented—resist labor exploitation. In 1995 and 1996, KIWA organized massive demonstrations against Korean restaurants that had failed to provide their employees with overtime and minimum wages, confronting the Korean Restaurant Owners Association (KROA).[64] Despite aggressive attacks combined with nasty tactics by KROA and conservative Korean merchant elites, KIWA has been successful in making KROA and many Korean restaurant owners concede to its wage equity demands and in restoring fired Korean and Latino workers.[65] Although KIWA has no financial resources, it does have the advantage in mobilizing people because it has involved both Korean and Latino workers in its collective actions. Because of its active role, KIWA is considered the primary adversary of Korean merchants in Los Angeles.

Because it has served so many Latino workers, KIWA has hired Latino staff. According to Angie Chung, KIWA's official activities are strongly bilingual and bicultural, incorporating both cultures and languages at the workplace. Moreover, Korean-Latino workers' solidarity, as shown in many demonstrations against Korean businesses, has contributed to strong Korean-Latino ties, even though it has weakened Korean solidarity. This shows the importance of grass-root labor organizations in mobilizing workers efficiently to protect their labor interests. Chung points out that KIWA has focused on empowering Korean and Mexican workers, helping start an independent organization—the Restaurant Workers Association— in Koreatown to resist owner abuse more effectively.[66] As shown in Peter Kwong's studies, Chinese restaurant workers in New York City's Chinatown, dissatisfied with Local 169, depended on the Chinese Staff and Workers Alliance, a grassroots organization, to organize picketing against Chinese restaurants.[67] He points out that, after several months of striking, employees of the Silver Palace in Manhattan's Chinatown organized their own union, called the 3-18 Independent Union, and signed a contract with more favorable terms and benefits than general union contracts.[68]

For the reasons discussed earlier, Korean employees of Korean stores in New York City as a whole must have enjoyed higher wages and better working conditions than both their Latino employees and Chinese employees of Chinese-owned stores in the same city. This does not mean, however, that no Korean employee has been abused or exploited by a Korean business owner. Some Korean women working in Korean restaurants, including international students' wives, and some undocumented Korean workers, whose numbers have greatly increased since the 1998 financial crisis in South Korea, are likely to have been abused. Korean immigrant worker labor issues had not surfaced in the Korean community in New York City until recently mainly because there was no community-based labor organization to help abused or exploited workers.

That trend changed in 2005 when the Young Korean American Service and Education Center, a Korean-American empowerment organization led by 1.5-generation Korean leaders, initiated the Korean Workers' Project in collaboration with the Asian American Legal Defense and Education Fund to help Korean workers with labor disputes. When the center publicized the project to the community, asking abused workers to report for aid, Yu Soung Mun, the executive director of the center, informed me that many Korean workers, including Korean Chinese, had visited it for assistance. The center has helped several Korean and Korean Chinese workers get back wages by initially suing the involved business owners and then agreeing to out-of-court settlements.[69] The center, however, has not expanded the program to Latino workers. When asked why, the executive director said that the center had neither the funds nor the manpower. For the first time in Korean history in New York City, in October 2006, a Korean employee joined Chinese and Vietnamese employees in picketing against a Korean nail salon in Manhattan in an effort organized by Chinese and local labor unions.[70]

Mutual Dependence and Personal Ties

We have noted that picketing by local unions and the investigations by former Attorney General Spitzer have more or less forced most Korean merchants to pay minimum wage and overtime since 2001. We have also noted that not many Latino employees participated in that picketing and that some Latino employees participated in counterdemonstrations. These points lead us to believe that most Latino employees at Korean businesses in New York City, as of 2006, are not terribly dissatisfied with how they are treated in the workplace.

To determine the extent to which they are satisfied, we need interviews with Latino workers. I have instead interviewed six Korean merchants who depended heavily on Latino employees to examine what kinds of relationships they maintain with Latino employees.

Chang Il Kim, a pioneer in the Korean produce business, has a store in Jamaica he has owned for twenty-seven years. He has seven employees, all Latino men—two Mexicans and five Guatemalans. He used to have several Korean employees, but said he replaced them with Latino workers because the Koreans had too many conflicts among themselves.[71] The Guatemalan cashier has worked for him for thirteen years and two other employees for ten years or more. Kim said that he did not worry about finding employees because "they do not leave my store unless they have to go back to their own country." He experienced some difficulty with Latino workers in the early years. "Some of them did not come to work on Mondays after drinking too much on weekends," he explained. As a result, he gave new employees a two-month training period during which he not only trained them but also dismissed those who had violated basic rules. When asked how he rewarded his Latino employees and kept them working for him for so many years, he answered this way:

> If they turned out to be good workers after the two-month training period, I tried to treat them nicely with reasonable wages and other benefits. I pay the cashier $550 for fifty hours of weekly work. All other employees who have worked for more than two years get wages involving more than minimum

wage and overtime pay. I give paid holidays each year and bonuses on important holidays. I give singles birthday parties by taking them to Korean restaurants. Since I do not pay rent, I can share some of my profits with employees.

I interviewed another Korean greengrocer, Dong-Sung Park, who had his store in a multiethnic neighborhood in Queens. Park is in his late fifties and had four employees, all Mexican men. When I asked him why he had all Mexican employees, he emphasized his strong preference for Mexican employees: "I have hired Mexican, Dominican, and Ecuadorian employees. But I have found Mexicans better than other Latino workers. They are very innocent, like untainted villagers, and listen to my work order closely." He added, however, that many recent Mexican immigrants came from cities and that some of them were thus "hard to handle." He also pointed out that in labor disputes in recent years some Mexican workers have taken legal action quickly because a Mexican labor organization helped them. In fact, he admitted to me that he once had trouble because a departing Mexican employee reported to the IRS that he had not paid his taxes. One day a few years ago, none of his Latino employees came to work. He found out that they had not come because the Korean cashier had been rude to them. He was able to keep the Latinos by persuading the Korean cashier to resign. I asked him whether he had close informal relations with Latino employees:

> Until several years ago, I had maintained close relations with Latino employees. I gave them bonuses on Christmas Day and I took them to Korean restaurants to celebrate their birthdays. But I have stopped all of that since I had legal trouble due to a Mexican employee's report to the IRS. If I maintain close relations with employees, they get more and more information about my business operation and they can hurt me. Now I only try not to violate labor laws.

Chun-Soo Lee owns five bagel and deli shops in Queens. According to him, 90 percent of about thirty employees working in his five shops are Latinos, mostly undocumented. They include Mexicans, a few Ecuadorians, a Peruvian and a Salvadorian. Eating bagels over coffee with him in one of his stores, I asked him why and how he had come to depend so heavily on Latino workers.

> I benefited a lot from Latino workers in my several stores. Once they start work, they continue. Most have worked for between four and six years for me. The Peruvian started work when she was in high school. She is married and attending college now. But she has continued to work here. Latino employees also work hard and do not complain. I used to have two white employees. When I gave instructions, they often talked back. I got tired. I had two Korean employees. But they often complained and demanded wage raises quickly. But Latino employees are simple and do not complain much.

Lee said that he also liked Mexican workers best. When I asked him why, he explained it this way:

> In addition to hard work and steadiness, Mexicans have two additional favorable characteristics as employees. One is their cultural similarities to Koreans. It is hard to pinpoint. . . . But we share many things to make us feel comfortable to talk to each other. I joke with a few Mexican workers like good friends. The other is their honesty. One time, by mistake I gave $70 more than I should have for his weekly wage. He brought the money back to me the next day.

This Mexican worker started in Lee's store four years ago when he was an undocumented resident. He has since become documented through his marriage to an American citizen. He gets $480 per week and two free meals a day for his forty-eight hours of work. Lee plans to train him as a manager for one of his bagel shops beginning next year. Lee explained that he had an Egyptian employee as well, working as a manager at another of his shops. Lee also invites each employee and his or her spouse to a Korean restaurant to celebrate his or her birthday every year and is willing to lend money to an employee in the event of an emergency.

Harry Min, a fifty-two-year-old Korean immigrant, has run a dry cleaning shop for ten years. He now owns two dry cleaners in Fort Lee, New Jersey, one run by his wife and the second by a Korean manager. He moves back and forth between the stores for overall supervision. He has ten employees, three Koreans and seven Latinos—four Mexicans, an Ecuadorian, a Salvadorian, and a Peruvian. He said all had worked for him for five to seven years. He inherited two black employees from the previous owner when he purchased his second store but could not keep them:

> They demanded too much money, $750 per week. It was also difficult to control them. Just as we have prejudice against blacks, they have prejudice against Koreans. They treated me as "old Chinese." I had a lot of stress in dealing with them. I could not work with them when they became a hindrance to the operation of my business.

He said Latinos are much better employees than blacks, and that Korean immigrants could not operate businesses without Latinos. He, too, emphasized the advantage of Mexican workers over other Latinos. He explained why: "Mexican workers are very innocent, follow my instructions closely, and do not make trouble. Other Latino employees like Ecuadorians and Salvadorians sometime give me trouble. They get late in the morning or do not come to work when they do not need money in the week."

Responding to my question about wages and other fringe benefits, Min said that he paid a Mexican worker with a college degree in Mexico $750 per week, the other two Mexican workers $600, and all others $500.

Everyone worked forty hours per week. He provides lunch for all employ-ees on Saturday and takes all employees to Korean restaurants a few times a year. He was happy to find that his Latino employees seem to like Korean food. He told me he felt as if his Latino employees were his chil-dren. He was willing to do even more for his employees:

> When my employees go to the hospital for emergency treatments and come up with big bills, I lend them money to pay for them and deduct certain amounts of money from weekly wages. I do not have to worry about their paying me back. Even if I forget about it they let me know about the weekly deduction. When they have personal problems, they often call me for help. For example, three employees have old cars. When their cars stop on the street, they call me for help. In addition, I sponsored a Korean employee and two Latino employees to help them apply for green cards.

I talked with In-Sook Nam, a Korean woman in her early fifties who co-owns, with her husband, a big twenty-four-hour deli-grocery in Manhattan. She is one of my wife's friends in her Catholic church. Twelve of her six-teen employees are Latinos, mostly Mexicans, the rest Koreans. I asked her how she felt about her Latino employees:

> All of them work hard and cause no trouble at all. I feel like they are my own children. It hurts me to think about their miserable situation. At ages when they should go to school and be under parental protection, they work menial jobs. And they work hard to keep their jobs. To help them, I have sponsored four of them for green cards in the order of employment. They don't know how to file green card applications. So I have done it for all of them. Helping them get green cards is similar to giving them two wings to fly in this coun-try. With their hard-working attitudes, they can do any thing here if they get green cards. I would feel happy if they find better jobs at another places after they get green cards. I have not done it to keep them in my business.

I interviewed an elderly Korean woman, named Myong Sook Min, who, along with her husband, lived with her married daughter. She told me about the relationships between her daughter and her Dominican maid-babysitter. Her husband and she originally immigrated to Brazil from Korea in 1966 and immigrated to the United States in 1985. The Dominican began to work at her daughter's home fourteen years ago when she was in her early forties. She, along with her daughter, took care of her two grandchildren and cooked at home while her daughter worked at her own tutoring company. Her daughter soon helped the maid invite her two children from Dominican Republic to live together and filed a peti-tion for her green card. All nine, six Korean Americans across three gener-ations and three Dominicans across two generations, lived together. They used four different languages: English, Spanish, Portuguese, and Korean.

One of the sons completed high school, went back to Dominican Republic, soon married a Dominican with whom he had two children, then separated from his wife, and came back to the United States alone. His mother, in her early sixties, had worked at the Mins for more than ten years. She invited her two grandchildren from Dominican Republic to live with her. The two families lived together for two years. Min and her daughter have considered the maid, her children, and her grandchildren as family members. Min's grandchildren call the maid *mama* and their mother *mommy*. Both Min and her daughter have always called the maid *senhora* to show their respect for her. When Min's children were in school, she arranged for the maid to take an English language course and to get a driver's license. Min has given the maid paid holidays for all American holidays, and helped her get a Medicaid card and low-income elderly housing in the Bronx, where the son currently lives and the maid lives on weekends.

This is a rare case. I asked Min how it was possible for them to live together harmoniously. She pointed out that her family had had no serious conflicts with the Dominicans and gave much credit to her daughter's considerate and compassionate nature. Min also emphasized that their both being devout Christians was an important factor.

I did not select merchants who treated their Latino employees well; I simply interviewed those who were willing to share their stories with me. Nevertheless, Korean merchants who treat Latino employees reasonably are more likely to have responded to my request for the interview, and those who exploited them are likely to have rejected it. My intent is not to generalize relationships between Korean business owners and Latino employees based on the six cases discussed here. These stories, however, do reflect a strong mutual dependence between Korean merchants and Latino employees and their informal, paternalistic relations. I am sure many other Korean merchants have similar informal relations with their Latino employees that are mutually beneficial. Korean business success is without question tied to such good relations. That the two groups share many values related to the conservative American dream ideology discussed earlier is also significant.

In her comparative study of employees of Chinese and Korean garment factories in New York City, Margaret Chin reports that Latino employees in Korean garment factories, most undocumented and all not unionized, are paid better than Chinese employees of Chinese-owned garment factories, mostly documented and almost all unionized workers.[72] No doubt, Korean business owners benefit more from the relations than Latino employees do. I also do not deny that these paternalistic relationships can be exploitative. That most of them have worked for a few or several years, however, suggests that they get some level of satisfaction in terms of wage and general treatment.

= Chapter 7 =

KPA Activities and Services

The Korean Produce Association (KPA) was established as a friendship and mutual aid organization (Sangjohe) among Korean greengrocers. It has organized many activities to facilitate fellowship and friendship networks among its members, and provided all kinds of services to its members, to the Korean community, and South Korea. Other Korean trade associations in the New York–New Jersey area provide services to its members and the Korean community, but cannot match the KPA in scope of services and money spent for the Korean community. In addition, no other Korean trade association in New York has done as much as the KPA to help South Korea export Korean agricultural products. Here we examine the KPA's various fellowship activities and multiple services.

Two Major Theoretical Perspectives

We have noted that middleman minority theory is most relevant to understanding Korean retailers' business-related conflicts with black residents and customers and their reactive solidarity and that the ethnic division of labor theory is most useful in explaining Korean greengrocers' conflicts with white suppliers and their use of ethnic collective action. Both theories are relevant to the KPA's overall mobilization to protect its members. Its service provisions to the Korean community, monetary and nonmonetary, and its efforts to help South Korea export agricultural products, which we will examine in detail, are linked to two theoretical perspectives: the positive relationship between immigrant-ethnic business and economic mobility, and transnational linkages.

Immigrant Business and Economic Mobility

Researchers interested in ethnic mobility and urban occupational structure long assumed that small business is the main avenue for economic mobility among minority groups, especially immigrant groups.[1] This assumption is perhaps most clearly reflected in Nathan Glazer and Daniel Moynihan's assertion that the "small shopkeeper, small manufacturer, or small entrepreneur of any kind played such an important role in the rise of immigrant groups in America that its absence from the Negro community warrants at least some discussion."[2]

Data collected in Europe and the United States in the 1970s, however, yielded findings that challenge this assumption. For example, based on survey research in Britain, Frank Bechhofer and his colleagues suggested that small business owners earned no more than blue collar workers, though the former worked longer hours.[3] In another British study, Howard Aldrich and his colleagues pointed out that Asian shopkeepers on the average earned less than they would earn by selling their labor in the open market.[4] Bonacich and Modell's data analysis based on second-generation Japanese Americans also largely supported the marginal characteristics of minority business owners. They reported that a greater proportion of Japanese small business owners (42 percent) earned $10,000 or less per year than those in the corporate economy (33 percent).[5]

Sociological studies conducted in the 1980s and later based on contemporary American immigrant samples generally showed economic advantages of self-employment over employment. Portes and his colleagues showed that Cuban workers in the ethnic economy—business proprietors and workers in Cuban-owned firms—received as great rewards from their human capital investments as those in the American primary economy.[6] To replicate the ethnic enclave economy thesis, two major empirical studies were conducted in the 1980s using the 1980 census. One study, by Jimmy Sanders and Victor Nee, focused on Cuban workers in Miami and Chinese workers in San Francisco showed that enclave entrepreneurs for both groups tended to be well rewarded for a given set of human capital investments, but that enclave employees do not receive as great rewards as those in the general economy.[7] The other, by Min Zhou and John Logan, focused on Chinese workers in New York City and produced mixed findings, neither supporting nor rejecting the enclave economy thesis. The authors concluded that "enclave economies are neither uniform nor static."[8]

However, George Borjas and other economists provided more or less opposite findings.[9] For example, Borjas concluded that "there is no evidence that immigrant entrepreneurs are particularly successful. The presumption that many immigrant entrepreneurs begin with small shops, and through their ability and hard work accumulate substantial wealth is a myth."[10] His data showed that self-employed immigrant workers drew higher earnings than salaried workers but that after controlling for human capital variables, their earnings advantage disappeared. Alejandro Portes and Min Zhou found that after controlling for human capital investments self-employed workers had higher annual earnings than salaried workers for three immigrant groups but that they earned lower hourly wages.[11] These findings suggest that self-employed immigrant workers' economic advantage over salaried workers is due mainly to their longer hours of work. The study by Portes and Zhou also revealed that self-employed workers were overrepresented in the exceptionally high-income category for all groups. Speaking about the implication of this finding, the authors remarked: "Hence, the presence of a cadre of successful immigrant entrepreneurs can have social and economic effects on their communities that go beyond purely individual success."[12]

These studies tried to measure economic rewards of immigrant entrepreneurship to human capital investments using self-employed people's individual earnings based on PUMS of the 1980 census. However, because self-employed people, whether immigrant or native-born, tend to underreport their earnings, we cannot measure the economic well-being of self-employed immigrants using reported earnings alone. We need another indicator.

The Korean Produce Association spends a great deal of money each year in providing different services to the Korean community, as do several other Korean business associations in New York City. Because Korean business associations use donations from their suppliers and their leaders for these services, the presence of many business owners in the Korean community and their establishment of business associations contribute to the economic welfare of the community as a whole. Moreover, supporting Portes and Zhou's claim, successful Korean businessmen also regularly donate monies individually to different social service and empowerment organizations, and to many churches in the Korean community. Because their donations are ultimately used for the needy members and the empowerment of the community, they contribute to the welfare of the community as a whole. Researchers who examine the economic benefits of immigrant businesses should pay attention to their social service role of business associations and successful merchants.

Transnational Linkages at the Organizational Level

The KPA's annual organization of the Korean Harvest and Folklore Festival and its efforts to help South Korea export Korean agricultural products to the United States are also theoretically related to the transnational literature. By virtue of technological advances in transportation and telecommunications, contemporary immigrants maintain strong and enduring ties to their homelands or home cities. This social phenomenon, often referred to as transnationalism, has received a great deal of scholarly attention from social scientists over the past twenty-five years or so.[13] *Ethnic and Racial Studies* and *International Migration Review* devoted special issues to transnationalism in 1999 and 2003, respectively. The fact that the two major international journals that specialize in immigration or ethnicity have devoted such attention to the topic is testimony to its popularity among researchers of contemporary immigrants.

These and other studies of transnationalism focus on four types of immigrants' ties to their homelands: social, economic, political, and religious. Most that focus on social or economic linkages with the home country, however, have examined individual immigrants' social networks or economic connections in the form of visits, long-distance telephone calls, remittances, and investments, whereas studies focusing on political linkages have examined measures for dual citizenship taken by several home countries of contemporary immigrants in the United States.[14] Only a few studies of transnational ties have paid special attention to organizational ties as well as individual ties, and these have focused on religious organizations.[15] Moreover, most studies on the United States focus on Caribbean and Latino immigrant groups, which maintain stronger transnational ties because of the proximity to their homelands. The existing literature on Asian immigrants' transnational ties is fragmentary, for the most part a book chapter or a section of a chapter.[16]

Several studies have examined immigrants' transnational entrepreneurial activities connecting the United States and their homeland or another diasporic community in the form of joint business ventures or transnational business networks.[17] No one, however, has examined an immigrant business association's linkages with organizations in the homeland. This chapter documents that the KPA has enhanced Korean immigrants' transnational ties to their homeland through the Korean harvest festival. It also shows that the KPA, in its efforts to help South Korea export agricultural products to the United States, has maintained strong transnational linkages with Korean central and local government agencies, and the Korean Farmers Cooperative.

KPA Structure and Activities

In 1991, the Korean Produce Association had 1,050 dues-paying members, but the membership dropped to 550 in 2005. The decline is phenomenal, given that the number of Korean produce stores slightly increased from about 1,800 in 1991 to approximately 2,000 in 2005, and that the KPA has formally expanded by merging with the Korean Produce Drivers' Association in 2002.[18] Until 2002, approximately 250 Korean produce delivery truck drivers had maintained a separate association. Because produce delivery drivers go to HPM almost every day, they are more likely to join the KPA than those who do not.

As noted earlier, business-related conflicts between Korean greengrocers and white suppliers and black customers have almost disappeared—one of the main reasons behind the decline in KPA membership. The other, as noted in chapter 4, is that most Korean greengrocers get produce delivered.

According to the 2005 annual meeting report, the KPA consists of the president, the lead vice president, nine other vice presidents representing different areas of the New York–New Jersey area, and about twenty other committee chairs. It also has a forty-five-member board of directors. Altogether, it has about seventy-five executives, staff, and board members, as well as two paid employees who work from 6 a.m. to 2 p.m. Special committees include the Committee on Aid to Members in Time of Accidents, the Scholarship Committee, the Publicity Committee, and the Election Management Committee. Most executive and board members become members of these special committees. In the spring, the KPA also establishes the committee for the Korean Harvest and Folklore Festival, a group made up of more than sixty that includes all former presidents and chairpersons of the board of directors as advisory members.

In its first ten years, dues-paying members of the KPA selected the president annually. Beginning in 1984, the selection shifted to every two years. The presidency of the KPA is considered one of the most prestigious positions in the Korean community's nonprofits, along with presidency of the New York Society of Korean Businessmen. Only the presidency of the Korean Association of New York, an umbrella organization, ranks higher. Thus two or three candidates for the presidency have usually engaged in excessive election campaigns, which have been widely publicized in Korean dailies in the New York–New Jersey area. These campaigns have on occasion contributed to intragroup conflicts among its leaders, one in 1995 included a court battle that disrupted the operation of the KPA for about two months (*Korea Times* 1996e). Because only dues-paying members can vote, the candidates for president have all made efforts to get the most likely supporters to register as members. This may be one of the reasons that, until recently, the KPA had more dues-paying members than any other Korean trade association in New York.[19]

The president spends at least a few hours a day at the KPA office about five times a week. In some situations, such as a beating of a Korean producer by employees of a produce store or a black boycott of a Korean produce store, he spends days and nights at the office, holding meetings with other staff members. A former KPA president, Chang Il Kim, put it this way: "The president considers it his workplace to attend every day." He works for nothing, and, in fact, also pays much higher dues than other members and makes significant donations for important KPA events. Bo Young Jung, who served as president of the KPA between 1989 and 1991, said:

> During my presidency, I went to the KPA office almost every day and might have worked in my store only about fifteen times during those two years.

For many days during the Church Avenue boycott, executive and board members of the KPA stayed in the office until after the midnight to discuss urgent issues to stop the boycott and to financially support the boycott victims. As the president I dealt with many stressful organizational issues for many days and had to attend so many community meetings. My stress and overwork took a toll on health. I have not yet completely recovered from the mild heart attack I had at the time.

When I asked him if as president of the KPA he also shouldered a significant financial burden, he said he had spent tens of thousands of dollars in the two years.

All staff and board members are supposed to participate in monthly meetings, which are held either at the KPA conference room or in a Korean restaurant. According to one former president, the majority fulfilled this obligation during the 1980s. As members of one or more special committees, they also spend a great deal of time at the KPA office. Attendance at special meetings to address business-related intergroup conflicts and other problems is also required. As association representatives, the president and other key staff members also participate in meetings and events organized by other Korean ethnic organizations.

Even if there is no formal meeting, many staff members often drop by the office when they come to HPM to buy produce. Many regular members also often visit the KPA office, whether for services and information or to meet friends. Korean greengrocers, whether affiliated with the KPA or not, usually meet with friends and colleagues at HPM early in the morning at one of the three coffee shops located there. The shops were run by Chung Won Cho, a greengrocer who served for the KPA for many years, until he died in February 2007. His daughter inherited all three and continues to operate them. Chang Il Kim, owner of a produce store for thirty-three years as well as former KPA president, recounts his experiences:

Back then, almost all Korean greengrocers visited HPM three or four times a week to buy green grocery items. It was a convenient place to meet and share our stories about problems and difficulties in immigrant life at the coffee shops. Since we engaged in the same business and had the same long hours of work and problems and risks in a strange environment, we maintained strong ties with one another. I often drank three or five cups of coffee each morning while visiting with my friends there.

Many Koreans who started their businesses in the 1970s have either recently retired or work on a part-time basis with managers running their stores. They still visit the KPA's office at HPM regularly to meet with their friends and enjoy memories of the early years. Chang Il Kim has had produce items delivered by a truck driver since the mid-1990s, thus does not have to visit HPM often. He still visits the KPA office every two weeks to meet his friends, however. When I visited the KPA office in 2005 and 2006, I usually found five to eight old-timers playing traditional Korean games (badeuk and hwatu). I talked with In Suck Whang, who served as president of KPA in 1991 and 1993, one day in 2006. He started his first produce business in Manhattan in 1976 and now has a produce store in New Hyde Park in Long Island. When I asked how often he visited the KPA office and why, he responded:

> I had merchandise delivered by a truck driver for ten years or so. When I did not come to HPM on a daily basis, I got too fat. To take more exercise, I changed the delivery system and visit HPM five days a week. Whenever I come here, I spend at least a few hours. I always visit the Korean Produce Association office and chat with my friends. For my health, I walk through the entire three HPM buildings. I have spent my life here for more than thirty years and cannot stop coming now.

Chang Il Kim informed me that he and others who were deeply involved in the KPA in the 1970s and early 1980s established Chunguhe, a green-grocery friendship association, in the early 1990s. The two major goals of the association are close friendship and mutual help. The twelve members[20] have regular meetings once or twice a month, playing golf and eating dinner in Korean restaurants, to maintain their friendships. They also take an out-of-the-city group tour for golfing and sightseeing in winter once or twice a year.

Because they are now financially stable, none of them usually need any financial assistance except possibly in the event of an accident or grave illness. Members of the association, for example, have agreed to organize the funeral and cover all funeral expenses when a member dies. Chung Won Cho, Chang Il Kim said, is one such example.

I have emphasized throughout the book that the KPA used more ethnic collective action than any other Korean business association because they encountered more business-related intergroup conflicts, especially with produce suppliers at HPM. It is also true that Korean produce retailers maintain stronger friendship ties among themselves than Korean merchants in any other business line because of their far more frequent meetings at HPM. Other Korean retail businesses, such as groceries and clothing shops, and hair-care establishments, have merchandise delivered. They do not have much time to meet one another because they work at their stores for long hours. The only other business line that involves a lot of contact among merchants at the wholesale market is the seafood retail business. Far fewer Korean immigrants—approximately 400—engage in that line of work, however. As noted earlier, only 40 percent of Korean greengrocers now visit HPM daily. This change has significantly reduced both KPA membership and Korean social interactions at HPM.

The KPA organizes several annual events that facilitate friendships and social interactions among its members. Employees and family members participate in summer picnics and enjoy various games, including traditional Korean wrestling (ssireum), and traditional Korean barbecue and gimchi, a popular Korean vegetable. On occasion, picnics were held jointly with another association, such as the Rockland State Park event in 1985, held with the Korean Seafood Association of New York. In the early years, attendance at the picnics was approximately 600, but that figure has dropped to around 300 in recent years.[21] In the early 1990s, when the KPA was most active, it spent considerable amounts on food, prizes, trophies, and shirts for the picnic. The event, however, did turn a slight profit, thanks to donations by produce suppliers and key staff members and prize raffles.[22] The KPA has often donated part of its profit to Korean community organizations.

The other significant annual event that the KPA organizes to enhance fellowship and social networks among members is the year-ending party held in a hotel ballroom, originally in December, but more recently in January. Guests include the KPA members, their spouses, and invited guests, heads of major Korean ethnic organizations, produce suppliers at HPM, high-ranking state and city government officials, and politicians. Attendance at this event also dropped from about 800 in the early 1990s to about 300 in 2005. The KPA has provided this event partly to provide Korean greengrocers and their family members with an opportunity to enjoy and relax with friends at a dinner dance. This dinner also helps publicize the organization and the contributions of greengrocers to New York City and the Korean community. At the dinner, scholarships are given to selected students and awards to prominent politicians and key government officials who have influenced Korean greengrocers' commercial activities.

Golf is an important part of Korean culture among government officials, politicians, and successful businessmen. It is well known that Korean immigrants make up a significant proportion of players at many golf courses in the New York–New Jersey area. Korean business and social service organizations usually organize tournaments as a way to collect donations, and many successful businessmen are ready to pay as much as $120 to participate. The KPA organizes at least four tournaments a year, two for an established scholarship fund, and two or more for recreation. About 100 members usually participate.

In earlier years, the KPA also had fishing and bowling contests every summer. About 100 members usually participated in each event. It often sent two or three teams, usually soccer and volleyball, to compete in community-wide athletic activities. These events provided more athletically oriented members with extra opportunity for fellowship and recreational activities. Until recently, approximately 100 members also participated in observing Independence Movement Day and Korean Independence Day at the HPM plaza each year. In addition, about thirty members of the Korean Harvest and Folklore Festival Committee have several days of meetings, usually in Korean restaurants, each year to prepare for the largest Korean ethnic festival in New York City. These meetings also provide the KPA's former and current key members with opportunities for social interactions and comradeship.

Because Korean produce stores are open for long hours, husband and wife coordination is critical to successful business operations. In fact, in the vast majority of cases, both partners are involved in the day-to-day operation of the business. However, the KPA is an all-male association and few women are involved. Only eight of 1,050 members in 1991 and seven of 550 members in 2005 were women.[23] By virtue of their financial ability and leadership positions, some KPA executives and board members have been able to serve similar roles at other Korean ethnic organizations. For example, Se Mok Lee served as president of the KPA between 2003 and 2005, then as president of the Overseas Advisory Board of the Korean Reunification between 2005 and 2007, and is currently serving as president of the Korean Association of New York, the umbrella Korean organization. He has devoted almost full-time work and donated generous sums to the Korean community.

The wives of these retailers have not enjoyed similar social and status rewards though they have worked just as hard for the businesses. In fact, many produce owners have been able to spend the time and money they did on fellowship, the trade association, and other ethnic organizations mainly because their wives have remained at their stores all the time. The patriarchal organizational culture is not limited to the KPA. Korean trade associations, for example, are always all-male clubs.[24] Moreover, the social rewards of business success are not limited to greengrocers. Business success has helped many other Korean men gain leadership positions in the Korean community, but not women.[25] The implications of the structure of Korean immigrant trade associations for gender issues are beyond the scope of this book, but the point is important to mention, even in passing.

I told four or five leaders of the produce business about women being underrepresented in the KPA and their lack of social rewards from their business success. Only one paid much attention to my concern. Bo Young Jung, who said he stayed in his store only about fifteen times during his two-year presidency, agreed and told me his personal story:

My wife died suddenly of stroke in 2000 just as we were about to come home from a trip to another city. I felt very guilty because she had sacrificed herself so much for our business when I was concentrating all my time and energy on the KPA. Mainly because she worked hard in the store every day during my absence, our produce business became successful. I spent large sums of money earned from the business for my organizational activities without helping her with our business. But she was so conservative on gender issues that she never complained. She seemed to feel good to see me satisfied with my organizational activities. Thinking about her sacrifice now, I feel that I cannot marry again.

Formal and Informal Member Services

All major nonprofessional Korean business associations in New York have offices and provide significant services to their members. Among the professional associations, however, none has an office and few services are offered.[26] Korean trade associations can maintain offices and hire paid employees to provide services mainly because they get significant donations from their suppliers and partly because key staff members donate significant amounts. When I conducted research in 1991, the KPA had the highest revenue and provided more services to its members than any other Korean business association. Since then, however, there has been a significant reduction in both revenue and services.

Business-Related Services

A trade association needs significant revenue to provide services for its members. In 1991, the KPA had an annual budget of $650,000 with three paid employees, a larger budget than any other Korean business association in New York.[27]

There were, and are, several revenue sources. First is annual dues, an important source of revenue for the KPA as well as other associations. Regular members pay $100 and board members pay $200. As mentioned earlier in regard to golf tournaments for scholarship funds, however, key executive and board members donate significant amounts of money several times a year for special events. In particular, according to the KPA's bylaws, the candidates for the president and his running mate, the lead vice president, should respectively deposit $15,000 and $5,000 in the KPA's account to formally register as candidates. The two who win the election are required to donate the deposited amounts to the KPA. In addition, the two highest-ranking executive members and the chair of the board of directors spend a great deal of money for several special events during their two-year term.

Donations by wholesalers are the largest source of revenue. Major produce suppliers at HPM donate significant amounts a few times a year for special events, such as the summer picnic, the New Year party, and the Korean Harvest and Folklore Festival. Other Korean business associations, such as the Korean-American Grocers Association of New York, the Korean Seafood Association of New York, and the Korean Apparel Contractors Association of Greater New York, also receive significant donations from their suppliers or manufacturers.[28] As we will see, the KPA and other Korean business associations use some of the donations from distributors and manufacturers for services to the community. Thus the Korean community in New York, as well as in other cities, benefits immensely from the presence of many Korean business associations. Earnings from advertisements in its newsletters, monthly or quarterly, and sales at the Korean Harvest and Folklore Festival are the third source of KPA revenue.

In the early years, many retailers joined partly for fellowship and partly for services. Two kinds of problems created service needs. Business-related conflicts with black customers, white suppliers, Latino employees, and white landlords, and business competition with Korean and non-Korean business owners were one type.

The other is related to various government regulations on business licensing, commercial parking, commercial leases, disposal of commercial wastes, sidewalk obstruction, and the sanitary conditions of stores. The New York City government in particular is notorious for imposing heavy penalties for various violations of business regulations to increase revenues.[29] Because most Korean produce retailers were ignorant of these regulations in the early years, they depended on the KPA for information, application forms, filing applications, and reducing penalties in case of violations. Of course, many other Korean greengrocers chose to become members of the Korean Small Business Service Center instead of relying on the KPA for these business-related services.

Most produce retail stores in New York City—as well as all peddlers, food vendors, and newsstands—have stoop-line (sidewalk) stands to display merchandise. Although longer and wider stoop-line tables contribute to greater sales, they inevitably lead to greater pedestrian and traffic congestion. The New York City government had had a law governing sidewalk obstruction for many years, but did not enforce it strictly until 1984. The 1984 revised regulations raised the fine from $50 to up to $3,000 (for repeated offenders) and gave the Department of Consumer Affairs the power to confiscate an offender's sidewalk fruits and vegetables.[30] Looking at reports of services by the KPA in the 1980s and 1990s reveals that the KPA helped its members most frequently with regulations and problems related to stoop-line stands. For example, the KPA established the stoop-line hotline at its office.[31] Staff members answered 750 telephone questions related to regulations and filled up 261 applications, renewals, or cancellations. Korean greengrocers have had more conflicts with government agencies than Korean merchants in any other type of business mainly because the majority of them use sidewalk tables to display produce outside the stores.

The KPA has lobbied city government officials and politicians and even organized mass rallies to moderate these strict sidewalk-obstruction regulations. In the following paragraphs, I trace these lobbying activities chronologically. In early summer 1983, the New York City government, specifically the Department of Consumer Affairs and the Department of Transportation, was planning to make regulations about stoop-line stands tougher to relieve sidewalk and traffic congestion. According to existing regulations at the time, peddlers, stores, and newsstands could establish stoop-line stands four feet long and ten feet wide after receiving licenses from the Department of Consumer Affairs. Tougher regulations included reducing the stands from four to three feet, expanding the number of neighborhoods with a complete ban on stands throughout the city, requiring permission from the landlords and local offices to get licenses, and confiscating all merchandise displayed on stoop-line stands and suspending licenses for repeat violations.[32]

In a letter to all produce retailers published in the KPA's monthly newsletter, Hak Sun Kim, president of the KPA at the time, said:

> I consider Korean produce stores having stoop-line stands a key weapon to increasing customers to compete with supermarkets successfully and an important source of business incomes to cover high rents. . . . Produce retail is the most important means of Korean immigrants' livelihood in New York City. The proposed regulations would be dangerous enough to destroy our produce business.

In late 1983 and early 1984, the KPA staff members actively lobbied several New York State assemblymen, New York City councilmen, and New York City government officials in Department of Consumer Affairs not to include produce stores in the categories of businesses the new regulations are applied to and to drop the requirement for getting permission from the district office for stands. As a result of their lobbying activities, city government officials eliminated produce stores, along with newsstands, from the four to three feet reduction regulation and dropped the requirement for getting permission from the local government.

Around the end of June 1984, in response to complaints about sidewalk congestion, the city government began a major campaign to crack down on violators of the stoop-line regulations. Many Korean merchants, mostly greengrocers, were among those whose displayed goods were confiscated, leading to losses of a few thousand dollars or more.[33] An especially common violation was extending the table beyond the limit or establishing it without permission. In response, the KPA tried to educate its members about the regulations by distributing fliers at Hunts Point Market. They also protested to governmental officials about the unfairness of confiscating goods without warnings and asked for more time (three months) to adapt to the new legislation.[34] They also lobbied city government officials and city council members to moderate the regulations by allowing the produce stores' sidewalk stands to extend beyond four feet.[35] Although city government officials were understanding about the request, Mayor Edward Koch killed the proposal.

The main reason that the KPA was able to so aggressively lobby government officials and local politicians was that Sung Soo Kim served as the executive director during that particular period. Mae M. Chung compared Sung Soo Kim to the biblical David fighting the Goliath of government bureaucracies.[36] As noted earlier, Kim resigned from his executive position at the KPA in early 1985 and established the Korean Small Business Service Center to help Korean and other small business owners in New York City. Since 1985, the Korean Small Business Service Center has taken a leading role in small business lobbying activities.

Later, when David Dinkins was elected mayor of New York in 1989, Sung Soo Kim, by then director of the Korean Small Business Service Center, again lobbied the city administration and the city council relentlessly, this time jointly with executive director of the KPA. In a hearing held in January 1993, Kim argued that many Korean produce and flower retail stores had been forced to close over the previous several years, and that strict enforcement of regulations on sidewalk stands had partly contributed to their business failure.[37] As a result, in April 1993 the city council passed a bill that increased the length of the sidewalk stand from four feet to five feet.[38] Kim estimated that about 70 percent of Korean greengrocers had paid penalties for violating one or another of the sidewalk stand regulations, and that this change would help many produce owners save significantly.

Retailers who violated stoop-line regulations had difficulty not only in finding time in attending hearings but also in communicating with hearing officers. Thus they usually asked the KPA to help them. Beginning in June 1984, the KPA's staff members began to negotiate with the Department of Consumer Affairs to explore the possibility of holding stoop-line stand hearings at HPM regularly for Korean violators. After a year and a half of intense lobbying, they succeeded: hearings would be held at HPM on the last Tuesday of every month. At the first, held on February 25, 1986, four greengrocers attended, with the KPA executive director serving as an interpreter.[39] Establishing the mobile administrative court at HPM helped Korean violators not only save time, but also clarifying their situation and often get their penalties reduced. Before the first hearings, the KPA had a big opening ceremony with about sixty members and three city government officials, including the administrative court judge. The system came to an end in June, however, when the operation of HPM was transferred from the New York City government to the cooperative association of produce suppliers.

Korean lobbies and collective action in connection with the sidewalk stands issue continued in the 1990s and 2000s. In 1995, Sung Soo Kim further lobbied city government officials to allow for a seasonal one-foot extension for vinyl-side awnings to protect fruits, vegetables, and flowers from freezing during the winter months, between December 1 and April 1. The City of New York Department of Sanitation responded favorably to his request, reinstating the extension, effective December 1, 1995.[40]

In June 2005, John Liu, the only Asian American City Council member in New York City and chair of the Transportation Committee, proposed a bill that would make every sidewalk stand go through a license renewal review by the Department of Transportation to ensure pedestrians' passage and security.[41] Leaders of the KPA, the Korean Small Business Service Center, and the Korean-American Grocers Association of New York mounted a strong protest, asking Liu to withdraw his proposal. When he refused to do so, they lobbied several city council members to reject it.[42] When the city council passed the proposal, the Korean community leaders organized a demonstration in front of Liu's office in Flushing, in which Korean, Chinese, and Latino business leaders all participated.[43] Kim and other Korean business leaders also met with Mayor Michael Bloomberg several times to present a position paper emphasizing the negative effects of the newly passed law on small business owners and the dwindling tax bases of the city government, asking him to veto it.[44] Mayor Michael Bloomberg did so in September.

The KPA also helped its members with other government regulations and violations, such as applications for food stamps, applications for food sanitation to the New York State Agricultural Department, application for possession of handguns, participation in administrative hearings for scale violations, Environment Control Board tickets (for violating the sidewalk litter law), and commercial parking tickets. It has also organized three to five seminars each year at HPM to teach its members about business regulations by inviting relevant officials from various government agencies to speak. In 1987, the KPA also arranged for Bronx Community College to provide commercial English and management courses for its members.[45] It also helped its members with other business-related matters: reports of robbery-related damages, choice of fire and liability insurances for the business, recommendations for accountants and lawyers, credit reviews, tax return filing, employee recommendations, advertisements of business sales, and interventions in business competition with neighboring stores. The KPA also purchased bullet-proof vests at reduced prices for its members.

Throughout the 1980s, KPA leaders discussed the need for a credit union. Finally, in 1992, the KPA purchased one that had carried a $50,000 debt. Three former KPA leaders operated it on a part-time basis. According to one, the credit union had had assets of about $200,000 at its peak, but because by law it could lend each member only up to $7,000, practical benefits to members were not great. As the KPA's membership began to dwindle in the mid-1990s, the credit union suffered financial difficulties and was forced to close in 2005 for its lack of business transactions.[46] Although the credit union was short-lived and not as beneficial to members as originally planned, it reflects the KPA leaders' great efforts to create multiple systems of services to Koreans. No other Korean trade association in the New York–New Jersey area has had a credit union for its members. The KPA's was one of only two created by Korean ethnic organizations in New York. The largest Korean Catholic church in New York, with approximately 7,000 members, started its (still active) credit union in 1983. It has three full-time employees and has served not only church members, but also those affiliated with the other twenty Korean Catholic churches in New York.

The KPA's budget in 2006 was about $600,000, which appears to be a slight decrease from the $650,000 for 1991. In terms of dollar value, however, the difference was significant. Additionally, the cost of the 2006 Korean Harvest and Folklore Festival was $400,000, whereas in 1991 it was only a little more than $150,000. The KPA has dramatically reduced business-related services for its members in recent years, because, according the executive director, Hahn-gyoung Jo, there is not much demand for these services. As of November 2005, he said, the KPA received only six or seven cases of complaints per month from its members. When I asked him about the little demand for services, he explained:

First of all, Korean greengrocers do not have much problem at HPM, no conflict with suppliers, not many parking tickets. They do not have much conflict with their customers either. Also, since they are well informed of government regulations, not many of them get tickets and fines nowadays. Those who violate government regulations are new immigrants. Even if greengrocers have problems, they have grown-up children who can help them. Some of them have their own lawyers.

In the 1980s and early 1990s, the KPA regularly published newsletters, quarterly magazines, and a member directory. They have ceased publication of all of them recently, except for the annual catalog on the Korean Harvest and Folklore Festival. In the early years, the KPA mobilized its members to picket and demonstrate by calling each member's business. Now this is impossible because there is no member directory. As noted, almost all group programs were initiated in the 1980s, but none exists now. Former presidents of the KPA reported that in the 1980s all executive and board members were very active participants in regular meetings with only two or three absentees per meeting. No doubt, their sense of threat from the outside world and of urgency to unite for self-defense at the time forced them to stick together. As of 2006, however, less than half of the members were attending regular meetings.

Nonbusiness Services and Financial Aid

Two-year reports of KPA activities reveal that the association also provided services for personal and family matters: parking tickets, information about changes in immigration law, children's applications for admissions to colleges, legal advice for the purchase and sale of houses, naturalization applications, and health and car insurance. On several occasions, the KPA provided free health clinics at its service room for members, employees, and family members.[47] In 1982, the KPA arranged discounted health insurance programs with the Sharon Agency and an agency representative worked at the KPA office to facilitate its members' choices of health insurance plans. That year, however, the KPA ended up losing about $25,000 because too few members joined the health insurance program. In 1988, the KPA successfully negotiated with Insurance System Unlimited to offer its members all types of insurance for discount prices. This lasted, a former president of the KPA informed me, only four or five years. The arrangement came to an end when, once again, the KPA could not recruit enough members to receive group insurance benefits. The association also provided car-towing services in the 1980s when its members had car problems. This too did not last long.

The KPA provided financial aid for its members and their family members in the events of accidents involving monetary losses, such as robberies and fire, and robbery-related injuries or deaths. In the early 1980s, the KPA established a special committee, called the Committee on Aids to Members in Time of Accidents to help victims of accidents among its members systematically. The committee collected donations from Korean greengrocers at HPM and deposited the monies in a special account to be used only to help victims of accidents. When accidents involved major financial losses, such as destructions of stores by fire or robbery-related deaths, the KPA collected donations at HPM from members.

The first major noteworthy aid to a member occurred in May 1982, when Si-Joong Yu was killed by a robber early in the morning on his way to HPM. The KPA organized a funeral preparation committee and held a funeral ceremony at HPM with about 150 members in attendance. Most of the KPA members participated in a donation campaign to help Yu's widow and children, collecting over $10,000.[48] Staff members also helped the wives of its members find meaningful jobs and get green cards. In the early 1990s, according to Chang Il Kim, he and four of his friends donated about $50,000 to a Korean produce owner to help establish a new produce store in a neighborhood in upstate New York when his previous landlord rejected his rental renewal. This donation activity, Chang Il Kim explained, led them to establish the *Chunguhe* to formalize mutual help and friendship among Korean greengrocers.

An article in a Korean daily, dated July 11, 1996, reported that the KPA collected donations at HPM to help two KPA members who had had accidents.[49] One member had to shut down his business in Yonkers temporarily after a wall collapsed on his business premises. The other member had his store in White Plains destroyed by a fire and his insurance company covered only about half of the losses. According to Hahn-gyoung Jo, executive director of the KPA, donations were collected most recently in January 2007, in the amount of about $12,000, to help a member who had lost his produce store through fire. These examples make it clear that despite the dramatic decrease in business-related services for members, the association still helps its members in a significant way.

Although the KPA organizes funerals when members die, the association itself does not cover funeral expenses. But, because each of the participants in the KPA-organized funeral—usually around 100—contributes between $100 and $300 to cover funeral expenses the surviving spouses do not have to shoulder much financial burden.[50] Once again, I observe that the association does not organize the funerals of wives of KPA members, even though many of them may have worked for their produce stores for longer hours than their husbands.

Services to the Korean Community

All major Korean business associations have played the role of social service agency for the Korean community.[51] They have created scholarship programs for students, held free health clinics, and regularly donated monies to Korean social service agencies. The KPA, however, seems to have played a bigger role than any other. Moreover, it is distinctive from others in that it has organized the Korean Harvest and Folklore Festival, the most important Korean ethnic festival in the area, each year. Here we examine the KPA's service activities to the Korean community in detail.

As soon as the KPA opened its office at HPM in 1980, it began to provide services to the Korean community. The most common form was regular (usually annual) donations of money to Korean social service agencies, such as the Young Women's Christian Association, the Korean Senior Citizens Association, and the Korean Association of New York. Former presidents of the KPA said that the association donated from about $10,000 to $15,000 per year. It also donated dozens of boxes of fruit to other Korean ethnic organizations for special events each year. For example, in 1983, it donated boxes of fruit for the Korean Seafood Association's outdoor picnic, a party for Korean elderly people organized by the Korean Association of New York, a donation bazaar organized by the Korean Senior Citizens Center, and a singles' party organized by a Korean restaurant in Manhattan in December 1983.[52] The KPA has also donated monies for the Korean Association of New York. Between 1982 and 1984, for example, when Ik Jo Kang, former president of the KPA, served as president of the Korean Association of New York, the KPA donated a great deal of money for the reconstruction of the KANY's building.[53]

Each November between 1979 and 1984, the KPA annually opened a one-day gimjang sijang (kimchi market) for Korean immigrant families in three areas of Queens—Flushing, Elmhurst, and Sunnyside. Kimchi is a traditional spicy pickled vegetable dish of Asian cabbages, radishes, onions, peppers, and garlic. Most Koreans eat it almost every day. In Korea, until twenty years ago, people purchased materials for kimchi (gimjang) in the gimjang sijang (the kimchi market) in late November and made enough batches to last throughout the winter.[54] In the early 1980s, Korean immigrants in New York City could purchase prepared kimchi from several Korean grocery stores, but had difficulty making it at home in large quantities because Asian cabbages and radishes were very expensive. For the one-day gimjang sijang service, KPA members could buy Asian cabbages and radishes directly from farms at low prices, and onions, peppers and other ingredients from HPM. On the advertised day and place, they sold these kimchi ingredients to Korean women for the same wholesale prices to help them make kimchi in large quantities at home. Chang Il Kim, who started the gimjang sijang, remembers the long line of Korean women wanting to purchase gimjang and that about thirty to forty KPA staff spent an entire day at the annual event. He explained that the KPA had to stop the service in the mid-1980s to avoid competition with Korean grocery stores that had begun to sell Asian cabbages and radishes.

The KPA established a scholarship program for Korean students in 1982. As of 2006, there are approximately twenty-five such programs in the Korean community in the New York–New Jersey area, most established by Korean trade and professional associations. The KPA's is one of the earliest. KPA leaders announced the program first at the 1981 year-end party and collected donations of more than $60,000 from about 600 guests, an average of more than $200 from each family.[55] This underscores both the immigrants' strong, semi-religious belief in the importance of education and produce leaders' commitment to the community. Jae Heung Choi, then president of the KPA, emphasized the importance of the KPA's establishment of the scholarship program:

Establishing the scholarship program is the most valuable of the KPA's social service activities. When we left Seoul, we were well aware of the significance of the second generation's education. In the United States, we have realized that our education is far more important than our wealth in improving our social status. We have also seen some excellent Korean students suffering from financial problems. These realizations have become the impetus for the development of our scholarship program.

Initially, the KPA Scholarship Committee awarded $1,000 each to seven to eight students per year. The program has expanded in recent years, and now awards scholarships to about twelve students. The awardees include about five or six black and Latino students. Three black students were added after 1992, following the long black boycott of two Korean stores, in the name of racial harmony. Two or three Latino students were then included among the awardees to improve Korean-Latino relationships. Most Latino student recipients in recent years have been children of Latino employees of produce wholesale companies at HPM.[56] The KPA has annually organized two scholarship banquets or golf tournaments to fill the coffers of the scholarship fund for the given year. The KPA's executive director told me that the tournament fee ($120 in 2005) is enough only to cover the expenses for the event, but that the donations made by produce suppliers, key staff members of the KPA, and golf-equipment stores supporting the event, contribute to the fund. KPA staff thus not only spend a great deal of time operating the scholarship program, but also donate significant amounts of money to the fund.[57]

The KPA's most significant contribution to the Korean community in New York is the Korean Harvest and Folklore Festival, which it has held since 1982 at Flushing Meadows–Corona Park in Queens, the home for the United Nations of cultural festivals.[58] According to one of its founders, the festival has three main goals. One is to provide opportunity for all Koreans in New York to celebrate Chuseok (the Korean Thanksgiving) together. In Korea, they celebrate Chuseok on August 15 on the lunar calendar to bless the rich harvest for the year and offer fresh crops and fruit to the spirits of the ancestors. It and New Year's Day are the two most delightful holidays in Korea. In the early years, the KPA held the festival on weekends in late September immediately after Chuseok. Because festival attendance has increased by leaps and bounds recently, the KPA has held it in the middle of October, after the regular baseball season is over, to avoid traffic congestion at Shea Stadium, which is adjacent to Flushing Meadows–Corona Park. The other two goals of the festival are to transmit Korean folk culture to the second generation and to publicize Korean cultural traditions to New Yorkers.

The festival includes traditional and contemporary Korean dances and music by performers from Korea, a major song contest organized by the Korean Broadcasting Station and broadcast to Korea, demonstrations of taekwondo and other traditional Korean folk games, ssireum (traditional Korean wrestling) competitions, demonstrations of traditional Korean wedding and ancestor worship, modeling of traditional Korean dresses (hanbok), a beauty contest to select Miss Apple, and vendor sales of Korean foods. The festival has become very successful in achieving all three of its goals. In 1985, only its fourth year, the festival drew approximately 20,000 Korean Americans and non-Korean New Yorkers.[59] Korean immigrants brought their children with them to the festival to help them experience their heritage and roots. New York City Mayor Edward Koch participated in the opening ceremony and proclaimed the day (September 29) Korean Greengrocers Day. The New York State Assembly also passed a resolution proclaiming the day the Korean Produce Association Day. Many other local politicians and government officials, as well as Korean politicians, participated in the festival.

The KPA expanded the one-day festival into a two-day weekend event in 1996, given the increase in both number of participants and support for the festival. According to the 2006 festival catalog, approximately 130,000 people participated in the 1996 festival and about 180,000 in 1998. These figures seem exaggerated. However, even assuming that only half that many attended, the Korean ethnic festival has had an amazing attendance record over the years that KPA founding members never imagined.

As younger Korean greengrocers have assumed leadership positions at the KPA over the last ten years or so, they have put more emphasis on the entertainment aspects of the festival by inviting dozens of celebrity singers and dancers from Korea. According to the association's executive director, most of the festival expenses in recent years have been spent on these entertainers.[60] Old-timers are somewhat concerned about the shift away from the original emphasis on Korean folk culture. They are not, however, too strongly opposed to the new direction because they know bringing top entertainers from Korea is effective in drawing a large audience. In 1997, the KPA added exhibitions of special Korean agricultural and manufacturing products to the festival. Several Korean provincial governments, between four and six, have participated. Additionally, because the festival has continued to draw the largest Korean crowd at one place in a given year, many American corporations, such as Pepsi Cola, Citibank, and Met Life, have recently begun participating in the exhibition. The widely distributed annual catalog includes the program for the festival, greetings from the United States and Korean presidents and prominent lawmakers and administrators in both countries, advertisements from produce suppliers, major American corporations and Korean immigrant businesses catering to mainly Korean customers, the companies from Korea and the United States participating in the exhibitions. It also introduces the KPA's annual activities.

About thirty KPA staff spend several months preparing for the festival each year. First, two KPA employees spend several months communicating with major corporations to secure booth rentals. Four executive members visit Korea in early May to negotiate with the Korean Agro-Fishery Corporation and provincial governments to send their products for exhibition, and with leading entertainers to perform. In August and September, the committee works at advertising the festival in Korean dailies; accepting applications for booth rentals from Korean food vendors and businesses; selling advertising space in the catalog to Korean businesses and American corporations; getting permission to use the park, microphones, and cooking equipment and to install special facilities (the stage) from the New York City government; and making arrangements with a travel agency and reservations with a hotel for entertainers, government officials, and politicians from Korea.

On the Friday before the festival, members of the Festival Preparation Committee spend nearly twenty hours setting up the main stage for various performances and the tents for the booths. Because the festival dates are set well in advance, they have no control over bad weather. Chang Il Kim remembered how the 2006 festival unfolded: "Last year at around four or five in the morning, a strong wind knocked down all the tents, and we had to set up everything all over again in a hurry to get everything ready by eight o'clock. Only tough Korean greengrocers can do it. No other Korean ethnic organization can undertake this kind of big event."

In the early years, KPA executive and board members' donations supported the festival. More recently, however, KPA has received significant financial support from the Overseas Korea Foundation, provincial governments, the Korean Agro-fishery Corporation, the Korean Farmers Cooperative, and Korean cultural organizations for publicizing Korean culture and Korean agro-fishery products in New York City. Additional funds come from booth rentals, catalog advertisements, and donations from produce suppliers.

The Korean Association of New York and the *Korea Times New York* newspaper have co-organized the Korean parade in Manhattan every October since 1980, and the Korean Association of New Jersey has held a major festival in the Fort Lee area since 2001. The KPA festival at Flushing Meadows-Corona Park was not only the first of its kind, but also is still the largest in the area in terms of both scale and attendance. In 2007, the Korean government donated $500,000 to the Korean community in New York in appreciation for its publicizing Korean culture through major cultural events. The KPA, the Korean Association of New York, and the Korean Association of New Jersey have equally divided the donations and earmarked them for their respective events.

Although the KPA was established as a trade organization, it has in recent years devoted more than two-thirds of its revenue and most time and energy to organizing the Korean cultural festival. Some Korean greengrocers, including a former KPA president, are critical of "the KPA's near-total devotion to the Korean cultural festival without doing what it was supposed to do." KPA leaders, however, intend to continue the festival, partly because in both Korea and New York City the KPA has been very much associated with it, and partly because the demand for services to its members has decreased so notably. As one KPA member said, "stopping the Korean cultural festival would be similar to destroying our pride and identity."

Two other factors inspire KPA leaders in continuing the festival. One is the social recognition that KPA leaders receive from holding such an important cultural event. As noted, every year key KPA leaders visit Korea and talk with provincial governors and leading entertainers, and, in the opening ceremony of the festival, all former and current KPA presidents sit with Korean and United States government executives and lawmakers. The second factor is the unusual loyalty of KPA leaders to their homeland and cultural traditions.

Research on the economic benefits of immigrant entrepreneurship has focused on self-employed immigrants' census-reported earnings and their ability to create jobs for family and community members. Because self-employed people usually underreport their earnings, however, it is difficult to measure economic advantage accurately using only census-reported earnings. Korean trade associations spend significant amounts of money on the Korean community providing various services. Successful Korean business owners also individually donate generously to community activities and social service agencies.[61] Most Korean social service agencies and community organizations, including many churches, thus cannot survive financially without the presence of many Korean business owners. Researchers have neglected to pay adequate attention to the social service functions of immigrant businesses and business associations.

By contrast, according to my research, Korean professional associations—lawyers, medical doctors, and accountants—have much smaller revenues than Korean business associations. Thus they do not provide monetary services, other than health clinics and professional seminars once or twice a year, to the Korean community. They have much smaller revenues partly because, unlike business associations, they do not get much in the way of donations from related associations. Additionally, Korean professionals typically do not donate much to their association or to Korean social service agencies and other ethnic organizations. They are much less willing to donate partly because as professionals they are less in need of the related status associated with professional organizations. Successful Korean immigrant merchants suffer what can be called status inconsistency, between their higher education or higher pre-migrant occupations and their livelihood in the United States.[62] Therefore they are more willing to spend money to gain status from positions in their business association and community organizations.

Korean immigrant professionals are also less interested in donating because they earn a living with less intergroup conflict than merchants. Self-employed Korean professionals depend heavily on Korean clients,[63] but the vast majority of self-employed Korean merchants depend on non-Korean customers. Professionals, whether employed or self-employed,

Table 7.1   A Comparison of Immigrants[a] in New York–New Jersey

	Korean	Filipino
Percentage of high school graduates	90	96
Percentage of college graduates	47	70
Percentage English fluency	19	70
Percentage of professional workers[b]	19	46
Percentage of workers in managerial, business, finance	17	13
Self-employment rate	28	5
Median household income for employed workers	$59,000	$92,000
Median household income for self-employed	$61,000	$110,000
Percentage below poverty	15.4	4.7

Source: Author's compilation from 5% Public Use Microdata Sample (PUMS) of the 2000 U.S. Census.

[a] Immigrants do not include 1.5-generation immigrants who came to the United States at age twelve or below.

[b] Workers include full-time workers who worked thirty-five hours or more per week for thirty-five weeks or more in 1999.

believe that they make a living using their credentials. Most Korean business owners, on the other hand, believe that not only hard work, but also ethnic unity are necessary for their economic success.

To show the advantage of the abundance of Korean-owned businesses to the Korean community, I briefly compare the Korean population with the Filipino. In 2005, the Filipino population in the New York–New Jersey CMSA (N = 192,978) was only slightly smaller than the Korean (N = 195,395). As shown in table 7.1, the 2000 census shows that economically active Filipino first-generation immigrants (twenty-five to sixty-four years old), have substantially higher educational levels (70 percent completing a college education) than their Korean counterparts (47 percent). Moreover, with no language barrier, almost all Filipino immigrants work in the general labor market, and only 5 percent of full-time workers were self-employed in 2000. By contrast, Korean immigrants with their severe language barrier are highly concentrated in small businesses. Self-employed Filipino immigrants are mostly in health, professional, and FIRE fields (finance, insurance, and real estate), but only a few self-employed Korean immigrants (16 percent) are. Filipino immigrants, whether self-employed or employed, do much better than Korean immigrants as measured by median household income.

Despite the huge economic advantage, the Filipino community has few ethnic organizations and most are professional associations. By contrast, there are approximately 1,000 Korean ethnic organizations, including about 600 Korean churches and more than thirty merchants' associations, in the New York–New Jersey area.[64] I suspect that the explanation for the low count of ethnic Filipino organizations is how few in the Filipino community are small business owners.[65] As noted, immigrant business associations tend to spend far more for the welfare of the community than their professional counterparts. Also, successful business owners tend to donate individually far more money to ethnic organizations than professionals. Because most of the few self-employed Filipino immigrants are professionals, the Filipino community may have difficulty finding sponsors or big donors for ethnic organizations. No one has conducted empirical research on the Filipino community in New York generally or on the relationship between the lack of small business owners and the lack of ethnic organizations in the Filipino community.

Loyalty to Homeland and Effort to Help It

Korean immigrants, as noted in chapter 3, are very loyal to their homeland. For example, in a 2005–2006 survey of Korean, Chinese, and Indian immigrants in New York City's five boroughs, I asked the respondents which team, the United States or homeland (Korean, Chinese, or Indian), they would cheer for in an Olympic soccer or cricket game. Ninety percent of Korean respondents, but only 40 percent of Chinese and 53 percent of Indian respondents, chose the category of "definitely the home country team." Korean greengrocers seem more loyal to their homeland than other Korean immigrants, including merchants in other types of businesses, mainly because they have had many business-related conflicts with other groups and government agencies. I discuss below the KPA's activities that reflect their loyalty to their homeland and efforts to help it.

The two important Korean national holidays are Independence Movement Day (March 1) and Independence Day (August 15).[66] The Korean Association of New York has formally observed both in recent years in its office in Manhattan, with more than 100 Korean immigrants attending each ceremony. In the 1970s and the early 1980s, however, when there was a small Korean population in New York City, it did not. According to my interviews and the biannual KPA reports on activities, it was KPA members who first started observing both national holidays in 1978, with about thirty members participating in each. As the number of Korean producer retailers increased, the number of participants in each national holiday ceremony also increased. To observe Independence Movement Day, the KPA president recited the Korean declaration of independence that the thirty-three leaders of the independence movement first read on Pagoda Park in Seoul on March 1, 1919. The Korean consul general and other staff members of the Korean Consulate in New York joined the ceremony, which was covered by Korean ethnic media. In 1984, two groups of Korean greengrocers, each with approximately fifty members, observed the March-First Independence Movement Day separately at HPM and the Brooklyn Terminal Market.[67]

The thirty-six years of Japanese colonization between 1910 and 1945 were among the most difficult periods in Korean history. Modern Korean nationalism developed primarily in response. Korean immigrants come to be more patriotic and more loyal to their homeland because of their experiences in an alien environment. The earlier Korean sugar-cane workers in Hawaii collected donations to support the independence movement during the colonization period.[68] Korean greengrocers seem to have begun observing the two Korean national holidays spontaneously in the late 1970s in response to the many hardships, including physical violence, they suffered.

No one remembers exactly what year the greengrocers' observance of two national holidays at HPM ended, but many suggest the late 1990s. Some produce old-timers are critical. Some young owners want to revive the practice. Kenny Pak, elected president of the KPA in 2007, is among them. When I talked with him in June 2007, he emphasized the importance of the KPA continuing the tradition. When I asked him in September whether the KPA had observed the Korean Independence Day, however, he said he had been unable to revive it because his staff members emphasized the logistical challenges. He lamented that many Korean produce retailers were happy to devote time for golf, and that few seemed interested in observing Korean national holidays.

Recall the exhibition of Korean local agricultural products at the annual harvest festival since 1997. The main goal, for all three parties (the KPA, provincial governments, and local companies of products), has been to publicize distinctive local Korean agricultural products to Korean immigrants and American citizens to promote export to the United States. The KPA's initiative did not appear in 1997 out of a vacuum, however. Instead, it reflects the business association's long-standing interest and efforts to help Korea export its products. As we saw in chapter 3, the Korean Businessmen's Association of New York (now called the New York Society of Korean Businessmen), an association of Korean importers and wholesalers of Asian-imported manufactured goods, made an important contribution to Korean exports of wigs, clothing, and other manufactured goods, especially in the 1970s and 1980s. The KPA, however, is the only Korean trade association that has significantly contributed to Korean exports of agricultural products to the United States.

To introduce the KPA and its activities, in February 1982, Jae Heung Choi, then KPA president, visited Korea and met with leaders of the Agricultural Cooperative Association and the New Village Movement's central office.[69] Their discussions explored the possibility of importing limited Korean fruit items to New York City and exporting American garlic to Korea through a few produce suppliers at HPM.[70] Two months later, four high-ranking officials from these two Korean organizations visited the KPA office at HPM. The KPA leaders invited four HPM business owners and the officials to a Korean restaurant to discuss import-export issues. Although the produce suppliers scheduled a business visit to Korea within a few weeks to check Korean fruits, the trip did not materialize.

In 1987, Ki Jung Kim, president of the KPA, visited the Seoul Produce Cooperative and came to agreement on exchanging produce information and cooperating to export Korean apples and pears to the United States and import American kiwis and papayas to Korea.[71] It was the Bo Young Jung team of the KPA (1989 to 1991), however, that took the most concrete action. Its efforts had much to do with the United States government's pressure on the Korean government to open its agricultural market after the Uruguay Round of negotiations began in 1986.[72] The KPA would be the bridgehead for exporting Korean agricultural products to the United States.

In early 1990, Bo Young Jung and Joo Tae Yoo, chair of the board of directors, and several other executive members visited Korea to explore the possibility of helping South Korea export selected flower and fruit items to the United States through HPM. They visited Garak Sijang, the largest agricultural and seafood market in Seoul, and met with officials from the Ministry of Agriculture and agricultural departments of two provincial governments, Kyungbuk and Taegu, home to the best apples in Korea. They gave information about prices and qualities of foreign-imported produce items at HPM and encouraged the Koreans to use greengrocers at HPM as intermediaries for their exports to the United States. In September 1990, they invited a group of Korean central and local government officials specializing in exports of Korean agricultural products and executive members of the Taegu Apple Cooperative to HPM. During that tour, the KPA leaders successfully negotiated with a produce supplier (A & J) to distribute Korean apples to New York State.[73]

Responding to the request from the Ministry of Agriculture in Korea, in early 1991, Jung, Yoo, and a few other KPA executives visited the U.S. Department of Agriculture to ask relevant officials to allow South Korea to export agricultural products to the United States and to obtain detailed information about the procedures of importing foreign agricultural products. Bo Young Jung spoke of his tour to the Department of Agriculture:

> In 1991 we visited the U.S. Department of Agriculture and talked with the Asian director dealing with the import and export of agricultural products to discuss the procedures of importing Korean fruits. He told us that most Korean fruit items had high levels (over 120) of insect damage. That level needed to be below 96 before Korean fruits could be imported to the United States. He explained that he and other American officials know that Asian countries, including Korea, use human manure to grow fruits. He said the U.S. government will not give permission to import Asian fruits until that practice changes. After the visit, we sent detailed information to a professor at Kyungbuk University helping the provincial government with export of Korean fruits. He in turn sent information to the governor, who relayed it

to the fruit farms. The next year, he sent two crates of apples to the KPA office as samples. To my knowledge, he sent one to a produce wholesaler at HPM and the other to the Department of Agriculture.

In March 1995, the KPA leaders, along with a few suppliers at HPM, visited Chejudo, the southernmost island in Korea, famous for its orange production.[74] In March 1996, the KPA again sent this Korean-American Agricultural Trade Promotion Mission to Korea. The ten-member team included eight KPA leaders and two American fruit experts, one president of a fruit-packing company and the other president of a produce supplier at HPM.[75] For two weeks, they toured several Korean apple, orange, persimmon, and ginseng farms, as well as major agricultural wholesale markets. Through special meetings and seminars with governmental officials and major fruit growers, the two American experts provided advice about the procedure for exporting Korean fruit to the United States: how to wrap fruit effectively and the need for using special equipment to maintain freshness during delivery. After the visit, the KPA displayed samples of key Korean agricultural products at the office, encouraging Korean produce retailers to order them.[76] That summer, it imported 80,000 cans of Korean apples and 40,000 cans of apple juice and distributed them to Korean greengrocers and some distributors at HPM.[77]

The KPA could not continue importing Korean agricultural products for distribution to Korean retailers because of the logistical difficulty in handling them. It has, however, arranged a few produce distributors at HPM to carry Korean fruits, such as apples, pears, and persimmons, so that Korean greengrocers could purchase them for retail. Since 1996, Korean supermarkets have been able to import fruits and vegetables from Korea. The exchanges of ideas and information between KPA staff members and government officials and company representatives in Korea was essential. No doubt the KPA has also benefited in terms of financial support from Korean government agencies and its publicity in Korea. KPA leaders, though, have made efforts to promote exports of Korean agricultural products primarily out of their loyalty to their homeland.

I asked Joo Tae Yoo, who joined the 1990 group tour to Korea, about the motivation of their effort. He said this in reply:

Hunts Point Market received agricultural products from all over the world. But it did not receive any product from Korea. We wanted to see some Korean fruit items distributed at Hunts Point Market. By helping to distribute Korean agricultural products at Hunts Point, we would help our homeland not only economically but also in cultural influence.

Bo Young Jung said much the same: "There were many foreign brands of fruits and vegetables in HPM. Korean greengrocers made up 75 percent of customers at HPM. But we could not see any Korean brand of fruits or vegetables. None of produce suppliers at HPM not carrying Korean brands hurt our ethnic pride. We wanted to distribute Korean apples and oranges from HPM to Korean and American customers." In their efforts to promote Korean agricultural products, the KPA has made an exhibition of selected Korean farm products at the Korean Harvest and Folklore Festival since 1997. Over the last few years, Korean products exhibited at the festival have included manufactured goods as well as farm products.

KPA leaders have undertaken several other successful efforts to help Korea. In 1986, it participated in the campaign initiated by the Korean Consulate to send books to schools in isolated rural areas in Korea, sending about $3,000 donations collected from Korean greengrocers at HPM.[78] The KPA under the leadership of Ki Jung Kim and his colleagues between 1987 and 1989 was engaged in three activities. First, the KPA leaders collected donations at HPM for two days to help flood victims in South Korea.[79] Second, the KPA co-organized with the (Korean) Young Women's Christian Association, a major Korean social service agency in the Korean community in New York, a seminar that focused on encouraging Korean immigrants to buy Korean rice and other Korean products instead of Japanese brands.[80] The tendency of most Korean immigrants to prefer Japanese rice over Korean rice at the time prompted the two organizations to hold a seminar on the issue. Third, the KPA sponsored the Korean-American amateur boxing match between New York and Seoul, organized by the *Daily News* and the *Korea Central Daily of New York* in 1988.[81]

According to Ki Jung Kim, KPA president, "the major goal of the boxing competition was to improve mutual understandings between Koreans and Americans on an equal basis through exchanges of sporting activities."[82] "I wanted to give Korean immigrants ethnic pride," Kim added, "by showing that Korean boxing champions compete with American champions on an equal basis."

In 1994, the KPA invited sixty-five Korean high school English teachers to New York City for tour and training, covering part of their travel expenses.[83] The teachers attended two-day classes at SUNY-Albany and spent the rest of the week taking tours to New York City, including HPM. Around 1994, the media and films in Korea portrayed Korean immigrants in the United States very negatively. The main reason KPA leaders invited a large number of Korean teachers to New York City at that time was, according to In Suck Whang, to "help shatter the negative images in Korea of Korean immigrants by showing them how hard Korean immigrants were working here and how much they were successful in businesses."

= Chapter 8 =

Conclusion

Because Korean immigrant merchants have used ethnic collective action mainly through their trade associations, it is effective for a systematic examination to focus on a particular association. As shown throughout this volume, because of the structure of their business and location of their stores, Korean produce retailers encountered more intergroup conflicts with white suppliers, black customers, and Latino employees, and more clashes with government agencies regulating small business activities than Korean merchants in any other type of business. Korean produce retailers and the Korean Produce Association were therefore the ideal choice and context in which to examine the positive effects of business-related intergroup conflicts on ethnic solidarity.

Korean produce retailers encountered more conflicts, including physical threats, with their white suppliers primarily because they had to buy produce at HPM. Many of them experienced discrimination as well. Their conflicts and the physical danger are the major contributing factors that led them to the KPA. They then used boycotts and demonstrations to challenge the white suppliers. To my knowledge, no previous work has detailed an immigrant trade association's conflicts and frequent use of ethnic collective action.

Both the ethnic division of labor theory and the middleman minority theory are important theoretical guides to understanding the positive effects of Korean immigrants' business-related intergroup conflicts on ethnic solidarity. The ethnic division of labor theory is more useful than middleman minority theory in understanding Korean greengrocers' conflicts with white suppliers and their use of ethnic collective action because the intergroup conflicts and collective action were confined to the two economically hierarchical groups at HPM. That is, the conflicts were based on the ethnic division of labor and therefore Koreans' use of collective action in self-defense at HPM had strong class elements. First, the KPA, as a trade association representing Korean produce retailers, organized the action against the suppliers. In addition, Korean produce retailers never framed their conflicts with produce suppliers as Korean-white conflicts. Finally, the emphasis on the critical role of an ethnic organization in mobilizing ethnic collective action provides critical insight into the KPA context. The KPA organized all major cases of produce retailers' collective action against white suppliers and government agencies.

Hechter's interpretation of collective action by an economically disadvantaged ethnic group as entirely rational, however, is problematic in understanding the nature of Korean produce retailers' boycotts and other forms of collective action. Although there are strong class elements, there is an ethnic element as well. The KPA was able to mobilize its members to demonstrations and boycotts effectively mainly because it emphasized racial discrimination and ethnic pride. Using the 1986 physical violence case as an example, we can see racial prejudice both in the ways the employees beat the retailer and in the manner in which the owner responded to the decision to boycott his store. The KPA-organized demonstrations and boycotts also include irrational, ethnic elements. First, the KPA could have taken legal action to help the Korean victims secure compensation for their humiliation and injuries. Yet the KPA instead focused on getting the involved distributor to make an apology, mainly to show the collective power and unity of Korean produce retailers and to restore their ethnic pride. Both the Korean media and staff members of the KPA defined the supplier's discrimination as racial and emphasized the ethnic elements of the retailers' solidarity.

By contrast, middleman minority theory—which focuses on the intermediary economic role of Korean immigrants in bridging white-black racial inequality—is more useful than any other in explaining black boycotts of Korean stores and Koreans' responses to boycotts (discussed in chapter 5). Middleman minority theory has advantages because it shows the inseparable connections between black boycotts and the factors that helped Koreans run businesses in black neighborhoods.

Changes in white-black racial inequality and racial segregation patterns helped Korean immigrants move into black neighborhoods in New York City for business ventures beginning in the early 1970s. Jewish and other white independent store owners were moving out of racially transitional areas, such as Harlem and many neighborhoods in Brooklyn, in the 1950s and 1960s, because of their retirements and the high crime rates there. By the 1970s, when these areas had become heavily lower-income black neighborhoods, big corporations were also reluctant to establish retail businesses there because of the residents' lower spending capacity and, again, the high crime rates. Korean immigrants took advantage of the small business vacuum created in these neighborhoods. Unlike typical middleman minorities, Korean immigrants in the United States were not encouraged by the government to run businesses in black neighborhoods. Nevertheless, similar structural factors, related to white-black racial inequality and racial segregation, helped Korean immigrants play the intermediary economic role distributing products to lower-income black customers.

When Korean retail stores in black neighborhoods became very visible in the 1980s and early 1990s, they were subjected to several long-term boycotts and other forms of rejection. Altercations between Korean store owners and employees and black customers were immediate grounds for action. The economic problems of blacks, including their underrepresentation in retail businesses in their own neighborhoods, and the Black Nationalist ideology were more fundamental. Black organizers thus emphasized economic autonomy as the goal of the boycotts. Just as emerging nationalism had rejected middleman merchants in other societies, Black Nationalism was used to reject Korean merchants in black neighborhoods in New York City.

The results of my survey of residents in the three black neighborhoods indicate that a much larger proportion of black respondents supported the Church Avenue boycott than white respondents. Moreover, a much larger proportion of black respondents accepted the statement stereotyping Korean merchants as overly concerned with making money, a typical characterization of middleman merchants. That Korean merchants were not boycotted in white neighborhoods points to the significant role of the Black Nationalist ideology in organizing and maintaining boycotts. Moreover, this consideration also helps us understand why Korean merchants in lower-income Latino neighborhoods did not have the same experience. Latinos in New York City have an entirely different ideology, given that they are a predominantly immigrant population.

The adequacy of middleman minority theory is further proved by the nature of Koreans' reactive solidarity. Responding to white produce distributors' discrimination against Korean produce retailers at HPM, the KPA singlehandedly organized boycotts and demonstrations with only Korean produce retailers participating. By contrast, other Korean merchants, the Korean Association of New York, the Korean ethnic media, and many other nonmerchant Koreans, as well as Korean produce retailers, participated in collective action against the boycotts. Although no Korean framed conflicts between Korean produce retailers and white suppliers as Korean-white conflicts, they did usually consider black boycotts as Korean-black conflicts.

The conflicts that climaxed in the victimization of many Korean business owners in the 1992 Los Angeles riots led to active research on the topic and the subsequent publication of a dozen books and many articles. Not much research, however, has been conducted to examine commercial activities of Korean immigrants in black neighborhoods in the era since the riots. As a result, people do not know the extent to which Korean immigrants reduced their commercial activities in black neighborhoods or the decrease in Korean-black conflicts since the early 1990s. Using comparative data collected in the early 1990s and 2006 and 2007, this volume provides important information about changes over time on both points.

My fieldwork reveals that the numbers of Korean stores in black neighborhoods were reduced by about two-thirds between the two periods. The movement of South Asian, Arab, Chinese and even African or Afro-Caribbean immigrants into business ventures in black neighborhoods, the emergence of mega-stores, and hikes of commercial rents in their neighborhoods—the latter two caused by changes in city zoning regulations—pushed out many Korean stores. Also, the reduction of the Korean immigrant flow and the entry of younger-generation Koreans into the mainstream economy have relaxed the Korean motivation to run businesses in lower-income black neighborhoods. What I call the serial middleman theory guided my 2006 data collection in black neighborhoods. The findings indeed indicate a succession of commercial activities in black neighborhoods from older to newer immigrant groups— from Jews to Koreans in the late 1960s and early 1970s, and from Koreans to South Asians and Arab immigrants in the late 1990s. Korean merchants in black neighborhoods encountered boycotts and other rejection in the 1980s and early 1990s because they were perceived as middleman merchants.

However, given the diversification of racial and ethnic compositions of business owners and the emergence of mega-stores in traditional black neighborhoods, black residents can no longer single out Korean or other immigrant entrepreneurial groups. Moreover, because of the gradual increase in the Latino and Caribbean immigrant populations in their neighborhoods, African American residents have almost lost their sense of territory. For these reasons, there has been no long-term black boycott of immigrant merchants in black neighborhoods in New York City in the past fifteen years or so. The influx of new immigrants and the city government's urban renovation efforts will continue to change the structure of black neighborhoods in New York City. We are in fact unlikely to witness either boycotts or riots in black neighborhoods in New York City in the future. Evidence indicates that inner-city black neighborhoods in other cities have gone through similar changes.

Korean immigrant business owners continue to depend heavily on Latinos, legal and illegal, for business operations, though the dependency has moderated in recent years. This dependence and related labor disputes have led to some picketing against Korean stores. Although Korean garment factories, dry cleaners, and restaurants also rely on Latino employees, only Korean produce stores in Manhattan encountered picketing, mainly because of their proximity to local unions.

Although Korean produce retailers had numerous conflicts with suppliers and customers in the 1980s and early 1990s, labor-related picketing against Korean-owned stores before 1998 was sporadic. It began to accelerate in 1998, however, and reached its peak between 1999 and 2002.

Local labor union pickets and the attorney general's aggressive investigations posed a threat to produce retailers and other Korean business owners in New York City, especially those in Manhattan. Several were forced to close their stores because of the pickets, and a few others were charged with heavy penalties for violations of minimum wage and overtime regulations. Korean business leaders were forced to educate Korean merchants about labor regulations. Some Korean produce stores went so far as to join a local union. In addition, the pressure on Korean business owners from the "twin attacks" of picketing and attorney general investigations seems to have led most to comply with labor laws, at least those involving minimum wage and overtime pay.

Labor disputes between Korean business owners and Latino employees in New York City have never taken the form of collective conflict. In fact, some Latinos participated in Korean-organized demonstrations against local unions and some who had organized picketing against Korean stores on behalf of Local 169 later picketed against the union headquarters. I have two suggestions to help make sense of these events.

First, because of their cultural and class differences, white labor union leaders had difficulty in successfully mobilizing Latino workers. Mexican or other Latino grassroots labor organizations would have done so more effectively. The Korean Immigrant Workers Advocate, a Koreatown-based leftist grassroots labor organization in Los Angeles, mobilized both Korean and Latino workers against Korean-owned businesses far more successfully than local labor unions had done in New York City. Peter Kwong's studies also show that restaurant workers in New York City's Chinatown, dissatisfied with Local 169, depended on the Chinese Staff and Workers Alliance, a grass-root Chinese labor organization, to organize pickets against the restaurants. Second, the reluctance of Latinos in picketing Korean stores and their conflicts with local unions also suggest that the unions tried to unionize Latino workers more to protect the union self-interest—expanding membership—than Latino workers.

Non-produce Korean merchants had conflicts with Latino workers over labor disputes as well. Accordingly, it is natural that other Korean business and community leaders joined the efforts of the KPA to resolve "targeting Korean produce retailers in Manhattan by local labor unions and Attorney General Spitzer" during the peak period.

The disputes with Latino employees involved more ethnic elements than those with white suppliers. Korean merchants, however, could not use ethnic collective action as effectively to resolve conflicts with labor unions and government agencies as they had a decade earlier with white suppliers and black customers. They could not mainly because failure to comply with labor laws is neither legally nor morally justifiable. In their conflicts with white suppliers and black customers, Korean produce retailers considered or presented themselves as victims. In disputes with Latino workers, however, the KPA had to emphasize its efforts to educate

Korean retailers about labor regulations because local unions and government agencies presented Latino workers as victims.

The two Korean organizations created in early 2001 reacted more radically, describing "Local 169 targeting only Korean merchants and Attorney General Spitzer targeting only Koreans" as "racist actions." They then organized several demonstrations against Local 169 in the spring of 2001. They mobilized about 1,000 people, including some Latino employees of Korean stores, to a demonstration staged in front of the headquarters of Local 169. They were able to mobilize such numbers mainly because there was no grassroots Korean labor organization in New York City at the time. Koreans in Los Angeles were more divided on Korean-Latino labor issues because the KIWA clarified them through the media, booklets, and press conferences (Chung 2007). With a few leftist 1.5-, and second-generation organizations active in the Korean community in New York, doing the same thing today would be difficult.

Personal interviews with Korean immigrant business owners provide qualitative insight about Korean-Latino employer-employee relations that other types of data cannot offer. Despite their significant class and ethnic differences, many Korean immigrant merchants and Latino employees maintain strong or moderate informal, paternalistic relationships because they are mutually beneficial to one another. Latino employees find stable employment as long as they work hard, and Korean merchants get a cheap but reliable work force. Moreover, as immigrants from Third World countries, the two groups share many values associated with the American dream ideology, which contributes to their personal bonds. Overall, Korean business owners evaluate Latino workers positively, which is why they depend on them. It would be interesting to see how Latino employees assess their relationships with their Korean employers.

Korean produce retailers maintain active friendship networks mainly through their regular visits to HPM to buy merchandise and to the KPA office. Given their long work hours, other Korean immigrant merchants do not have the same opportunity to meet with Koreans in the same line of business. In the early years, hundreds of produce retailers visited HPM every day and many encountered discrimination or physical violence almost every week. The KPA also had no difficulty in mobilizing for collective action. An occupationally specialized ethnic group is more likely to develop solidarity than one not specialized, partly because the members' activities facilitate their social interactions.[1] This generalization is not applicable to other types of specialized businesses, such as groceries and dry cleaners.

The KPA developed a sophisticated system of providing business-related and non-business family services to its members in the early 1980s. In the first half of the 1980s, KPA employees seem to have spent most of their time and energy in helping its members deal with government regulations regarding sidewalk stands. Between 1983 and 1985, the association lobbied city government agencies successfully to exempt Korean produce retailers from a new law on the length of sidewalk stands. Sung Soo Kim, the executive director of the KPA at the time, established his small business service center independently of the KPA in 1985 and has continued to lobby government agencies and politicians relentlessly to moderate government regulations of small business activities. Political lobbying is just one example of the significant role the leaders of a trade association can play.

KPA leadership tried to establish a number of group systems for the welfare of its members in the 1980s—a produce group-purchase system, a group health insurance plan, a credit union, and a group purchase of bullet-proof vests. It was successful in creating them, but was unable to sustain them because of shortages of manpower and funds. Nevertheless, it is impressive that it created so many collective programs. The KPA's services to its members have dropped dramatically, mainly because of a lack of demand. Yet the KPA has maintained the system of assistance to victims of accidents and the group funeral service system in the event of a member's death, two traditional forms of mutual help that were popular in Korea before modern insurance systems emerged.

As noted in chapter 2, Korean immigrants are characterized by their cultural homogeneity and highly nationalistic sentiments. No doubt, these qualities facilitated group solidarity among produce retailers in protecting their business interests against government agencies and external interest groups. However, it was their business-related conflicts that determined their ethnic solidarity. The causal relationship between the conflicts and the solidarity is demonstrated by the fact that as their conflicts have been reduced to almost nothing in recent years, the KPA's membership and collective activities have also declined. As its external threats have disappeared, the KPA has grown much more loosely organized. Ethnic solidarity has waned and waxed, but their business-based ethnic attachment has been stable.

As reviewed in chapter 7, the KPA provides many monetary and non-monetary services to the Korean community in New York every year. These include a scholarship program, donations to particular ethnic organizations and the Korean Association of New York, and, most important, the Korean Harvest and Folklore Festival. This annual celebration is the most important of Korean cultural and social events and is unmatched in scope, expense, and impact in the New York-New Jersey area. All major Korean business associations, however, provide some services to Korean social service agencies and other ethnic organizations. Further, researchers interested in the economic effects of immigrant entrepreneurship have examined only self-employment earnings compared to employment earnings. But we also need to consider the collective benefits of immigrant entrepreneurship, that is, its economic effects on the community. We may be able to discern these more clearly by comparing the Korean community in New York with its abundance of small businesses with another immigrant community with an exceptionally low self-employment rate, such as the Filipino community. Filipino immigrants individually earn much higher incomes than their Korean counterparts, but the Filipino community does not have business owners able and willing to donate monies for community organizations.

Korean produce retailers have showed their loyalty to Korea by observing Korean national holidays at the HPM plaza, their sense of being discriminated against and their struggles as small business owners in an alien environment seeming to have led them to pay homage to patriotic ancestors. The KPA has done much to help Korea. Ongoing efforts to help Korea export agricultural products to the United States are the most significant. In those efforts, the KPA has established and maintained ties with several governmental and nongovernmental organizations in Korea, visiting them and inviting their leaders to New York on numerous occasions. Korean immigrant churches, provincial organizations, and many other ethnic organizations in the New York area maintain some level of exchange with similar organizations in Korea. Transnational studies have neglected to examine such relationships.

══ Notes ══

Chapter 1

1. Geertz 1963.
2. A. Cohen 1969.
3. A. Cohen 1969.
4. Bonacich and Modell 1980; Kim and Hurh 1985; Light and Bonacich 1988, 247–59; Light and Rosenstein 1995; Light and Gold 2000; Lovell-Troy 1980; Min 1988; Portes 1995; Sanders and Nee 1996; Zhou 1992.
5. Light 1984; Light and Gold 2000; Marger and Hoffman 1992; Min and Bozorgmehr 2000.
6. Light 1979; Light and Sanchez 1987; Min 1984a.
7. Waldinger 1985, 1986.
8. Bonacich 1975; Bonacich and Modell 1980; Fong and Ooka 2002; Fugita and O'Brien 1991; Goldscheider and Zuckerman 1984, 95–96, 160–61; Light 1986; Light and Bonacich 1988, chapter 12; Min 1991, 1996; Min and Bozorgmehr 2000; Olzak 1986; Reitz 1980.
9. Ivan Light (1972) and other researchers (Light and Gold 2000) consider family ties as one of the major components of ethnic resources.
10. Min 1996, 5.
11. For example, Larry Shinagawa and Gin Pang (1996) argue that the increase in pan-Asian solidarity has contributed to the increase in pan-Asian intermarriage. It is true that members of various Asian ethnic groups—Chinese, Korean and Indian American—have made broad pan-Asian coalitions to protect common interests based on their collective consciousness of a common fate as Asian Americans. This does not mean, however, that Chinese or Korean Americans maintain close personal interactions with Indian or other South Asians in the forms of friendship, dating and intermarriage. Intermarriages among Asian Americans occur within particular pan-ethnic boundaries, like East Asian and South Asian boundaries.
12. Modell 1980.
13. Reitz 1980.
14. I. Kim 1981, 118–19, 257–59; Light and Bonacich 1988, chapter 12; Min 1996; Min and Bozorgmehr 2000; Olzak 1986.
15. Min 1996.

16. D. Y. Kim 1999; Light and Bonacich 1988; Min 1996; Yoon 1997.
17. Abelmann and Lie 1995; Joyce 2003; C. J. Kim 2000; K. C. Kim 1999; J. Lee 2002; Min 1996; Yoon 1997.
18. Min 1996.
19. Min 1996.
20. Min 1997; Shin and Yu 1984.
21. Korean National Bureau of Statistics 1977.
22. Shin and Yu 1984.

Chapter 2

1. Korean Association of New York 1985, 54.
2. Alien spouses of American citizens are eligible for naturalization only after three years of immigration. Other immigrants can apply for naturalization after five years of residence. Thus wives of U.S. servicemen can invite their parents and siblings faster than other immigrants.
3. During the period, Korean adoptees were admitted to the United States at the rate of about 3,000 per year. The annual number of Korean adoptees admitted to the United States has dropped significantly, however, to less than 1,500 per year, as fewer and fewer children have been abandoned and more and more children have been adopted in Korea. China has supplied the largest number of children for adoption by American parents in recent years, more than 7,000 each year.
4. I. Kim 1981, 73–79.
5. Yoon 1997.
6. Ong and Hee 1993.
7. I. Kim 1981, 153–55; Liu, Ong, and Rosenstein 1991.
8. Khandelwal 2002; Liu, Ong, and Rosenstein 1991.
9. I. Kim 1981, 148, 157. Korean and other Asian medical professionals in New York filled vacancies in the periphery specialties and low-income minority neighborhoods, not attractive to native-born white professionals (I. Kim 1981, 155–56; Rosenthal 1995; Shin and Chang 1988). They usually worked for second- or third-rate public hospitals, which recruited "cheap" foreign medical professionals (I. Kim 1981, 157).
10. Before 1976, foreigners with medical certificates were eligible for immigration to the United States. The 1976 revision required foreign medical professionals to get job offers from American companies to be eligible for immigration. They also needed to take TOEFL (Test of English as a Foreign Language) to get medical licenses in the United States.
11. Institute on International Education 2007.
12. Min 2006a.
13. Min 2001; Oh 2007.
14. See Min 2006b.
15. Beveridge 2002.
16. For example, one Korean immigrant who moved to Bay Terrace (a heavily Jewish neighborhood) in 1985 reported that he got flat tires a few times from nails carefully placed in front of his tires by neighbors. He said he reported the incidents to the police, who did not take any action.

17. Only 2,221 Indian Americans were settled in this community district, though Asian Indians in Queens outnumbered Koreans by a large margin.
18. Asian Indians have established their enclaves in Jackson Heights, Richmond Hills, and Eastern Queens.
19. Kibria 2002.
20. New York City and Zuccotti 1973.
21. Min 2001; Zhou 2001.
22. Min 1996, 54–55.
23. Min 2001, 180.
24. U.S. Bureau of the Census 2002.
25. Hein 2006.
26. Min 1998, 67.
27. Park and Cho 1995.
28. Hurh and Kim 1990; Min 1992.
29. Kim and Kim 2001.
30. Korea National Statistical Office 2005, 270.
31. Significant numbers of Chinese have come to the United States illegally, and a large proportion of them are settled in New York City (Liang 2001). Table 2.6 shows that 40 percent of mainland Chinese immigrants have not completed a high school education. A large proportion seem to be undocumented residents.

Chapter 3

1. Yoon 2004.
2. Beveridge 2002; Min 2002a.
3. Min 2007.
4. Min 2007.
5. As noted in chapter 3, under the impact of globalization, many Koreans, as well as people of other nationalities, have come to the United States in non-immigrant status, either as international students, temporary workers, visitors or trainers, during recent years (see Min 2006c).
6. Min 2006a, 2007.
7. Remember that immigrants are more likely to have two jobs than native-born Americans.
8. Workers in the ethnic economy include all self-employed people, unpaid family workers, and co-ethnic employees (see Light et al. 1994). The census question on class of work, however, has not included categories of whether employed workers are in the ethnic economy or the general economy.
9. Light et al. 1994.
10. Min 1984a, 1988.
11. Light 1984; Light and Gold 2000; Min 1987; Waldinger, Aldrich, and Ward 1990.
12. Yoon 1997, 125.
13. Min 1988, 57.
14. Min 1986–1987.
15. Park et al. 1990.
16. Min 1984b.
17. Min 1998.

18. Min 1988, 88.
19. National Federation of Independent Business 1979.
20. Kwon 1997.
21. Oh 2007.
22. Min 1996, 54.
23. Fifteen of the 109 self-employed Korean respondents (14 percent) reported that they engaged in the nail salon business.
24. Park 1997.
25. Chin 2005, 29.
26. Min 1996, 54.
27. *Korea Times New York* 2006a.
28. Oh 2007.
29. Bonacich and Modell 1980; Min 1991; Reitz 1980.
30. Min 1991.
31. Korean women employed in Korean nail salons depend on tips from their customers for a significant proportion of their daily earnings. To establish as many regular customers as possible, they need to talk with their customers constantly during service deliveries, asking about the customers' children and other personal matters. To do so effectively, they need to remember non-Korean customer names and to give those customers their American (rather than their Korean) names.
32. Min 1991.
33. All Korean immigrants can read Korean-language dailies and listen to Korean-language TV and radio programs. For this reason, the Korean community in New York, as well as in other Korean communities, has developed active Korean-language media.
34. Min 1991, 1998, chapter 4.

Chapter 4

1. Simmel 1955; Coser 1964.
2. Portes 1984.
3. Olzak and West 1991.
4. Espiritu 1992.
5. Bakalian and Bozorgmehr forthcoming.
6. Hechter 1975, 1978.
7. Hechter 1978, 300.
8. Hechter 1978, 298–99.
9. Hechter 1987; Hechter, Friedman, and Appelbaum 1982.
10. Hechter, Friedman, and Appelbaum 1982.
11. Aldrich 1975.
12. I. Kim 1981, 114.
13. To my knowledge, Philadelphia is the only other city where Korean immigrants, some of them transplants from New York, have established a significant presence in retail produce (about 200 stores in 2006).
14. Min 1996, 54.
15. Because of this tendency of each Korean business association to overestimate the number of Korean-owned shops, I decided not to itemize the number of stores in each business type.

16. Hunts Point Terminal Produce Cooperative Association 1987, 2.
17. To start a wholesale business at Hunts Point Market, one needs permission from members of the Hunts Point Market Cooperative Association.
18. *Sage Gae Times* 1996b.
19. *Korea Central Daily* 1986c.
20. Harney 1984.
21. Harney 1984; *Korea Times* 1984a.
22. *Korea Central Daily* 1987a.
23. KPA 1985.
24. *Dong-A Ilbo* 1982.
25. *Korea Central Daily* 1986a, 1986b.
26. *Sage Gae Times* 2002. A few middlemen suffered losses of up to several hundreds of thousands of dollars. The KPA and the Korean Produce Truck Drivers Association took measures to eliminate business owners who defaulted on their credit (*Sage Gae Times* 2002). It is not clear, however, what measures they took and whether the measures were effective.
27. *Sage Gae Times* 1996b.
28. *Korea Times* 1996d.
29. KPA 1989, 16.
30. *Korea Times* 1996a, 1987a, 1996c; KPA 1996.
31. KPA 1982, 14.
32. *Korea Times* 1991.
33. *Sage Gae Times* 1995b.
34. Moritz 1982.
35. Kramer 1982.
36. Kang, Yu, and Riew 1982.
37. White 1982.
38. KPA 1989.
39. *Korea Central Daily* 1986a, 1986b.
40. *Korea Central Daily* 1986a.
41. *Korea Central Daily* 1986a.
42. Korean seafood retailers at the Fulton Fish Market were sympathetic to Korean produce retailers because they too were subjected to racial discrimination and physical violence, the Fulton market being operated in much the same way as Hunts Point.

Chapter 5

1. Abelmann and Lie 1995; Joyce 2003; C. J. Kim 2000; K. C. Kim 1999; Light and Bonacich 1988; H. Lee 1999a, 1999b; J. Lee 2002; Min 1996; Yoon 1997.
2. Abelmann and Lie 1995, 162–80.
3. C. J. Kim 2000, 11.
4. Andreski 1963; Blalock 1967, 79–84; Bonacich and Modell 1980; Eitzen 1971; Turner and Bonacich 1980; Zenner 1991.
5. Willmott 1966.
6. University of Natal 1961; Moodley 1980.
7. Bonacich and Modell 1980; Cobas and Duany 1997; Light and Bonacich 1988, 17–18; Light and Gold 2000, 6–7.

8. Bonacich and Modell 1980; Turner and Bonacich 1980; Zenner 1991.
9. Caplan 1970; Cohen 1970; Eitzen 1971; Hunt and Walker 1974; Palmer 1957.
10. Light and Bonacich 1988, 18–19.
11. Rinder 1958–1959.
12. Loewen 1971.
13. Joyce 2003; Min 1996.
14. Cohen 1970; I. Kim 1981, 110–11; J. Lee 2002, 50–52; Min 1996; Waldinger 1986–1987, 1996, 260.
15. Light and Bonacich 1988, 325.
16. Aldrich 1975; Aldrich and Reiss 1976; I. Kim 1981, 110–11; Waldinger 1986–1987.
17. Blalock 1967, 69–74; Bonacich 1973; Bonacich and Modell 1980; Turner and Bonacich 1980; Zenner 1991, 22–25.
18. Bonacich 1973; Eitzen 1971; Hunt and Walker 1974.
19. Blalock 1967, 84; Zenner 1991, 23.
20. Capeci 1985; Cohen 1970; Weisbord and Stein 1970, 45.
21. Marx 1969; Reddick 1942; Tsukashima and Montero 1976.
22. Loewen 1971, 175–76.
23. Bonacich 1973.
24. Stryker 1974.
25. Zenner 1991, 49.
26. Haley and Malcolm X 1964.
27. Carmichael and Hamilton 1967.
28. Eitzen 1971, 153.
29. I. Kim 1981, 111.
30. Noel 1981.
31. Min 1996, 67.
32. I. Kim 1981, 110; H. Lee 1993, 67–68.
33. *Sage Gae Times* 1992.
34. Douglas 1985.
35. *Miju Mail* 1984.
36. J. Lee 2002, 24–25.
37. H. Lee 1993, 69.
38. I. Kim 1981, 110–14.
39. Joyce 2003; Min 1996.
40. Joyce 2003, 147.
41. See also Joyce 2003, 70.
42. Joyce 2003, 70; Min 1996.
43. *Sage Gae Times* 1995a.
44. Abelmann and Li 1995, 159–80; Cho 1993.
45. Joyce 2003.
46. J. Lee 2002, 5–7.
47. K. C. Kim 1999; H. Lee 1999a, 1999b; Min 1996.
48. In 1984, a Korean immigrant was picketed by several white residents in an upscale white neighborhood in midtown Manhattan when he tried to remodel a closed flower shop into a delicatessen. Those who opposed it feared that a delicatessen would spoil the community's reputation as an upscale neighborhood. The Korean, however, ultimately succeeded in establishing the

store with the support of other white residents, local politicians, and the mainstream media (Geist 1985; Min 1996, 82). Also, Korean merchants in Flushing and other Queens neighborhoods encountered white residents' complaints about Korean-language commercial signs (*Korea Central Daily* 1989c; Min 1996, 81).

49. Douglas 1985; *Korea Times* 1984b.
50. Mathews 1984.
51. Mathews 1984, 4.
52. *Amsterdam News* 1984.
53. *Amsterdam News* 1984.
54. C. J. Kim 2000; H. Lee 1993, 1999a; Joyce 2003; Min 1996; Yoon 1997.
55. Farber 1990.
56. Farber 1990.
57. Infoshare Online n.d.
58. H. Lee 1999a; *Sage Gae Times* 1990a.
59. *The New York Times* 1990.
60. H. Lee 1999a, 98.
61. *Sage Gae Times* 1990b.
62. Purdum 1990.
63. *Sage Gae Times* 1991c.
64. *Sage Gae Times* 1991a.
65. Foderaro 1990; Terry 1990.
66. *Korea Times* 1990a, 1990b.
67. *Sage Gae Times* 1991b, 1991d.
68. *Sage Gae Times* 1990e; see Joyce 2003, 114.
69. *Korea Central Daily* 1992b; *Sage Gae Times* 1990d.
70. *Korea Central Daily* 1992a; Tabor 1992.
71. *Korea Central Daily* 1992a.
72. H. Lee 1999b.
73. J. Lee 2002, 64.
74. Noel 1981.
75. Jamison 1988, 6.
76. Stryker 1974; Zenner 1991, 49.
77. Drake and Cayton 1945, 430–32.
78. C. J. Kim 2000; Min 2005.
79. *Sage Gae Times* 1990c.
80. For example, Father Lawrence Lucas, a Harlem-based black priest, said in an essay contributed to *The New York Amsterdam News* during the 1990 Church Avenue boycott: "Koreans get loans from banks and other financial institutions and insurance, as well as commercial sites from the City and privately owned businesses while the same system systematically denied in general to Africans located in America." Brenda Bell, chair of the Flatbush Coalition for Economic Empowerment, the neighborhood empowerment group that organized the boycott, was also quoted as saying: "All of a sudden, they are everywhere. . . . They are given money to establish themselves. How can poor people like that just come to this country and do that unless they have been given a 'fund.' There's no one that does that for black people" (English and Yuh 1990, 6).
81. Min 1988, 80; 1996, 102; Yoon 1997, 142.

82. When a riot occurred in Washington Heights in July 1992 after the shooting death of a Latino boy by police, three Korean-owned stores were destroyed, though this had not been planned (see Min 1996, 52).
83. Cheng and Espiritu 1989.
84. Yoon 1997, 212–18.
85. Yoon 1997, 217.
86. Yoon 1997, 220–21.
87. Chang and Diaz-Veizadez 1999, 43; Cheng and Espiritu 1989; S. Cho 1993; Lim 1982.
88. Remember that Korean immigrants chose self-employment in small business mainly because they could not find meaningful professional occupations. Remember too that many chose to open retail shops in lower-income black neighborhoods with high crime rates mainly because they did not have enough capital for middle-class white neighborhoods. We need, however, to also understand the unhappy situation of black customers. Between the 1970s and the early 1990s, they were forced to pay more for produce, grocery, and clothing items in Korean-owned shops because there were no supermarkets or department stores in their neighborhoods and because they had no cars, thus preventing them from getting to malls in white, middle-class neighborhoods.
89. Blumer 1958; see also Bobo, Kluegel, and Smith 1996.
90. Yoon 1997, 217.
91. See also Stewart 1997, 35.
92. Min 1998.
93. Waters 1999; Zhou and Bankston 1998.
94. Portes and Zhou 1993.
95. Mainly because of its conservative implications for understanding the situation of African Americans and other disadvantaged minority groups, many social scientists have negative views of segmented assimilation theory.
96. Committee for Resolution of Conflicts with Residents in Harlem 1985.
97. Committee for Resolution of Conflicts with Residents in Harlem 1985.
98. Joyce 2003, 77–80; H. Lee 1999a; Min 1996, 75–79; Yoon 1997, 179–83.
99. KPA 1991.
100. *Korea Central Daily* 1990a.
101. *Sage Gae Times* 1990b.
102. *Korea Central Daily* 1990b.
103. Because Korean immigrants in New York concentrate in several business lines, strong competition between two or more Korean stores in the same line of business, located close to one another, is inevitable.
104. He worked as executive director of the Korean Produce Association of New York on a temporary basis in 1984 and 1985, intending to go to law school. His keen awareness of Korean greengrocers' problems during the period, however, led him to give up his plans for law school and to establish the Korean Small Business Service Center instead.
105. *Korean Journal U.S.A.* 1990.
106. *Korea Central Daily* 1990c.
107. *Sage Gae Times* 1990d.
108. There was one more long-term black boycott of a Korean store in New York, in 1995, but, as noted, the hats store, the target of the boycott, was located in Greenwich Village, a white neighborhood, in Manhattan.

109. I identified only one major boycott of a Korean store—a woman's hat shop—in a black neighborhood in Los Angeles in 1996. It was organized by Brotherhood Crusade and Nation of Islam in January 1996, after the owner had asked a black male customer, who was a minister, to leave the store on the grounds that it was a women's hat store. The minister was looking for a hat for his wife and considered the request racially motivated. He then consulted two Black Nationalist organizations to organize a boycott, which forced the owner to close the store. Korean and black church leaders helped it reopen later in summer (see *Sage Gae Times* 1996a).

110. At least five Korean organizations in New York City, including the Korean-American Grocers Association of New York and the Korean Produce Association, have established scholarship programs for black children. The Organization for African American Korean American Solidarity, established in 1993, also has held several annual social and cultural activities to bridge the two communities (Bell 1998). Won Duk Kim, a long-time Korean businessman in Harlem, organized the Korean African Association for Friendship in 1990 and guided thirty-seven African American pastors on a friendship visit to Korea in October 1991. In addition, Korean Association of New York, several Korean churches, and the Council of Korean Churches of New York have helped the black community in a number of ways (see Min 1996, 129–35).

111. Allen 1996; Firestone 1996; Serant 1996.

112. Allen 1996; *Sage Gae Times* 1996a.

113. Fireston 1996.

114. Given this, it is not surprising that three of the fourteen surviving Korean-owned stores in Harlem were beauty supply stores.

115. Some of 74,643 native-born blacks were children of Caribbean and African immigrants who would not consider them African Americans.

116. Choi 2005.

117. Grant, Oliver, and James 1996, 382.

118. Min 2006a.

119. Kibria 2006.

120. Goldscheider and Kobrin 1980; Goldscheider and Zuckerman 1984, 160–61, 187; Light and Roach 1996.

121. Light and Roach 1996.

122. D. Y. Kim 2004; E. Y. Kim 1993; Min 1998, 71–72.

123. D. Y. Kim 2004; Min 1988; Waldinger 1989.

124. Waldinger 1989, 67.

125. Gold 1992, 85; 1995, 35; Gold and Phillips 1996.

126. Gold 1995, 35.

127. Min 2006a; Sakamoto and Xie 2006, 61.

128. Gold and Phillips 1996; Simon 1997.

Chapter 6

1. Chang and Diaz-Veizadez 1999; Cheng and Espiritu 1989; Chung 2007; D. Y. Kim 1999; Light and Kim 1999; Yoon 1997.

2. Massey 2000, 34.

3. Rumbaut 1996.

4. Waldinger and Lichter 2003, chapter 9.
5. Waters 1999.
6. Bobo et al. 1996.
7. Bonacich 1994; Light and Kim 1999.
8. Light 2006.
9. Min 1987.
10. Yoon 1997, 213.
11. Min 1996, 114. That Korean merchants in black neighborhoods did not hire enough black employees is one of the major complaints black community leaders have.
12. One Korean owner said that the black employee had become a good friend, which is a somewhat atypical interracial relationship.
13. Yoon 1997, 209. Almost all respondents who chose blacks were found to have businesses in heavily black neighborhoods in south central Los Angeles. This indicates a sense of obligation to hire black employees because of the black customer base.
14. Yoon 1997, 211.
15. Min 1996, 114–15.
16. Min 1996, 115.
17. Yoon 1997, 211.
18. The random surname sampling technique was used for the survey. Indian Christians and Muslims who were not included in Indian surnames were located through personal channels and interviewed separately. In all, 370 Chinese, 282 Indians, and 277 Korean immigrants who had a job at the time of the interview or within five years before it were interviewed. The numbers of Chinese, Indian, and Korean respondents in row 1 in the table indicate those who were self-employed.
19. Liang and Morooka 2004.
20. D. Y. Kim 1999.
21. Yoon 1997, 215.
22. Smith 2001.
23. *Korea Central Daily* 1989a, 1989b.
24. *Korea Central Daily* 1989d, 1989e; *Sage Gae Times* 1989b.
25. *Sage Gae Times* 1989b.
26. *Sage Gae Times* 1989a.
27. *Korea Central Daily* 1989d.
28. *Sage Gae Times* 1995a, 1995b.
29. *Sage Gae Times* 1995a.
30. *Sage Gae Times* 1997.
31. Kershaw 2001.
32. The KPA provided a copy of the letter.
33. Jacobs 2000.
34. Jacobs 2000.
35. Kershaw 2001; *Korea Times* 2001b, 2001f.
36. *Korea Times* 2001d; *Sage Gae Times* 2001c.
37. Kershaw 2001.
38. *Korea Times* 2001h.
39. *Korea Times* 2001k.

40. *Sage Gae Times* 2000.
41. *Sage Gae Times* 2000.
42. KPA public file.
43. *Korea Central Daily* 2001a, 2001b; *Korea Times* 2001a.
44. *Korea Times* 2001c.
45. *Korea Times* 2001e.
46. *Korea Times* 2001e; *Sage Gae Times* 2001a.
47. *Korea Times* 2001g.
48. *Korea Times* 2001i.
49. *Korea Central Daily* 2001b.
50. Leslie Casimir (2001), a reporter of *Daily News*, reported that Jacob Han, a brother of Josephine Kim, established the Korean Anti-Discrimination Association.
51. Casimir 2001.
52. Casimir 2001; *Sage Gae Times* 2001b.
53. Casimir 2001, 5.
54. *Korea Times* 2001i.
55. *Korea Times* 2001j.
56. *Korea Central Daily* 2001b, 2001c.
57. Greenhouse 2002.
58. Greenhouse 2002.
59. Greenhouse 2002.
60. Latinos comprise close to half of the population in Los Angeles and the majority in Koreatown. Koreans make up only 20 percent of that population (Yu et al. 2004).
61. Beveridge and Weber 2003, 75.
62. Yu et al. 2004.
63. Cho 1992; Chung 2007, 158–59; Saito and Park 2000.
64. Chung 2007, 161–63.
65. Chang and Diaz-Veizadez 1999, 89–90; Chung 2007, 160–62.
66. Chung 2007, 192.
67. Kwong 1987, 1997, 198–99.
68. Kwong 1997, 199.
69. *Korea Central Daily* 2007; *Korea Times* 2006c, 2007.
70. *Korea Times* 2006b.
71. According to Kim, conflicts among Korean employees are primarily attributable to the senior employee's trying to control more recent hires.
72. Chin 2005, 34–36.

Chapter 7

1. Glazer and Moynihan 1963, 30; Goldscheider and Kobrin 1980; Lipset and Bendix 1966, 101, 102, 177–81; Light 1972; Ritterband and Cohen 1984; Sowell 1981.
2. Glazer and Moynihan 1963, 30.
3. Bechhofer et al. 1974.
4. Aldrich et al. 1981, 1983.
5. Bonacich and Modell 1980, 128.
6. Portes 1987; Portes and Bach 1985; Wilson and Portes 1980.

7. Sanders and Nee 1987.
8. Zhou and Logan 1989, 817.
9. Borjas 1990; Bates 1989; Bates and Dunham 1991.
10. Borjas 1990, 163.
11. Portes and Zhou 1996.
12. Portes and Zhou 1996, 228.
13. Foner 1997; Schiller, Basch, and Szanton Blanc 1992; Levitt 1999; Portes 2003; Portes, Guarnizo, and Landolt 1999.
14. Guarnizo 1998; Smith 2003.
15. Levitt 1999, 2001, 2007.
16. Chen 2002; Min 1998; Ong 1999; Wong 1998; Yang 2006.
17. Chen 2002; Guarnizo 2003; Itzigsohn et al. 1999; Landolt, Autler, and Baires 1999; Ong 1992; Portes 2003; Wong 1998; Yang 2006.
18. *Korea Times* 2002.
19. The Korean Nail Salon Association had about 1,200 members as of 2005, the largest membership among all Korean business associations in New York.
20. According to Kim, to maintain harmony and prevent conflict among members, all existing members should approve the application of any Korean greengrocer to join the organization. Kim said that because of this strict rule, its membership has not increased much since.
21. KPA 1987.
22. KPA 1991.
23. Min 1997, 187.
24. Min 1997.
25. See Min 1998, chapter 4.
26. Min 1996, 203.
27. Min 1996, 203.
28. Because part of these donations are used for the Korean community as a whole, the presence of many business owners in the Korean community contributes to the community welfare in general.
29. Breznick 1991.
30. Collins 1985.
31. KPA 1985.
32. KPA 1984.
33. Collins 1985; *Mijoo Mail* 1984.
34. *Dong-A Ilbo* 1984.
35. KPA 1984.
36. Cheng 1995, 23–24.
37. *Sage Gae Times* 1993a.
38. *Sage Gae Times* 1993b.
39. *Korea Times* 1986.
40. *Korea Central Daily* 1996.
41. *Korea Central Daily* 2005.
42. *Korea Times* 2005a.
43. *Sage Gae Times* 2005.
44. *Korea Times* 2005b.
45. KPA 1989.
46. *Korea Central Daily* 1992b.

47. *Korea Times* 1987b.
48. KPA 1982.
49. *Korea Times* 1996b.
50. It was a Korean custom to donate money when people participated in memorial or funeral services. Not only Korean produce retailers, but also other Korean immigrants usually donate to help the surviving family members cover funeral expenses.
51. Min 2001.
52. KPA 1985.
53. *Korea Times New York* 1996a.
54. Kimchi used to be stored underground in earthenware jar that aided the fermentation process. Today special containers and refrigerators have been developed to help women make smaller batches year around.
55. KPA 1982.
56. The KPA has chosen children of Latino employees of produce suppliers at HPM because they have directly served Korean produce retailers and delivery truck drivers who visit HPM.
57. Operating the scholarship program involves organizing fundraising events a few times a year, advertising the scholarship program in Korean dailies to accept applications, selecting awardees, and holding the award ceremony.
58. Brawarsky 2002.
59. Velez and Leahy 1985
60. He said that due to popularity of Korean culture in other Asian countries Korean entertainers currently charge much greater amounts of money to perform in the United States than twenty years ago.
61. Most Korean ethnic organizations depend on donations from board members for their revenues. Korean merchants are the vast majority of board members for various Korean ethnic organizations.
62. Hurh and Kim 1990; Min 1988.
63. Oh 2007, 145–46.
64. Min 2001.
65. The internal diversity and division among Filipino immigrants may also be significant factors for the lack of ethnic Filipino organizations.
66. First Independent Movement Day is the day—March 1, 1919—on which thirty-three Korean representatives declared independence against Japanese colonization in Seoul, which led to nationwide anti-Japanese demonstrations. The Japanese military government ruthlessly repressed the movement, killing more than 6,000 Korean participants. Independence Day is the day—August 15, 1945—that Korea was liberated from Japanese occupation at the end of World War II.
67. KPA 1985.
68. Choy 1979.
69. Chung-Hee Park, a military general who became the president of Korea in 1962 in a coup d'état, made an important contribution to industrializing South Korea through his multiyear economic planning. He started the New Village Movement to modernize farming and village life.
70. KPA 1982.

71. *Korea Central Daily* 1987c.
72. The Uruguay Round was a trade negotiation from September 1986 to April 1994 that transformed the General Agreement on Tariffs and Trade, the World Trade Organization. The main goal was to reduce agricultural subsidies, put restrictions on foreign investment, and begin the process of opening trade in banking and industry.
73. *Korea Times* 1990c.
74. KPA 1995.
75. *Chosun Ilbo* 1996a.
76. *Chosun Ilbo* 1996b; KPA 1996.
77. *Chosun Ilbo* 1996c.
78. KPA 1986.
79. *Korea Central Daily* 1987b.
80. *Korea Central Daily* 1987c.
81. *Chosun Ilbo* 1988.
82. *Chosun Ilbo* 1988.
83. KPA 1994.

Chapter 8

1. Hechter 1978.

═ References ═

Abelmann, Nancy, and John Lie. 1995. *Blue Dreams: Korean Americans and the Los Angeles Riots.* Cambridge, Mass.: Harvard University Press.

Aldrich, Howard. 1975. "Ecological Succession in Racially Changing Neighborhoods: A Review of the Literature." *Urban Affairs Quarterly* 10(3): 327–48.

Aldrich, Howard, and A. Reiss. 1976. "Continuities in the Study of Ecological Succession: Changes in the Race Composition of Neighborhoods and Their Businessmen." *American Journal of Sociology* 81(4): 846–66.

Aldrich, Howard, John Carter, Trevnor Jones, and David McEvoy. 1981. "Business Development and Self-Segregation: Asian Enterprise in Three British Cities." In *Ethnic Segregation in Cities*, edited by Ceri Peach, Vaughn Robinson, and Susan Smith. London: Croom Helm.

———. 1983. "From Periphery to Peripheral.: The South Asian Petite Bourgeoisie in England." In *Research in the Sociology of Work*, vol. 2, edited by I. H. Simpson and R. Simpson. Greenwich, Conn.: JAI Press.

Allen, Michael O. 1996. "Small Shops Blast Big Store Zones." *New York Daily News*, May 1, 1996.

Amsterdam News. 1984. "Korean Women in Coma after Fight with Picketers." November 13, 1984.

Andreski, Stanislav. 1963. "An Economic Interpretation of Anti-Semitism in Eastern Europe." *Jewish Journal of Sociology* 5(3): 201–13.

Bakalian, Anny, and Mehdi Bozorgmehr. Forthcoming. *Backlash 9/11: Impact and Reaction of Middle Eastern and Muslim Americans.* Berkeley, Calif.: University of California Press.

Bates, Timothy. 1989. "The Changing Nature of Minority Business: A Comparative Analysis of Asian, Non-Minority, and Black-Owned Businesses." *The Review of Black Political Economy* 18(1): 25–42.

Bates, Timothy, and Constance Dunham. 1991. "The Changing Nature of Business Ownership as a Route to Upward Mobility of Minorities." Paper presented at the conference on Urban Labor Markets and Labor Mobility, sponsored by the Urban Institute, Arlie House, Virginia, March 7–8, 1991.

Bechhofer, Frank, Brian Elliot, Monica Rushforth, and Richard Bland. 1974. "The Petit Bourgeoisie in the Class Structure: The Case of Small Shopkeepers." In *The Social Analysis of Class Structure*, edited by Frank Parkin. London: Tavistock.

Bell, Bill. 1998. "Black, Korean Union." *New York Daily News*, June 26, 1998.

Beveridge, Andrew. 2002. "Immigrant Residence and Immigrant Neighborhoods in New York: 1910 and 1990." In *Mass Migration to the United States: Classical and Contemporary Periods*, edited by Pyong Gap Min. Walnut Creek, Calif.: AltaMira Press.

Beveridge, Andrew, and Susan Weber. 2003. "Race and Class in the Developing New York and Los Angeles." In *New York and Los Angeles: Politics, Society, and Culture*, edited by David Halle. Chicago, Ill.: University of Chicago Press.

Blalock, Herbert. 1967. *Toward a Theory of Minority Group Relations*. New York: John Wiley & Sons.

Bobo, Lawrence, James R. Kluegel, and Ryan A. Smith. 1996. "Laissez-Faire Racism: The Crystallization of a 'Kinder, Gentler' Anti-Black Ideology." Unpublished paper. New York: Russell Sage Foundation.

Bonacich, Edna. 1973. "A Theory of Middleman Minorities." *American Sociological Review* 38(5): 583–94.

———. 1975. "Small Business and Japanese American Ethnic Solidarity." *Amerasia Journal* 3(1): 96–112.

———. 1994. Asians in the Los Angeles Garment Industry. In *The New Asian Immigration in Los Angeles and Global Restructuring*, edited by Paul Ong, Edna Bonacich, and Lucie Cheng. Philadelphia, Pa.: Temple University Press.

Bonacich, Edna, and John Modell. 1980. *The Economic Basis of Ethnic Solidarity: Small Business in the Japanese American Community*. Berkeley, Calif.: University of California Press.

Borjas, George. 1990. *Friends or Strangers: The Impact of Immigrants on the U.S. Economy*. New York: Basic Books.

Brawarsky, Sandee. 2002. "For Koreans, Feast and Thanks." *The New York Times*, October 4, 2002.

Breznick, Alan. 1991. "City Squeezing Business for Fees." *Crain's New York Business*, July 22, 1991.

Capeci, Dorminic, Jr. 1985. "Black-Jewish Relations in Wartime Detroit: The Marsh, Loving, and Wolf Surveys and Race Riots of 1943." *Jewish Social Studies* 26(1): 56–73.

Caplan, Nathan. 1970. "The Negro Ghetto Man: A Review of Recent Empirical Studies." *Journal of Social Issues* 26(1): 56–73.

Carmichael, Stokely, and Charles Hamilton. 1967. *Black Power: The Politics of Liberation in America*. New York: Vintage Books.

Casimir, Leslie. 2001. "Village Labor Unrest: Local 169 and Greengrocers Square Off." *New York Daily News*, May 20, 2001.

Chang, Edward, and Jeannette Diaz-Veizadez. 1999. *Ethnic Peace in American Cities: Building Communities in Los Angeles and Beyond*. New York: New York University Press.

Chen, Yong. 2002. "Chinese American Business Networks and Transpacific Economic Relations Since the 1970s." In *The Expanding Role of Chinese Americans in U.S.-China Relations*, edited by Peter Koehn and Xiao-huang Ying. Armonk, N.Y.: M. E. Sharpe.

Cheng, Lucie, and Yen Le Espiritu. 1989. "Korean Business in Black and Hispanic Neighborhoods: A Study of Intergroup Relations." *Sociological Perspectives* 32(4): 521–34.

Cheng, Mae M. 1995. "A Giant Slayer: A Face of the City." *New York Newsday*, March 19, 1995: 23–24.

Chin, Margaret. 2005. *Sewing Women: Immigrants and the New York City Garment Industry.* New York: Columbia University Press.

Cho, Namju 1992. "Check Out, Not In: Korean Wilshire/Hyatt Take-Over and the Los Angeles Korean Community." *Amerasia* 18(1): 131–9.

Cho, Sumi. 1993. "Korean Americans vs. African Americans: Conflict and Construction." In *Reading Rodney King/Reading Urban Uprising,* edited by R. Cooding-Williams. New York: Routledge.

Choi, In Chul. 2005. "The South Side: The End of Korean Frontier?" In *Koreans in the Windy City,* edited by Hyock Chun, Kwang Chung Kim, and Shin Kim. New Haven, Conn.: East Rock Institute.

Chosun Ilbo. 1988. "Newyork-suh Hanmichinsun Jumokdaegyul" ["A Korean-American Friendship Boxing Match in New York City"]. June 30, 1998.

———. 1996a. "Hanmi Nongteuksanmul Gyoryu Chokjindan Banghan" ["The Korean-American Agricultural Trade Promotion Mission Visits Korea"]. March 17, 1996.

———. 1996b. "Sintobuli Hankuk Nongsanmul Mokeupsida" [" 'Sintobuli' Let's Eat Korean Agricultural Products"]. April 30, 1996.

———. 1996c. "Sintobuli Hanguknongsanmul Mokeupsida" ["Let's Use Korean Agricultural Products"]. July 13, 1996.

Choy, Bong-Youn. 1979. *Koreans in America.* Chicago, Ill.: Neilson Hall.

Chung, Angie Y. 2007. *Legacies of Struggle: Conflict and Cooperation in Korean American Politics.* Stanford, Calif.: Stanford University Press.

Cobas, José A., and Jorge Duany. 1997. *Cubans in Puerto Rico: Ethnic Economy and Cultural Identity.* Gainesville, Fla.: University of Florida Press.

Cohen, Abner. 1969. *Customs and Politics in Urban Africa: A Study of Hausa Migrants in Yoruba Towns.* London: Routledge & Kegan Paul.

Cohen, Nathan. 1970. *The Los Angeles Riots: A Sociological Study.* New York: Praeger.

Collins, Gail. 1985. "Picking a Street Fight." *Tuesday Business,* October 1, 1985.

Committee for Resolution of Conflicts with Residents in Harlem. 1985. "The Efforts to Resolve the October 1984 Conflicts with Harlem Residents." Unpublished committee report.

Coser, Lewis. 1964. *The Functions of Social Conflict,* 2nd ed. Glencoe, Ill.: Free Press.

Dong-A Ilbo. 1982. "Chonggwasang Choissi Jipdan Pokhaengdanghae" ["Greengrocer Choi Beaten by a Group at Terminal Market"]. April 3, 1982.

———. 1984. "Newyork-Si Jwadaedansok Sichungbangmun Yuboyochung Gurbu" ["New York City Government Reject Postponing Crackdown on Sidewalk Tables"]. July 28, 1984: 4.

Douglas, Carlyle. 1985. "Korean Merchants Are Targets of Black Anger." *The New York Times,* January 19, 1985.

Drake, St. Clair, and Horace R. Cayton. 1945. *Black Metropolis: A Study of Negro Life in a Northern City.* New York: Harcourt, Brace.

Eitzen, Stanley. 1971. "Two Minorities: The Jews of Poland and the Chinese in the Philippines." In *Ethnic Conflicts and Power: A Cross-National Perspective,* edited by Donald Gelfand and Russell Lee. New York: John Wiley & Sons.

English, Merle, and Ji-Yeon Yuh. 1990. "Black-Korean Conflict Simmers." *The New York Newsday,* February 13, 1990.

Espiritu, Yen Le. 1992. *Asian American Pan-Ethnicity: Bridging Institutions and Identities.* Philadelphia, Pa.: Temple University Press.

Farber, M. A. 1990. "Black-Korean Who-Pushed-Whom Festers." *The New York Times,* May 7, 1990.

Firestone, David. 1996. "Zoning Plan for Warehouse-Style Stores Is Approved and Sent to Council in Close Vote." *The New York Times,* October 24, 1996.

Foderaro, Lisa. 1990. "As One Grocery Boycott Ends, One Drags On." *The New York Times,* September 9, 1990.

Foner. Nancy. 1997. "What's New about Transnationalism? New York Immigrants Today and the Turn of the Twentieth Century." *Diaspora* 6(3): 355–75.

Fong, Eric, and Emi Ooka. 2002. "The Social Consequences of Participating in the Ethnic Economy." *International Migration Review* 36(1): 125–36.

Fugita, Stephen, and David O'Brien. 1991. *Japanese American Ethnicity: The Perspective of Community.* Seattle, Wash.: University of Washington Press.

Geertz, Clifford. 1963. *Peddlers and Princes: Social Change and Economic Modernization in Two Indonesian Towns.* Chicago, Ill.: University of Chicago Press.

Geist, Williams. 1985. "The Deli on the Park Avenue Is Starting to Fit In." *The New York Times,* February 20, 1985.

Glazer, Nathan, and Daniel P. Moynihan. 1963. *Beyond the Melting Pot: Negroes, Puerto Ricans, Jews, Italians, and Irish of New York City.* Cambridge, Mass.: The MIT Press.

Gold, Steven J. 1992. *Refugee Communities: A Comparative Field Study.* Newbury Park, Calif.: Sage Publications.

———. 1995. *From the Workers' State to the Golden State: Jews from the Former Soviet Union in California.* Boston, Mass.: Allyn & Bacon.

Gold, Steven, and Bruce Phillips. 1996. "Mobility and Continuity among Eastern European Jews." In *Origins and Destinies: Immigration, Race, and Ethnicity in America,* edited by Silvia Pedraza and Rubén Rumbaut. Belmont, Calif.: Wadsworth Publishing.

Goldscheider, Calvin, and Francis Kobrin. 1980. "Ethnic Continuity and the Process of Self-Employment." *Ethnicity* 7(2): 256–78.

Goldscheider, Calvin, and Alan S. Zuckerman. 1984. *The Transformation of the Jews.* Chicago, Ill.: University of Chicago Press.

Grant, David, Melvin L. Oliver, and Angela D. James. 1996. "African Americans: Social and Economic Bifurcation." In *Ethnic Los Angeles,* edited by Roger Waldinger and Mehdi Bozorgmehr. New York: Russell Sage Foundation.

Greenhouse, Steven. 2002. "Korean Grocers Agreed to Double Pay and Improve Workplace Condition." *The New York Times,* September 18, 2002.

Guarnizo, Luis Eduardo. 1998. "The Rise of Transnational Social Formation: Mexican and Dominican State Responses to Transnational Migration." *Political Power and Social Theory* 12(1): 45–94.

———. 2003. "The Economics of Transnational Living." *International Migration Review* 37(3): 666–99.

Haley, Alex, and Malcolm X. 1964. *The Autobiography of Malcolm X.* New York: Ballantine Books.

Harney, James. 1984. "Efforts Bear Fruit: 2 Nabbed and 1G." *New York Daily News,* April 29, 1984.

Hechter, Michael. 1975. *Internal Colonialism: The Celtic Fringe in British National Development.* Berkeley: University of California Press.

———. 1978. "Group Formation and the Cultural Division of Labor." *American Journal of Sociology* 84(2): 293–318.

———. 1987. *Principles of Group Solidarity.* Berkeley, Calif.: University of California Press.

Hechter, Michael, Debra Friedman, and Malka Appelbaum. 1982. "A Theory of Ethnic Collective Action." *International Migration Review* 16(2): 212–34.

Hein, Jeremy. 2006. *Ethnic Origins: The Adaptation of Cambodian and Hmong Refugees in Four American Cities.* New York: Russell Sage Foundation.

Hunt, Chester, and Lewis Walker. 1974. *Ethnic Dynamics: Patterns of Inter-group Relations in Various Societies.* Homewood, Ill.: Dorsey.

Hunts Point Terminal Produce Cooperative Association. 1987. "Market History." Unpublished report.

Hurh, Won Moo, and Kwang Chung Kim. 1990. "Religious Participation of Korean Immigrants in the United States." *Journal for the Scientific Study of Religion* 29(1): 19–34.

Immigration and Naturalization Service. 1965–1978. Annual Reports. Washington: Government Printing Office.

———. 1979–2002. Annual Reports. Washington: Government Printing Office.

Infoshare Online. n.d. Home page. Accessed at http://www.infoshare.org.

Institute on International Education. 2007. *Open Doors 2007: The Annual Report on International Education.* New York: Institute on International Education. Accessed at http://opendoors.iienetwork.org.

Itzigsohn, Jose, Carlos D. Cabral, Esther H. Mendina, and Obed Vázquez. 1999. "Mapping Dominican Transnationalism: Narrow and Broad Transnational Practices." *Ethnic and Racial Studies* 22(2): 316–39.

Jacobs, Andrew. 2000. "Produce Market Owners Allow Workers to Unionize." *The New York Times,* January 1, 2000.

Jamison, Harold. 1988. "Vann's Try to Settle Korean Fights Hits Snag." *Amsterdam News,* October 8, 1988.

Joyce, Patrick D. 2003. *No Fire Next Time: Black-Korean Conflicts and the Future of America's Cities.* Ithaca, N.Y.: Cornell University Press.

Kang, Ik Jo, Duk Jong Yu, and Hackjong Riew. 1982. "Korean Businessmen Protest a News Column." *New York Daily News,* August 8, 1992.

Kershaw, Sarah. 2001. "Union Drive Collides with Korean Grocers." *The New York Times,* February 25, 2001.

Khandelwal, Madhulika S. 2002. *Becoming American, Being Indian: An Indian Immigrant Community in New York City.* Ithaca, N.Y.: Cornell University Press.

Kibria, Nazli. 2002. *Becoming Asian American: Second Generation Chinese and Korean American Identities.* Baltimore, Md.: Johns Hopkins University Press.

———. 2006. "South Asian Americans." In *Asian Americans: Contemporary Trends and Issues,* 2nd ed., edited by Pyong Gap Min. Thousand Oaks, Calif.: Pine Forge Press.

Kim, Claire Jean. 2000. *Bitter Fruit: The Politics of Black-Korean Conflict in New York City.* New Haven, Conn.: Yale University Press.

Kim, Dae Young. 1999. "Beyond Co-Ethnic Solidarity: Mexican and Ecuadorian Employment in Korean-Owned Businesses in New York City." *Ethnic and Racial Studies* 22(3): 581–605.

———. 2004. "Leaving the Ethnic Economy: The Rapid Integration of Second-Generation Korean Americans in New York." In *Becoming New Yorkers:*

Ethnographies of the New Second Generation, edited by Philip Kasinitz, John H. Mollenkoph, and Mary C. Waters. New York: Russell Sage Foundation.

Kim, Eun Young. 1993. "Career Choice Among Second-Generation Korean Americans: Reflections on a Cultural Model of Success." *Anthropology and Education Quarterly* 24(3): 224–48.

Kim, Illsoo. 1981. *New Urban Immigrants: The Korean Community in New York.* Princeton, N.J.: Princeton University Press.

Kim, Kwang Chung, editor. 1999. *Koreans in the Hood: Conflict with African Americans.* Baltimore, Md.: Johns Hopkins University Press.

Kim, Kwang Chung, and Won Moo Hurh. 1985. "Ethnic Resources Utilization of Korean Small Businessmen in the United States." *International Migration Review* 19(1): 82–111.

Kim, Kwang Chung, and Shin Kim. 2001. "Ethnic Roles of Korean Immigrant Churches in the United States." In *Korean Americans and Their Religions: Pilgrims and Missionaries from a Different Shore*, edited by Ho-Youn Kwon, Kwang Chung Kim, and R. Stephen Warner. University Park, Pa.: Pennsylvania University Press.

The Korea Central Daily New York (*Korea Central Daily*). 1986a. "Injongchabyul, Pokhaeng Jungdanhara" ["Stop Racial Discrimination and Beating"]. March 14, 1986.

———. 1986b. "Hengpoe Shidalida Terjinbunno" ["Anger Burst After Suffering from Monopoly"]. March 18, 1986.

———. 1986c. "Gyopo Chonggwasang 40% Gangdodeung Danghae" ["40% of Korean Produce Retailers Encountered Robbery"]. December 5, 1986.

———. 1987a. "Nosanggando Gyuktookkute Bupjapa" ["A Robber Caught after Fighting"]. February 25, 1987.

———. 1987b. "Chonggwa Sangjohe Sujae Euiyongeum Mogeum" [KPA Collects Donations for Flood Victims], March 22, 1987.

———. 1987c. "Guksanpum Aeyong Gwonjang Semina" ["Seminar on Love of Korean Products"]. March 30, 1987.

———. 1989a. "Jugujiyoksurdo Haninbacheuk Umjikim" ["Residents Too Start to Boycott Korean Merchants"]. April 12, 1989.

———. 1989b. "Gyopochonggwasang-e Nojogaeip Apryok" ["Korean Produce Stores Pressured to Join Labor Union"]. April 26, 1989.

———. 1989c. "Flushing Ganpanbungyu Haninupso Biwhajojim" ["Controversy over Foreign-Language Commercial Signs Spread"]. July 14, 1989.

———. 1989d. "4-Gae Hain Chonggwasang-suh Sikpumnojo Gaip" ["Four Korean Produce Stores Joined Labor Union"]. August 5, 1989.

———. 1989e. "Minojo Gaipapryuk Bongyukhwa" ["Pressure to Join Labor Unions Accelerated"]. July 14, 1989.

———. 1990a. "Sotbureun Hwahae-boda Janggijok Daechaek Ganggu" ["Looking for a Long-Term Solution Rather than a Risky Temporary Harmony"]. February 5, 1990.

———. 1990b. "Gyopo Eupso 24-Sigan Chejero" ["Korean Stores Start 24-Hour Service"]. April 4, 1990.

———. 1990c. "Hanin Inkwon Onghowi Baljok" ["Korean-American Civil Rights Committee Established"]. May 25, 1990.

———. 1992a. "Nuguege Hosohaeya Hapnigga?" ["Whom Can I Ask for Help?"]. February 19, 1992.

———. 1992b. "Hanin Gagaeso Heugin Jipdanguta" ["Blacks Attack in a Korea-Owned Store"]. July 4, 1992.

———. 1996. "Chunggwa Jwadae Chungmak Yonjangsulchi Seungin" ["Extension of An Extra Foot for Produce Sidewalk Stands for Vinyl-Side Awnings Approved"]. November 29, 1996.

———. 2001a. "2-He Isang Nodongbup Wiban Hyungsachobol" ["Criminal Punishment against Violations of Labor Laws Twice or More Often"]. February 23, 2001.

———. 2001b. "Daegyulgukmyun Akhwallro" ["Confrontations Getting Worse and Worse"]. April 6, 2001.

———. 2001c. "Hanindeul Satae Mugwansim Bansunghaeya" ["Koreans Should Reflect on Their Indifference to Pickets"]. April 6, 2001.

———. 2005. "Jwadae Umgyuk Gyujehamyon Sosangin Dajuku" ["If Sidewalk Stands Are Strictly Regulated, All Small Business Owners Will Disappear"]. August 17, 2005.

———. 2007. "Chosunjok Nodongja Chebulimguem Badanaetda" ["Korean Chinese Workers Receive Back Wages"]. April 29, 2007.

Korea National Statistical Office. 2005. *2005 Social Indicators in Korea*. Seoul: Korea National Statistical Office.

The Korea Times New York (*Korea Times*). 1984a. "Kimsungsoossi-e Yonggamhan Shiminsang" ["Sung Soo Kim Awarded the Courageous Citizens Award"]. April 30, 1984.

———. 1984b. "Blacks Began to Boycott Korean Stores in Harlem." October 31, 1984.

———. 1986. "Jwadaewiban Gyopo Chutjaepan" ["Violators of Stoop-line Stand Law Had Hearings First Time"]. February 27, 1986.

———. 1987a. "Gongdonggumae Ggum Iruotda" ["The Dream of Group Purchase Achieved"]. August 17, 1987.

———. 1987b. "Chonggwa Sangjohe Muryo Gongangjindan" ["Korean Produce Association Provides Free Health Clinic"]. September 25, 1987.

———. 1990a. "Haninsangdae Heuginhaengpae Hwaksanjojim" ["Blacks' Harassment and Violence Against Korean Business Owners and Employees Have Increased"]. August 12, 1990.

———. 1990b. "Manhattan Haninsangga Heuginnodong" ["Blacks in Korean Stores in Manhattan"]. August 19, 1990.

———. 1990c. "NewYork Chedae Yutong Domaesang Hwakbo" ["The KPA Secures the Largest Distributor for Korean Apples"]. September 26, 1990.

———. 1991. "Beating One Korean Produce Retail Is The Same as Beating All Koreans." July 27, 1991.

———. 1996a. "Old Timer: My Way, My Life." March 23, 1996.

———. 1996b. "Sangjohe Joochook Uhryoumdanghan Dongryo Dopneunda" ["The KPA Help Its Members in Difficulty"]. July 11, 1996.

———. 1996c. "Chunggwasangjohe Wongajolgamundong" ["Korean Produce Association Tries to Lower Unit Prices"]. October 29, 1996.

———. 1996d. "Huntspoint Sijang Shi-jikyong Yogu" ["Demand Hunts Point Market Be Run by New York City"]. November 11, 1996.

———. 2001a. "Nodongbup Joonsooddaen Gwagu Jalmot Yongso" ["If Korean Merchants Observe Labor Laws, Their Past Violations Will Be Absolved"]. February 23, 2001.

———. 2001b. "8-Gae Haninupsodaesang Siwi" ["Picketing against Eight Korean Stores"]. March 30, 2001.

———. 2001c. "Nojo 'Siwi Yulhulgan Joongdan' " ["Local Union Plans to Stop Pickets for Ten Days"]. April 11, 2001.

———. 2001d. "17-Nyon-gan Piddamheulnin Tojon Nojo-ga Asagatseupnida" ["A Business Based on 17 Years of Blood and Tears Destroyed by the Union"]. April 13, 2001.

———. 2001e. "Hinin Nojodaechaekwi Jaegusung" ["The Korean Task Force for Resolution of Labor Disputes Being Restructured"]. April 16, 2001.

———. 2001f. "Uriga Wonhanun Guteun Geunroja Kwonikppun" ["All We Want Is Workers' Rights"]. May 5, 2001.

———. 2001g. "Deli-Upso Satae Chongchejok Daeeung" ["All-Around Measures to Pickets Against Deli Stores"]. May 5, 2001.

———. 2001h. "Joo-Bupmuguk 3-Gae Hanindeli Goso" ["The Attorney General Sues Three Korean Produce Retailers"]. May 5, 2001.

———. 2001i. "Local 169 Injongchabyuljok Haengwi Gyutan" ["Picketing to Protest Local 169's Racist Pickets"]. May 24, 2001.

———. 2001j. "Hanin 1,000-Yumyong Chamga" ["About 1,000 Participated"]. June 4, 2001.

———. 2001k. "Upjoodeul 31-Man 5-Chun Dollar Jibeul Hapeui" ["Business Owners Agree to Pay $315,000"]. November 23, 2001.

———. 2002. "Chongghwa Unsonghyuphe Tonghap Jamjong Hapeui" ["Korean Produce and Truck Drivers' Associations Have Reached a Tentative Agreement to Unify the Two Associations"]. February 21, 2002.

———. 2005a. "Gwanryon Hanindanche Moongchimyon Jwadaegyujong Muhyohwa Ganeung" ["If Korean Ethnic Organizations Are United, It Is Possible to Nullify Regulations on Sidewalk Stands"]. August 25, 2005.

———. 2005b. "Jwadaegangwha Gobugwon Haengsa" ["Mayor Vetoes Enhanced Regulations on Sidewalk Stands"]. September 16, 2005.

———. 2006a. "Jamaica Domaesanga Gaebal Gibon Yoongag Deulerna" ["An Outline of Wholesale Market Development Surfaced"]. September 9, 2006.

———. 2006b. "Neil Upgedo Nodongbungyu" ["The Nail Salon Business Too Encounters Labor Disputes"]. October 26, 2006.

———. 2006c. "Hanin 2-Myong Mijigeup Imgeum Batgede" ["Two Koreans Get Unpaid Wages"]. November 11, 2006.

———. 2007. "Milin Imgeum 3-Man 2-Chun Dollar Badanae" ["Settlement for Accumulated $3,200 Back Wages Reached"]. January 24. 2007.

Korean Association of New York. 1985. *History of the Korean Association of New York.* New York: The Korean Association of New York.

The Korean Journal U.S.A. 1990. "Hanincheuk Ipjang Jonjok-euro Jijihanda" ["I Strongly Support the Korean Side"]. June 16, 1990.

Korean National Bureau of Statistics. 1977. *Population Composition by Surnames: A Report on the Data of the 1975 Korean Census of Population.* Seoul: The Korean Economic Planning Board.

Korean Produce Association (KPA). 1980–1996. Annual and Biannual Reports on Activities. New York: The Korean Produce Association.

Kramer, Marcia. 1982. "Korean Merchants Protest." *New York Daily News,* August 7, 1982.

Kwon, Victoria Hyonchu. 1997. *Entrepreneurship and Religion: Korean Immigrants in Houston, Texas.* New York: Garland Publishing.

Kwong, Peter. 1987. *The New Chinatown.* New York: Hill and Wong.

——. 1997. *Forbidden Workers: Illegal Chinese Immigrants and American Labor.* New York: The New Press.

Landolt, Patricia, Lilian Autler, and Sonia Baires. 1999. "From Hermano Lejano to Hermano Mayor: The Dialectics of Salvadoran Transnationalism." *Ethnic and Racial Studies* 22(2): 290–315.

Lee, Heon Cheol. 1993. "Black-Korean Conflict in New York City: A Sociological Analysis." Ph.D. dissertation, Columbia University.

——. 1999a. "The Dynamics of Korean-Black Conflict: A Korean-American Perspective." In *Koreans in the Hood: Conflict with African Americans,* edited by Kwang Chung Kim. Baltimore, Md.: Johns Hopkins University Press.

——. 1999b. "Conflicts between Korean Merchants and Black Customers: A Structural Analysis." In *Koreans in the Hood: Conflict with African Americans,* edited by Kwang Chung Kim. Baltimore, Md.: Johns Hopkins University Press.

Lee, Jennifer. 2002. *Civility in the City: Blacks, Jews, and Koreans in Urban America.* Cambridge, Mass.: Harvard University Press.

Levitt, Peggy. 1999. "Local-Level Global Religion: The Case of U.S. Dominican Migration." *Journal for the Scientific Study of Religion* 37(1): 74–89.

——. 2001. *The Transnational Village.* Berkeley, Calif.: University of California Press.

——. 2007. *God Needs No Passport: Immigrants and the Changing American Religious Landscape.* New York: The New Press.

Liang, Zai. 2001. "Demography of Illicit Emigration from China: A Sending Country's Perspectives." *Sociological Forum* 16(4): 677–701.

Liang, Zai, and Hideki Morooka. 2004. "Recent Trends of Emigration from China: 1982–2000." *International Migration* 42(3): 145–64.

Light, Ivan. 1972. *Ethnic Enterprise in North America: Business and Welfare among Chinese, Japanese, and Blacks.* Berkeley, Calif.: University of California Press.

——. 1979. "Disadvantaged Minorities in Self-Employment." *International Journal of Comparative Sociology* 20(1): 31–45.

——. 1984. "Immigrant and Ethnic Enterprise in North America." *Ethnic and Racial Studies* 7(2): 195–216.

——. 1986. "Ethnicity and Business Enterprise." In *Making It in America,* edited by Mark Stolarik and Murray Friedman. Lewisburg, Pa.: Bucknell University Press.

——. 2006. *Deflecting Immigration: Networks, Markets, and Regulation in Los Angeles.* New York: Russell Sage Foundation.

Light, Ivan, and Edna Bonacich. 1988. *Immigrant Entrepreneurs: Koreans in Los Angeles 1965–1982.* Berkeley, Calif.: University of California Press.

Light, Ivan, and Steven Gold. 2000. *Ethnic Economies.* San Diego, Calif.: Academic Press.

Light, Ivan, and Rebecca Kim. 1999. "Immigrant Incorporation in the Garment Industry in Los Angeles." *International Migration Review* 33(Spring): 5–26.

Light, Ivan, and Elizabeth Roach. 1996. "Self-Employment: Mobility Ladder or Economic Lifeboat." In *Ethnic Los Angeles,* edited by Roger Waldinger and Mehdi Bozorgmehr. New York: Russell Sage Foundation.

Light, Ivan, and Carolyn Rosenstein. 1995. *Race, Ethnicity, and Entrepreneurship in Urban America*. New York: Aldine de Gruyter.

Light, Ivan, and Angel A. Sanchez. 1987. "Immigrant Entrepreneurs in 272 SMSAs." *Sociological Perspectives* 30(4): 373–99.

Light, Ivan, Georges Sabagh, Mehdi Bozorgmehr, and Claudia Dermartirosian. 1994. "Beyond the Ethnic Enclave Economy." *Social Problems* 41(1): 601–16.

Lim, H. 1982. "Acceptance of American Culture in Korea: Patterns of Cultural Contact and Koreans' Perception of American Culture." *Journal of Asiatic Studies* 25(1): 25–36.

Lipset, Seymour, and Reinhard Bendix. 1966. *Social Mobility and Industrial Society*. Berkeley, Calif.: University of California Press.

Liu, John, Paul Ong, and Caroline Rosenstein. 1991. "Dual Chain Migration: Post-1965 Filipino Immigration to the United States." *International Migration Review* 25(3): 487–513.

Loewen, James. 1971. *The Mississippi Chinese: Between Black and White*. Cambridge, Mass.: Harvard University Press.

Lovell-Troy, L. A. 1980. "Ethnic Occupational Structures: Greeks in the Pizza Business." *Ethnicity* 8(2): 82–95.

Lucas, Lawrence. 1990. "Seeing Through Smoke Screen of the Boycott." *Amsterdam News*, October 6, 1990.

Marger, Matin, and Constance A. Hoffman. 1992. "Ethnic Enterprise in Ontario: Immigrant Participation in the Small Business Sector." *International Migration Review* 26(3): 268–81.

Marx, Gary. 1969. *Protest and Prejudice*. New York: Harper and Row.

Massey, Douglass S. 2000. "Why Does Immigration Occur?" In *The Handbook of International Migration: The American Experience*, edited by Charles Hirschman, Philip Kasinitz, and Josh DeWind. New York: Russell Sage Foundation.

Mathews, Les. 1984. "Harlem Pickets Demand Respect for Customers." *Amsterdam News*, October 27, 1984.

Mijoo Mail. 1984. "Jwadae Jipjungdansok Boryu Gangryuk Gwoneui" ["Asked To Delay Crackdown on Violations of Sidewalk Stand Regulations"]. July 28, 1984.

Min, Pyong Gap. 1984a. "From White-Collar Occupations to Small Business: Korean Immigrants' Occupational Adjustment." *Sociological Quarterly* 25(3): 333–52.

———. 1984b. "An Exploratory Study of Kin Ties Among Korean Immigrant Families in Atlanta." *Journal of Comparative Family Studies* 15(1): 59–75.

———. 1986–1987. "Filipino and Korean Immigrants in Small Business: A Comparative Analysis." *Amerasia Journal* 13(1): 53–71.

———. 1987. "Factors Contributing to Ethnic Business: A Comprehensive Synthesis." *International Journal of Comparative Sociology* 28(3-4): 173–93.

———. 1988. *Ethnic Business Enterprise: A Case Study of Korean Small Business in Atlanta*. Staten Island, N.Y.: Center for Migration Studies.

———. 1991. "Cultural and Economic Boundaries of Korean Ethnicity: A Comparative Analysis." *Ethnic and Racial Studies* 14(2): 225–41.

———. 1992. "The Structure and Social Functions of Korean Immigrant Churches in the United States." *International Migration Review* 26(4): 1370–94.

———. 1996. *Caught in the Middle: Korean Communities in New York and Los Angeles*. Berkeley and Los Angeles, Calif.: University of California Press.

———. 1997. "Korean Immigrant Wives' Labor Force Participation, Marital Power, and Status." In *Women and Work: Exploring Race, Ethnicity, and Class*, edited by Elizabeth Higinbotham and Mary Romero. Thousand Oaks, Calif.: Sage Publications.

———. 1998. *Changes and Conflicts: Korean Immigrant Families in New York*. Boston, Mass.: Allyn & Bacon.

———. 2001. "Koreans: Institutionally Complete Community in New York." In *New Immigrants in New York*, revised and updated, edited by Nancy Foner. New York: Columbia University Press.

———. 2002a. "Introduction." In *Mass Migration to the United States: Classical And Contemporary Periods*, edited by Pyong Gap Min. Walnut Creek, Calif.: AltaMira Press.

———. 2005. "Review of Bitter Fruits: The Politics of Black-Korean Conflict in New York City." *Amerasia Journal* 31(2): 187–90.

———. 2006a. "Korean Americans." In *Asian Americans: Contemporary Trends and Issues*, edited by Pyong Gap Min. Walnut Creek, Calif.: AltaMira Press.

———. 2006b. "Major Issues for Asian American Experiences." In *Asian Americans: Contemporary Trends and Issues*, edited by Pyong Gap Min. Walnut Creek, Calif.: AltaMira Press.

———. 2006c "Immigration: History and Trends." In *Asian Americans: Contemporary Trends and Issues*, edited by Pyong-Gap Min. Walnut Creek, Calif.: Altamira Press.

———. 2007. "Korea." In *The New Americans: A Guide to Immigration Since 1965*, edited by Mary C. Waters and Reed Ueda. Cambridge, Mass.: Harvard University Press.

Min, Pyong Gap, and Mehdi Bozorgmehr. 2000. "Immigrant Entrepreneurship and Business Patterns: A Comparison of Koreans and Iranians in Los Angeles." *International Migration Review* 34(3): 707–38.

Moodley, Kogila. 1980. "Structural Inequality and Minority Anxiety: Responses to Middle Groups in South Africa." In *The Apartheid Regime: Political Power and Racial Domination in South Africa*, edited by Robert M. Price and Carl G. Rotberg. Berkeley, Calif.: University of California, Institute of International Studies.

Moritz, Owen. 1982. "In the Korean Shadow of Yankee Stadium." *New York Daily News*, August 9, 1982.

National Federation of Independent Business. 1979. "How Small Business Begin?" Unpublished paper.

New York City, and John E. Zuccotti. 1973. *Community Planning District Profiles, Part 1: Population and Housing*. New York: New York City Planning Commission.

The New York Times. 1990. "Sonny Carson, Koreans and Racism." May 8, 1990.

Noel, Peter. 1981. "Will Black Merchants Drive Koreans from Harlem?" *New York Amsterdam News*, July 11, 1981.

Oh, Sookhee. 2007. "Immigrant Communities and Ethnic Linkages: Suburban Koreans in the New York-New Jersey Metropolitan Area." Ph.D. dissertation, New School University.

Olzak, Susan. 1986. "Competition Model of Ethnic Collective Action in American Cities." In *Competitive Ethnic Relations*, edited by Susan Olzak and Joane Nagel. New York: Academic Press.

Olzak, Susan, and Elizabeth West. 1991. "Ethnic Conflicts and the Rise and Fall of Ethnic Newspapers." *American Sociological Review* 56(4): 458–74.

Ong, Aiwha. 1992. "Limits to Cultural Acculturation: Chinese Capitalist on the American Pacific Rim." *Annals of the New York Academy of Science* 645:125–45.

———. 1999. *Flexible Citizenship: The Cultural Legacy of Transnationality.* Durham, N.C.: Duke University Press.

Ong, Paul, and Suzanne Hee. 1993. *Losses in the Los Angeles Civil Unrest, April 29–May 1, 1992.* Los Angeles, Calif.: UCLA Center for Pacific Rim Studies.

Palmer, Mabel. 1957. *The History of Indians in Natal.* Natal Regional Survey, vol. 10. Oxford: Oxford University Press.

Park, Insook Han, and Lee-Jay Cho. 1995. "Confucianism and the Korean Family." *Journal of Comparative Family Studies* 26(1): 117–35.

Park, In-Sook Han, James Fawcett, Fred Arnold, and Robert Gardner. 1990. *Korean Immigrant to the United States: A Pre-Departure Analysis.* Occasional Paper no. 114. Honolulu, Hawaii: East-West Center, Population Institute.

Park, Kyeyoung. 1997. *The Korean American Dream: Immigrants and Small Business in New York City.* Ithaca, N.Y.: Cornell University Press.

Portes, Alejandro. 1984. "The Rise of Ethnicity: Determinants of Ethnic Perceptions among Cuban Exiles in Miami." *American Sociological Review* 49(3): 389–97.

———. 1995. "Economic Sociology and the Sociology of Immigration: A Conceptual Overview." In *The Economic Sociology of Immigration,* edited by Alejandro Portes. New York: Russell Sage Foundation.

———. 1987. "The Social Origins of the Cuban Enclave Economy of Miami." *Sociological Perspectives* 30(4): 467–85.

———. 2003. "Conclusion: Theoretical Convergencies and Empirical Evidence in the Study of Immigrant Transnationalism." *International Migration Review* 37(Fall): 874–91.

Portes, Alejandro, and Robert Bach. 1985. *Latin Journey: Cuban and Mexican Immigrants in the United States.* Berkeley, Calif.: University of California Press.

Portes, Alejandro, and Min Zhou. 1993. "The New Second Generation: Segmented Assimilation and Its Variants among Post-1965 Immigrant Youth." *Annals of the American Academy of Political and Social Science* 530 (November): 74–98.

———. 1996. "Self-Employment and the Earnings of Immigrants." *American Sociological Review* 61(1): 219–30.

Portes, Alejandro, Luis E. Guarnizo, and Patricia Landolt. 1999. "The Study of Transnationalism: Pitfalls and Promise of an Emergent Research Field." *Ethnic and Racial Studies* 22(2): 217–37.

Purdum, Todd. 1990. "Dinkins Supports Shunned Grocers." *The New York Times,* September 22, 1990.

Reddick, L. D. 1942. "Anti-Semitism Among Negroes." *Negro Quarterly* 1(Summer): 111–5.

Reitz, Jeffrey G. 1980. *The Survival of Ethnic Groups.* Toronto: McGraw-Hill.

Rinder, Irwin. 1958–1959. "Stranger in the Land: Social Relations in the Status Gap." *Social Problems* 6(3): 253–60.

Ritterband, Paul, and Steven Cohen. 1984. "The Social Characteristics of the New York Area Jewish Community, 1981." *American Jewish Yearbook* 84: 128–64.

Rosenthal, Elizabeth. 1995. "Competition and Cutbacks Hurt Foreign Doctors in U.S." *The New York Times,* November 7, 1995.

Rumbaut, Rubén. 1996. "Origins and Destinies: Immigration, Race, and Ethnicity." In *Origins and Destinies: Immigration, Race, and Ethnicity in Contemporary America,* edited by Silvia Pedraza and Rubén Rumbaut. Belmont, Calif.: Wadsworth Publishing.

The Sage Gae Times (Sage Gae Times). 1989a. "Chonggwasang Nojogaip Apryuk-eun Budang" ["Pressuring Korean Produce Stores to Join Labor Union Is Not Justified"]. July 25, 1989.

———. 1989b. "Misikpumnojo Haninchonggwasang-e Ggeunjilgin Gongse" ["Food Labor Union Tirelessly Pressures Korean Produce Stores to Join Labor Union"]. July 28, 1989.

———. 1990a. "Shiwi iggeunseryok Deulunatda" ["The Groups Who Control the Church Avenue Boycott Unveiled"]. February 8, 1990.

———. 1990b. "Saebyok Iseul Nogin Hanindul-eui Onjong" ["Koreans' Charity Has Melted Early Morning Dew"]. February 10, 1990.

———. 1990c. "Heuginbulmaeshiwi Jijineun 13%bbeun" ["Only 13% of Respondents Support the Brooklyn Boycott of Korean Produce Stores"]. June 16, 1990.

———. 1990d. "Haningyungyoung Super Bulmaeundong Geuksung" ["A Korean-Run Supermarket Encounter A Severe Boycott"]. November 2, 1990.

———. 1990e. "Brooklyn-so Hanin Pokhaengdanghae Joongtae" ["A Korean Was Viciously Attacked in Brooklyn"]. November 3, 1990.

———. 1991a. "Jangbongjaessee Gage Ijon Chujin" ["Mr. Jang Planning to Transfer His Store"]. March 16, 1991.

———. 1991b. "Harlem-sodo Bulmaesiwi Wihyup" ["Threat of Boycott in Harlem Too"]. April 13, 1991.

———. 1991c. "Jangbongjaessee Red Apple Maedo" ["Jang Bong Jae Sold Red Apple"]. May 25, 1991.

———. 1991d. "Bulmaesiwi Bilmi Heugindeul Geumpoom Yogu" ["Blacks Ask for Money with Threat of Boycott"]. May 28, 1991.

———. 1992. "Newyorksi Supermarket Binminga Talpi" ["New York City Supermarkets Move out of Poor Minority Neighborhoods"]. June 8, 1992.

———. 1993a. "Jwadae Gyujehamyon Sosangin Saengjon Bulganung" ["If Sidewalk Stands Are Restricted Too Much, Small Business Owners Cannot Survive"]. January 27, 1993.

———. 1993b. "Jwadae 7 Wol-butir 5 Feet-ro Hwakjang" ["Sidewalk Stands to Be Extended to Five Feet in July"]. April 28, 1993.

———. 1995a. "Heukinsiwi Teujipjapgi Yangsang" ["Black Demonstration"]. February 6, 1995.

———. 1995b. "Chonggwasangjohe Hangeuisiwi Dolip" ["KPA Starts Picketing"]. February 22, 1995.

———. 1996a. "Han-Heuk Gyoge Joongjae-e Nasotda" ["Korean and Black Church Leaders Intervene for Reconciliation"]. May 31, 1996.

———. 1996b. "Domaesangchimtu Jojikbumje Ppurippobnunda" ["To Eliminate Organized Crimes from Hunts Point Market"]. June 27, 1996.

———. 1997. "Haninbonjeupche Nosabungyu" ["A Korean Garment Factory Encountering a Labor Dispute"]. February 13, 1997.

———. 2000. "Siwidaehang Tujaenggigeum 5-Manbul Josung" ["A $50,000 Fund Established to Counter Pickets"]. October 5, 2000.

———. 2001a. " 'Haninhe Gigu Pyonip' Tajin" ["Explores the Possibility of Being Incorporated in the Korean Association of New York"]. March 27, 2001.

———. 2001b. "Donbatgo Haningage Pyojoksiwi" ["Paid Picketing against Korean Stores"]. May 12, 2001.

———. 2001c. "Ilbuinsa Gongmyongshim-euro Munje Bokjap" ["The Problem Has Become More Complicated by the Intervention of Some Koreans"]. July 3, 2001.

———. 2002. "Mulgungap Ttemugnun Upso Choljohi Ungjing" ["Plan to Punish Harshly Produce Retailers Who Have Avoided to Pay Debts to Delivery Companies and Suppliers"]. January 28, 2002.

———. 2005. "Sosangin Baesinhan John Liu Sieuiwon Gaksunghara" ["Awaken John Liu Who Turned against Small Business Owners"]. August 31, 2005.

Saito, Leland T., and Edward J. W. Park. 2000. "Multiracial Collaborations and Coalitions." *Transforming Race Relations: A Public Policy Report*, edited by Paul Ong. Los Angeles, Calif.: LEAP Asian Pacific American Public Policy Institute and UCLA Asian American Studies Center.

Sakamoto, Arthur, and Yu Xie. 2006. "The Socioeconomic Attainments of Asian Americans." In *Asian Americans: Contemporary Trends and Issues*, edited by Pyong Gap Min. Thousand Oaks, Calif.: Pine Forge Press.

Sanders, Jimmy, and Victor Nee. 1987. "The Limits of Ethnic Solidarity in the Enclave Economy." *American Sociological Review* 52(6): 745–67.

———. 1996. "Immigrant Self-Employment: The Family as Social Capital and the Value as Human Capital." *American Sociological Review* 61(2): 231–49.

Schiller, Nina Glick, Linda Basch, and Cristina Szanton Blanc, editors. 1992. *Towards a Transnational Perspective on Migration: Race, Class, Ethnicity, and Nationalism Reconsidered*. New York: The New York Academy of Science.

Serant, Claire. 1996. "Megastore Plan Hit." *New York Daily News*, August 7, 1996.

Shin, Eui-Hang and K. S. Chang. 1988. "Peripherization of Immigrant Professionals: Korean Physicians in the United States." *International Migration Review* 22(4): 609–26.

Shin, Eui-Hang, and Eui-Young Yu. 1984. "Use of Surname in Ethnic Research: The Case of Kim in the Korean American Population." *Demography* 21(3):347–59.

Shinagawa, Larry H., and Gin Young Pang. 1996. "Asian American Panethnicity and Intermarriage." *Amerasia Journal* 22(2): 127–52.

Simmel, Georg. 1955. *Conflict and The Web of Group Affiliations*, translated by K. H. Wolff and R. Bendix. Glencoe, Ill.: Free Press.

Simon, Rita J. 1997. *In The Golden Land: A Century of Russian and Soviet Jewish Immigration in America*. Westport, Conn.: Praeger.

Smith, Robert C. 2001. "Mexicans: Social, Educational, Economic, and Political Problems and Prospects in New York." In *New Immigrants in NewYork*, rev. ed., edited by Nancy Foner. New York: Columbia University Press.

———. 2003. "Migrant Membership as an Instituted Process: Transnationalization, the State and the Extra-Territorial Conduct of Mexican Politics." *International Migration Review* 37(2): 297–343.

Sowell, Thomas. 1981. *Ethnic America: A History*. New York: Basic Books.

Stewart, Ella. 1997. "Communication between African Americans and Korean Americans: Before and After the Los Angeles Riots." In *Los Angeles: Struggle Toward Multiethnic Community: Asian American, African American, & Latino*

Perspectives, edited by E. T. Chang and R. Leong. Seattle, Wash.: University of Washington Press.

Stryker, Sheldon. 1974. "A Theory of Middleman Minorities: A Comment." *American Sociological Review* 38(2): 281–2.

Tabor, Mary. 1992. "Unfulfilled Promises: 2 Koreans Seek Justice and Dream." *The New York Times*, October 26, 1992.

Terry, Don. 1990. "Dinkins Responds to 2nd Boycott of a Korean Store." *The New York Times*, August 28, 1990.

Tsukashima, Ronald T., and Darrel Montero. 1976. "The Contact Hypothesis: Social and Economic Contact and Generational Changes in the Study of Black Anti-Semitism." *Social Forces* 55(1): 149–65.

Turner, Jonathan, and Edna Bonacich. 1980. "Toward a Composite Theory of Middleman Minorities." *Ethnicity* 71(1): 144–58.

U.S. Census Bureau. 1972. *1970 Census of Population, Subject Reports: Chinese, Japanese, and Filipinos in the United States*. Washington: Government Printing Office.

———. 1983. *1980 Census of Population, General Population Characteristics, United States Summary* (PC80-1-B1). Washington: Government Printing Office.

———. 1993. *1990 Census of Population, General Population Characteristics, United States* (CP-1-1). Washington: Government Printing Office.

———. 2002. *Census 2000 Summary File 1* (SF 1). Washington: Government Printing Office.

University of Natal. 1961. *Studies of Indian Employment in Natal*. Cape Town, South Africa: Published for the University of Natal by Oxford University Press.

Velez, Carlos, and Jack Leahy. 1985. "Koreans Thankful at Fest." *New York Daily News*, September 30, 1985.

Waldinger, Roger. 1985. "Immigrant and Industrial Change in the New York City Apparel Industry." In *Hispanics in the U.S. Economy*, edited by George Borjas and Marta Tienda. Orlando, Fla.: Academic Press.

———. 1986. *Through the Eye of the Needle: Immigrants and Enterprise in New York's Garment Trade*. New York: New York University Press.

———. 1986–1987. "Changing Ladders and Musical Chairs: Ethnicity and Opportunity in Post-Industrial New York." *Politics and Society* 15(4): 369–401.

———. 1989. "Structural Opportunity or Ethnic Advantage? Immigrant Business Development in New York." *International Migration Review* 23(1): 48–72.

———. 1996. *Still the Promised City?* Cambridge, Mass.: Harvard University Press.

Waldinger, Roger, and Michael I. Lichter. 2003. *How the Other Half Works: Immigration and the Social Organization of Labor*. Berkeley, Calif.: University of California Press.

Waldinger, Roger, Howard Aldrich, and Robin Ward, editors. 1990. *Immigrant Business in Industrial Societies*. Newbury Park, Calif.: Sage Publications.

Waters, Mary. 1999. *Black Identities: West Indian Immigrant Dreams and American Realities*. Cambridge, Mass.: Harvard University Press.

Weisbord, Robert, and Arthur Stein. 1970. *Bitter Sweet Encounter: The Afro-American and the American Jew*. Wesport: Conn.: Negro Universities Press.

White, Joyce. 1982. "Pride—and Prejudice." *New York Daily News*, August 9, 1982.

Willmott, W. E. 1966. "The Chinese in Southeast Asia." *Australian Outlook* 20 (December): 252–62.

Wilson, Kenneth, and Alejandro Portes. 1980. "Immigrant Enclaves: An Analysis of the Labor Market Experiences of Cubans in Miami." *American Journal of Sociology* 86(2): 295–319.

Wong, Bernard. 1998. *Ethnicity and Entrepreneurship: The New Chinese Immigrants in the San Francisco Bay Area.* Boston, Mass.: Allyn & Bacon.

Yang, Q. Philip. 2006. "Future Prospects of Asian Americans." In *Asian Americans: Contemporary Trends and Issues,* edited by Pyong Gap Min. Thousand Oaks, Calif.: Pine Forge Press.

Yoon, In-Jin. 1997. *On My Own: Korean Businesses and Race Relations in America.* Chicago, Ill.: University of Chicago Press.

———. 2004. *The Korean Diaspora.* Seoul: The Korea University Press.

Yu, Eui-Young, Paul Choe, S. I. Han, and K. Yu. 2004. "Emerging Diversity in Los Angeles Koreatown, 1990–2000." *Amerasia Journal* 30(1): 25–52.

Zenner, Walter. 1991. *Minorities in the Middle: A Cross-Cultural Analysis.* Albany, N.Y.: State University of New York Press.

Zhou, Min. 1992. *Chinatown: The Socioeconomic Potential of an Urban Enclave.* Philadelphia, Pa.: Temple University Press.

———. 2001. "Chinese: Divergent Destinies in Immigrant New York." In *New Immigrants in New York,* rev. ed., edited by Nancy Foner. New York: Columbia University Press.

Zhou, Min, and Carl L. Bankston, III. 1998. *Growing Up American: How Vietnamese Children Adapt to Life in the United States.* New York: Russell Sage Foundation.

Zhou, Min, and John Logan. 1989. "Returns on Human Capital in Ethnic Enclaves." *American Sociological Review* 54(4): 809–20.

= Index =

Boldface numbers refer to figures and tables.

Abelmann, Nancy, 68, 77
African American Coalition Against
 Racism, 76
African Americans: Black
 Nationalism, 72, 81–82, 149; boycotts of Korean businesses by (see
 black boycotts); as employees,
 98–100; Korean-owned stores in
 neighborhoods of, 73–75; middleman merchants, antagonistic
 relations with, 71–72; racial
 stereotyping by, 82–83; racial
 stereotyping of, 84–86; traditional
 neighborhoods, changes in the
 racial composition of, 91–94, 150
Agricultural Cooperative Association,
 143
Aldrich, Howard, 120
American dream ideology, 84, 86, 99,
 118
Asian American Legal Defense and
 Education Fund, 113
Asian Americans: businesses owned
 by, types of, 36–37; Chinese
 (see Chinese Americans); educational attainment of, 26–27;
 Filipinos (see Filipino immigrants);
 Indian (see Indian Americans);
 Korean (see Korean Americans);
 self-employment rates among,
 28–29; settlement patterns of,
17–19 (see also settlement
 destinations)
Association of Mexican Workers, 104

Bechhofer, Frank, 120
black boycotts: decline of, reasons for,
 89–96, 149–50; ethnic collective
 action and, 4; ethnic solidarity and,
 86–89; explanations for, 80–86;
 Korean businesses, impact of
 decline in, 94–96; of Korean-owned
 stores in New York City, 76; mega-
 stores moving into urban neighborhoods, impact of, 89–91; middleman
 minority theory as an explanation
 of, 68–73, 148–50; prevalence and
 process of, 75–80; racial composition of black neighborhoods, impact
 of, 91–94; reactive solidarity and,
 72–73
Black Nationalism, 72, 81–82, 149
Bloomberg, Michael, 132
Blumer, Herbert, 85
Bobo, Lawrence, 98
Bonacich, Edna, 3, 69–72, 120
Borjas, George, 120
Broadway Korean Businessmen's
 Association, 40
Bronx Korean Merchants Association,
 64–65
Bronx Terminal Market, 55, 64–65

185